PROFESSIONALISM AND SOCIAL CHANGE

From the Settlement House Movement to Neighborhood Centers,
1886 to the Present

PROFESSIONALISM
and
SOCIAL CHANGE

FROM THE
SETTLEMENT HOUSE MOVEMENT
TO NEIGHBORHOOD CENTERS
1886 TO THE PRESENT

JUDITH ANN TROLANDER

New York   COLUMBIA UNIVERSITY PRESS   1987

The Andrew C. Mellon Foundation, through a special grant, has assisted the Press in publishing this volume.

Library of Congress Cataloging-in-Publication Data

Trolander, Judith Ann, 1942–
  Professionalism and social change.

  (Columbia history of urban life)
  Bibliography: p.
  Includes index.
  1. Social settlements—United States—History—19th century.   2. Social settlements—United States—History—20th century.   I. Title.   II. Series.
  HV4194.T74   1987   362.5'57'0973   87-6414
  ISBN 0-231-06472-1

OCLC# 15366038

Book designed by Laiying Chong.

Columbia University Press
New York   Guildford, Surrey
Copyright © 1987 Columbia University Press
Printed in the United States of America

This book is Smyth-sewn.

CONTENTS

PREFACE

In the summer of 1985, a group of settlement house executives and others gathered at Martin Luther King Center of Hallie Q. Brown House Association to plan a conference celebrating one hundred years of the social settlement movement in the United States. Hallie Q. Brown House is fairly indicative of what is happening nationally to settlement houses in the mid-1980s. Located in a racially mixed neighborhood undergoing gentrification near downtown St. Paul, Minnesota, Hallie occupies a modern low, sprawling, concrete fortress that appears to have been built with resistance to vandalism uppermost in mind. Listed above the receptionist's desk, Hallie's programs are all direct service in nature, being oriented toward solving specific problems for individuals, such as unemployment, day care, tutoring, juvenile delinquency prevention, and crime victim assistance.

During the planning meeting, when someone mentioned featuring ethnic entertainment at the anniversary conference in commemoration of the movement's past success with immigrants, Hallie's director admitted that his settlement had no muscial groups. He also doubted how many settlement-connected people today would relate to an ethnic evening. Concerned over the much-diminished role of recreation in the settlements, the group added a conference session on "Why was 'basketball' important?" While discussing another session, "Social reform vs. direct services," one of the settlement leaders observed that they were all doing direct services, but what they believed in was social reform. The settlement executive directors present—a Hispanic woman, a black male, and a white male who had grown up using his neighborhood settlement house—are representative of today's settlement leaders nationally.[1]

So much of the settlement movement in 1986—the neighborhoods, the buildings, the programs, and the staff—are in sharp contrast to Jane Addams' Hull House and other settlements nearly one hundred years ago. Yet the mix of interest in reform with immediate services to their neighborhoods is at the heart of the original settlement house idea. Most of what historians have written specifically about the settlement movement focuses on the Progressive Era, and much of it emphasizes the reform tradition. The best-known settlement historian, Allen Davis, described the early houses as "spearheads for reform" in a book of that title.[2] With reference to the 1920s, Clarke Chambers told of settlement workers holding on to their reform ideals in the face of political conservatism.[3] I have detailed the settlements' contributions to reform, in spite of United Way and government bureaucracy, in the New Deal.[4] While historians have produced almost nothing on the last forty-five years of the movement, they have explored various factors that influenced settlement houses. Social welfare historians have stressed the twentieth-century trend toward professionalization. Urban historians have written about demographic changes in slums and ghettos, and women historians are exploring gender as a factor in shaping institutions. What remains is to bring these elements—professionalism, race, gender, and reform—together while explaining how and why the settlement movement in the United States changed from 1886 to the present and to evaluate its recent signifcance.

This study focuses primarily on the last four decades of the settlement house movement. Historians have already explored the earlier years, and chapter 1 presents a summary of their findings while outlining the main controversies surrounding the settlement house. To what extent and in what ways was it a democratic agency or an institution of social control? Did it significantly increase opportunity for its neighbors? How effective was it as an instrument of reform? Why has it changed and declined in influence and prestige? Has it outgrown its usefulness? The bulk of the study explores the roles of professionalism, race, and gender in relation to these questions. Given the lack of historical studies covering the post–World War II settlement house, these chapters are almost entirely based on original research.

The recent decades were an exciting period to study. One sees an institution rapidly professionalizing, as men replaced women staff and then black staff replaced whites. Neighborhoods undergo cataclysmic change with urban renewal, public housing construction, and the black migration to the cities. During these years, the settlement house was probably more shaped by social changes than it influenced them. As such it reflected much that went on in cities following the Great Depression.

Bringing this study up to 1986 has involved the difficult task of assessing current trends. Historians rely heavily on archival sources, which are virtually nonexistent for the 1980s. Consequently, I have supplemented the abundant manuscript collections for the earlier decades with interviews and other contacts with settlement house workers. These contacts have included attendance at the 1984 International Federation of Settlements Conference in London, the 1986 International Federation Conference in New York, participation with settlement workers and academics in the Midwest American Settlement House Centennial, and the teaching of a course on settlement houses in the University of Minnesota's School of Social Work. It is my hope that such activities along with this book will bring the academic and settlement house communities into closer and more beneficial contact with each other.

Many individuals and organizations have contributed to this study. The University of Minnesota provided me with a Summer Faculty Research Appointment, a Grant-in-Aid of Research, a single-quarter leave, and travel expenses for attendance at the 1984 Toynbee Hall Centenary and International Federation of Settlements Seminar in London. The Minnesota Humanities Commission generously funded a panel presentation I organized on the theme "Were settlement houses democratic agencies or institutions of social control?" The panel's cosponsors were Pillsbury United Neighborhood Services and the University of Minnesota's Duluth campus, Humphrey Institute, and School of Social Work (Twin Cities campus). Among the historians who made suggestions regarding the manuscript and/or the panel were Robert Fisher, Louise Wade, Clarke Chambers, Patricia Mooney Melvin, and Walter I. Trattner. My graduate students offered a number of thought-provoking comments, particularly Dawn Baker and Diane Morlan. Among those individuals who were especially helpful were Margaret Berry, retired head of the National Federation of Settlements; Camillo DeSantis, former settlement head, currently with United Way of Minneapolis; and Tony Wagner, head of Pillsbury United Neighborhood Services. Numerous archives have gone to considerable expense housing and processing settlement house collections. The leader in this area is the Social Welfare History Archives Center at the University of Minnesota, currently presided over by Dave Klaassen. The book's editors, Kate Wittenberg and Joan McQuary, have been especially helpful with their support and suggestions. Finally, I wish to thank my typists, particularly Beth Kwapick and Barb Williams. Without the help of all these people and organizations, this manuscript would not have been possible. I do, of course, take full responsibility for the material presented here.

PROFESSIONALISM AND SOCIAL CHANGE

*From the Settlement House Movement to Neighborhood Centers,
1886 to the Present*

INTRODUCTION

The year 1986 marks the hundredth anniversary of the settlement house movement in the United States. From their beginnings, the purpose of settlement houses has been to meet the needs of the low-income neighborhoods in which they are located. Settlements have fulfilled their purpose in two ways. The first is by providing immediate services, usually of an educational/recreational nature. The second is by working to bring about social reform, thus alleviating the underlying causes of social problems in their neighborhoods. By having twin objectives—immediate services and basic reform—settlement houses have had the flexibility to survive conservative as well as reform periods. When reform is "out," settlements may appear on the surface to be simply service-oriented agencies. When reform is "in," settlements are ready to openly play a role. This flexibility is fundamental to the definition of the settlement house.

The common thread uniting settlement houses over time and distinguishing them from similar social agencies is their multifaceted focus on, and ties to, low-income neighborhoods. Other agencies, like the Y's, have neighborhood branches but are essentially franchise operations with a national headquarters. Still other kinds of neighborhood organizations of a grass-roots variety lack the breadth of issues, programs, and varied people involvement of the settlement house. These grass-roots neighborhood organizations will occasionally criticize the settlement house as being "for, not of" the neighborhood. However, that is precisely the point—settlement house workers have over time either been well-to-do college graduates or professional social workers who, combined with their predominantly well-to-do boards, have brought an outsider's perspective to their focus on low-income neighborhoods. As such, they may be labeled paternalistic and charged with social control, but they also bring a broader vision of society to the neighborhoods along with promoting a greater awareness of their neighborhoods in the rest of society. It is this mix of outsiders with the neighborhoods that gives settlement houses a certain uniqueness, dynamism, and significance, and also makes them fascinating to study.

The early social settlement workers, who consciously combined a commitment to reform with daily services, had as their method actually living in the settlement house and developing a "neighborly," as opposed to a professional, relationship with the surrounding low-income people they sought to help. The name "settlement house" refers to this practice of well-to-do outsiders "settling" or residing in the agency. Sufficiently active as reformers to be characterized by their Progressive Era historian, Allen Davis, as "spearheads for reform," they are also commonly credited with being the major institutional example of the social reform side of early social work.

Social welfare historians generally regard professionalism as being responsible for social work turning away from its early commitment to reform. However, professionalism is a broad concept, and its content is not static. Social work is a professional field that is influenced by shifting political winds and fads, partly in response to available jobs and grant money. For example, the 1920s emphasized psychological concepts and casework; the 1930s saw a revolution in public welfare; the 1950s stressed delinquency; the 1960s promoted direct action, confrontation, and community organization; and the 1970s and 1980s feature almost exclusively direct services and therapy. Each professional social work emphasis has different implications for settlement houses and for what is feasible in the realm of social action. Also, at any given time, the concept of professionalism has a series of facets—an organized body of literature, a set of ethics or values, control over entry into or status within it, a teachable discipline, and professional organizations. These facets may, at times, work toward different and, perhaps, contradictory goals. For example, a professional settlement organization may be promoting social action while social work schools are ignoring social action techniques in their curricula. Professionalism has had its greatest impact on settlements during the post–Great Depression decades. That was when M.S.W.s (holders of the master of social work degree) joined settlement staffs for the first time in significant numbers, and the practice of settlement workers living in the settlement houses disappeared. A "professional" relationship replaced a "neighborly" one.

An even broader concept than professionalism is social change. It refers to changing neighborhoods, such as blacks displacing whites, and physical disruption of neighborhoods through urban renewal. Social change also includes social reform. Settlement houses have participated in the three reform periods of this century—the Progressive Era, the New Deal, and the Great Society—plus, they have contributed to other reform movements, such as feminism and civil rights. Thus, social change represents a variety of external forces operating on settlement houses, which in turn have a traditional commitment to respond as catalysts for reform.

Historically, settlements have constituted a movement. However, part of what is disappearing is a sense of common identity and shared goals among the houses. Also, the total number of neighborhood centers identifying with the traditional settlement house movement is declining, although a number of agencies remain major operations. Another problem in assessing the significance of the declining numbers of settlement houses is the trend of settlements to merge with each other and of branch operations to proliferate. Settlement houses in recent decades have rarely gone out of business. Instead, a settlement house in trouble will merge with another settlement, which may, temporarily or permanently, continue some settlement operations at the newly absorbed house. Thus, it is difficult to be precise about numbers and still convey the strength of the movement.

The peak of settlement house prestige and, perhaps, of numbers of independent settlement houses was just prior to World War I. At that time, the movement consisted of around four hundred houses, although perhaps half of these had religious sponsorship and, depending on the individual house, may have functioned somewhat like a church mission. The National Federation of Settlements, founded in 1911, denied membership to houses that proselytized extensively. As long as the remaining houses were eager to be part of the national organization, membership in the National Federation provided a convenient means of identifying an agency as a settlement house.

Membership in the National Federation was relatively stable until

the 1970s. For example, in 1946, 203 independent houses belonged.[1] Over half were located in the seven major metropolitan areas
of the Northeast and Midwest (New York had 18, Chicago 18, Cleveland 12, Boston 24, Detroit 14, Philadelphia 15, and the Twin Cities
11). However, smaller cities like Peoria and Cedar Rapids each had
a settlement house. Altogether, twenty-five states and the District of
Columbia had at least 1 settlement house, although the South only
had 8 houses in the national organization and the West Coast had
just 6 (all in California). Some of these houses were full-fledged, dynamic operations with extensive daily programming and an active
commitment to reform. Others had only a couple of staff members,
focused completely on providing daily activities for their neighbors,
and had little involvement in social reform. The National Federation, however, bound them all together with its national, reform-
oriented focus.

During the 1950s and 1960s, the concern for juvenile delinquency
and the War on Poverty stimulated the expansion of settlement operations. By 1957, membership in the National Federation stood at
256 houses in thirty-one states, the District of Columbia, and Hawaii.[2] Membership shrank slightly to 253 in 1967;[3] but by then, the
merger trend as well as the move toward decentralization with pro-
liferating branch operations was well under way. Expansion had occurred in formerly underrepresented areas with California now up
to 15 independent settlements and Texas going from 1 in 1946 to 9
by 1967. Expansion had also occurred in more traditional strong-
holds, with New York up to 26 houses, not counting branches.

With the 1970s, it becomes difficult to gauge the strength of the
movement by membership in the National Federation of Settlements. Blacks took over the national organization, interagency politics became chaotic, and agencies suffered funding cutbacks. Thus,
a number of major houses dropped out of the national organization,
leaving membership at approximately 110 in 1980.[4] However, a
number of the houses which dropped out continued to operate major programs much as before; and even though they were not members, they would occasionally participate in settlement conferences
and continue to identify themselves with the settlement house tradition. Given the neighborhood roots of the settlement house, they
don't need a national organization to survive. Thus, my impression

is that, while considerably fragmented today, the actual strength of settlement house operations has been remarkably stable over time.

The significance and impact of settlement houses has probably fluctuated more than their numbers. Each house may serve a couple hundred to a couple thousand neighbors in programs that are usually of a general educational/recreational nature, although today a number of settlements are becoming more specific-problem-oriented with a greater emphasis on direct services. However, settlements have never served more than a small fraction of the urban poor. Their greater significance lies in their social change function. They played a role in formulating our social welfare structure by seeking legislation and by experimenting with social services. They have also provided a window on poverty for the rest of society. Thus, their daily program of education, recreation, and direct services gives them viability over time; their reform role gives them significance. However, given the mushrooming growth of other social agencies, including social change ones, the relative influence or impact of settlement houses has declined.

This study has essentially three themes related to this decline in influence. The first is how professionalism affected and sometimes hurt the settlement houses. The second is the growing impact of blacks on the settlement house, first in the neighborhoods and then in the evolution from white female to black male leadership in the settlement movement itself. Finally, the role of settlements have played in social reform, although reflecting a varying commitment, deserves recognition and analysis.

Although this study covers the years from 1886 to 1986, the focus is on the post–World War II settlement house. Other scholars and other books have covered the earlier period, and their findings are summarized in chapter 1. The remaining chapters are based on original research, mostly in the voluminous manuscript collections available. In looking at the settlement house over the last four decades, almost half its history, one sees major change in staff and method, in clientele, and in ability to influence social change. The settlement house becomes a new kind of neighborhood center.

RESIDENTS IN
LOW-INCOME NEIGHBORHOODS:
SETTLEMENT HOUSE WORKERS
FROM 1886 TO 1945

I N ORDER TO MEASURE THE DECLINE OF THE TRADI-
tional settlement house movement and to determine how the
neighborhood center of today is different, one should look first at
the settlement house in its heyday, the Progressive Era, and then
consider the impact of the conservative 1920s, the liberal New Deal,
and the dislocations of World War II. Over these decades, one sees
an innovative institution rapidly expanding, then stabilizing as other
social agencies proliferate. The reform environment, the changing
population of low-income neighborhoods, and the emergence of
professional social work were some of the factors behind the settlements' growth pattern. In turn, these factors affected such questions
as to what extent the settlement house was a democratic agency or
an institution of social control. How effective was the settlement
method in achieving reform and in increasing opportunity for its
neighbors? During these years, the method of residence in the settlement house remained intact as settlement workers sought to meet
the needs of their neighbors.

Settlement houses enjoyed the most prestige and influence during
the early twentieth-century reform period, the Progressive Era. Most

settlements were founded during those years. At that time, the public and the infant social work profession regarded settlement houses as innovative, successful in helping immigrants adjust to life in the United States, useful in meeting the needs of low-income neighborhoods, and effective in bringing about a wide variety of reforms. A number of leading reformers were on settlement house staffs or connected with them as volunteers or residents. In fact, the Progressive Era settlement house was a center that attracted reformers, facilitated their exchange of ideas, and provided a congenial, supportive atmosphere for their efforts.

The very earliest settlement houses in the United States predated the Progressive Era by only a little over a decade. In 1886, an American philosopher and Ethical Culture Society leader, Stanton Coit, began the settlement house movement in the United States when he opened Neighborhood Guild on New York's Lower East Side. Previously, while a graduate student at Columbia University, Coit had chosen to live in the slums. He then went to Europe, earned a Ph.D. from the University of Berlin, and spent three months as a resident at London's Toynbee Hall, the first settlement house in the world, which was established in 1884.

The idea for Toynbee Hall grew out of some English social welfare experiments and was closely tied to the universities. Edward Denison, a young Oxford graduate, moved into a London slum in 1867 and for two years worked for housing and sanitation reform. He was followed by Arnold Toynbee, another Oxford graduate, who moved into London's destitute East End and began a program of lectures and discussions for the slum dwellers. He soon died; but Canon Barnett, the vicar for the neighborhood, established Toynbee Hall as a center where university students could live, share their learning, study slum life, and work for reform. The settlement was "to be a kind of glue," pulling different elements of society together.[1]

Like the neighborhood around Toynbee Hall, that surrounding Coit's Neighborhood Guild was crowded with Jewish immigrants and the very poor. Since Coit and his co-workers came from a Protestant background, religion was a barrier between the settlement workers and the poor they sought to help. By emphasizing the secular nature of the American settlement movement, Coit and the settlement workers who followed him minimized this religious barrier.

The traditional settlement house method included a unique feature. Coit and some other socially minded college graduates "settled" or took up residence in Neighborhood Guild and invited their neighbors from the surrounding ghetto in for theatricals, lectures, and clubs. An average day at the settlement around 1900 began at 9:00 A.M. with the kindergarten. A Legal Aid Society and a loan office were open all day. After school let out at 3:00 P.M., the club rooms, study room, library, and rooftop playground came alive. In the evening, teenagers gathered for clubs or games, and a trade union might meet. People also used the settlement's public baths, the first in New York.[2] Through providing these activities and by living in the settlement house, the settlement workers tried to replace the typical nineteenth-century charity worker's air of superiority with one of neighborliness. They also hoped that residence in the slums would make them more effective social reformers.

Unlike most of the settlement workers, Coit consciously sought to empower the poor in agitating for reforms. His plan was to organize working-class people into clubs. Each club would consist of approximately one hundred families living on a particular block or street. Clubs in the same neighborhood would unite to form a neighborhood guild. Other neighborhood guilds would also have clubs forming additional neighborhood guilds. The guilds would then join together to form a huge working-class network that would agitate for reform.[3] However, Coit failed to make the neighborhood guild idea workable. Within two years of founding Neighborhood Guild, he left the settlement movement and the United States to become an Ethical Culture minister in England. His settlement almost collapsed, but in 1891, two other founders of Neighborhood Guild, Edward King and Charles B. Stover, reorganized it along more traditional lines as University Settlement.

The best example of the "guild" approach was Hudson Guild, founded in 1895 by another Ethical Culture Society leader, John Lovejoy Elliott, in the Chelsea neighborhood of New York. Elliott used block clubs as the basis for a self-governing house council that set house rules, oversaw maintenance, allocated club space, and had the power with a two-thirds majority to fire the house director. The block clubs also formed a district committee to deal with other charities and city departments. Finally, each block club had a representative whose duty was to keep the settlement staff informed of neighborhood problems, such as who needed to see a charity doctor. Eventually, the block club concept broke down over the failure of each block club to find and maintain adequate leadership. Also, the block clubs never had as much power as Hudson Guild's well-to-do board. However, Elliott went on to organize his own and other New York settlements' mothers' clubs into the League of Mothers' Clubs, which did effectively lobby for various welfare measures. Hudson Guild was unique among early settlements in the extent to which it empowered the poor.[4]

It was the traditional settlement house concept of the well-to-do interpreting the poor that spread rapidly in the late nineteenth and early twentieth centuries. Neighborhood Guild was followed in 1889 by College Settlement in New York, established by a group of women graduates of Eastern colleges, and by Jane Addams' Hull House in Chicago. So little publicity had accompanied Neighborhood Guild that when Jane Addams laid her plans for Hull House, she thought she was establishing the first settlement house in the United States. By 1895, the United States had around fifty settlement houses, including Lillian Wald's Henry Street Settlement in New York, which developed the visiting-nurse way of caring for the poor at home. By World War I, settlement houses numbered between two hundred and four hundred, depending on how rigorously one applies nonsectarian criteria. Industrial, cultural, and social trends contributed to this rapid expansion.

Early social settlements were established while the United States was going through major industrialization. As cities expanded, they divided into neighborhoods along social class lines. Immigrants entered the United States at a heavy rate. In some years, they numbered a million or more. Hampered by broken English and ethnic rivalries, they crowded into urban slums. There they found a variety of ethnic organizations, ranging from mutual aid societies to foreign language churches, to help them adjust. Among these institutions, the settlement house was unique in that immigrants of all nationalities were welcome to come together. Furthermore, in the settlement house, immigrants could meet well-to-do settlement volunteers from other parts of the city along with the college-educated residents. Most immigrants shared the dream of America as the land of opportunity, which was real because of the economic expansion of the times. Within the settlement house, they were, to a certain extent, willing to defer to the well-to-do residents and volunteers in part because they saw an open class system. The settlement house could help them assimilate and move up in American society. The acculturation activities of the early settlement house workers might be regarded as paternalistic, but these activities were eagerly sought by the settlements' clientele. Thus, in an increasingly fragmented city, the settlement house provided a meeting ground for different ethnic groups and for the well-off and the poor to come together, to bridge class differences, and to work together on resolving social problems.

Men formed a significant minority among the early settlement leaders and demonstrated the influence of the Social Gospel on the movement. Social Gospel ministers believed in trying to solve such problems as poverty. Among the early settlement house leaders who studied for the ministry were Graham Taylor, Robert A. Woods, and George Bellamy. However, for these ministers to have emphasized their Protestant religion in what were increasingly Catholic and Jewish slums would have been to invite defeat.[5] A true settlement house was a secular institution, but it was also dedicated to the same kind of humanitarian concerns as the Social Gospel. Thus, a number of young men, who had trained for the ministry but who had a strong desire to work with the poor, found the settlement house a more effective setting than the church.

Also, most of the early settlement workers were relatively young college graduates. As such, they had been exposed to the intellectual concept of Reform Darwinism, which emphasized the environment, as opposed to individual character defects, as being at the root of social problems. The new social sciences were emerging in colleges, and the slum was worthy of study. Thus, settlement houses developed university ties, providing a base for those doing studies and a laboratory experience for students seeking firsthand knowledge of slum conditions. Some settlements emphasized their university ties by naming themselves University Settlement, College Settlement, or after a specific college such as Hiram House (Hiram College), University of Chicago Settlement, and Northwestern University Settlement.

These youthful college graduates were also receptive to Progressive Era reform. While one can cite humanitarian and religious motives, self-interest also played a role. In the early years of the twentieth century, many so-called "nice people" supported Progressive reforms because they felt threatened by hordes of "foreigners" with alien ideologies. Certainly, the settlement house movement fit into this desire to Americanize foreign immigrants as well as to increase or reestablish the influence of the well-to-do in the slums.

Most of the early settlement house workers were also women. The movement coincided with the first generation of women to graduate from colleges in significant numbers. They faced problems such as, what careers were available to them? How could they establish their independence from their parents when society said it was improper for single women, even if they were college graduates, to live alone? Finally, how could they be influential when they didn't even have the vote? Jane Addams' resolution of these questions illustrates the self-interested appeal settlement work had for the single, female college graduate.

When Jane Addams founded Hull House in 1889, she was twenty-nine, independently wealthy, and without any prospects of marriage. A graduate of Rockford College, she shared with other women college graduates of her generation a sense of being special and an obligation to prove that they could do something with their college education. In Jane Addams' case, she wasn't interested in teaching; and after six months, she dropped out of medical school. Her stepmother involved her in an endless round of tea parties and urged her to put their family's interests first, to play the maiden aunt, and help out relatives when needed—what Jane Addams called the "family claim." The settlement house offered a solution to both her occupational and personal dilemmas.

Since a high percentage of these women college graduates did not marry, they sought not only an occupation but a substitute for traditional family life. What they were familiar with was the college dormitory. Residence in the settlement house was a lot like that. Furthermore, since the stated purpose was to help the poor, young women who eschewed family obligations to be settlement residents could hardly be accused of selfishness. The semi-protected environment of the settlement house was respectable, and the camaraderie among the residents provided an alternative to family life.[6]

The settlement house also offered women a career. Other than teaching and medicine, few professional opportunities existed for women. The settlement house was new and part of the larger, emerging occupational field of social work, which welcomed women. Finally, in a world where women still couldn't vote, settlement work gave them the opportunity to influence public policy. Not surprisingly, many women settlement workers, like Jane Addams, were active in the feminist movement.

So many women flocked to the settlement movement that they quickly came to dominate it, both in terms of numbers as well as leadership positions. Women were, therefore, primarily responsible for shaping the settlement house movement in the United States. The movement they led generally rejected the more aggressive style of neighborhood organizing that Stanton Coit proposed, that is, going out into the neighborhood and organizing the men into block clubs. Instead, the women residents preferred to invite their neighbors into the settlement house. Once there, many, if not most, of the activities revolved around children. The women settlement workers did not try to foist their feminism onto their neighbors. However, they freely engaged in the feminist movement from an institutional base that they controlled. Thus, certain aspects of the settlement movement, such as residence in the house, a passive approach to neighborhood organizing, a consensus style of seeking reform, emphasis on children's work, and a feminist commitment, were well adapted to the fact that either women dominated the movement or the settlement house reflected their influence.

The practice of settlement workers living in the settlement house was more than personal convenience for single women. It was at the heart of the original settlement method and a unique concept for both men and women. Usually college graduates, many residents had full-time jobs outside the house; but in return for the privilege of living there, they gave a portion of their time to house activities. They might lead a club, teach a class, or use the house as a base to engage in more innovative projects. Florence Kelley, for example, moved into Hull House in 1891. A divorced mother with three

youngsters, she set up her own household near Hull House the following year. With Hull House connections she campaigned for in-
vestigations of working conditions and tough factory inspection, and
then served as the head factory inspector for Illinois. She praised
Hull House for enabling her to learn more about working-class life
and had a high opinion of the intelligence and efficiency of the women
residents there.[7] Later, as head of the National Consumers League,
she found settlement workers to be strong allies in her efforts to
improve working conditions. Thus, settlement house residents provided support groups for the reformers in their midst.

Residence in or near the settlement house had several other advantages. In place of the traditional condescension of the ordinary
charity workers, settlement residents aimed for a more egalitarian
relationship with those they were trying to help, specifically that of
neighbor. They also hoped that by living in the slums, they would
gain added insight into the causes of poverty.[8] Furthermore, when
they did complain about social problems, their complaints had an
added legitimacy. To illustrate, Jane Addams might be a well-bred
college graduate; but when she objected to the lack of garbage collection in her neighborhood, it was *her* garbage-filled neighborhood
that needed better service. When the authorities offered to make her
garbage inspector, she accepted the challenge; and garbage pickup
improved.[9] These advantages of residence helped the settlement
workers function more effectively as advocates for their neighborhoods.

In doing so, just how much settlement workers were advocates for
their own values rather than the values of their neighbors is debatable. Historian Thomas Lee Philpott criticized the settlement workers for being "not of, but for" the neighborhood.[10] Since almost all
settlement residents chose to live in the settlement house itself rather
than in a neighborhood tenement, they did emphasize a certain
apartness from the neighborhood. However, as one of my students
pointed out, this apartness had a certain honesty about it. Theoreti-
cally, the settlement workers could have moved into tenements and
claimed to be more like their neighbors, but it wouldn't have been
true. In other words, the settlement residents were probably more
honest and open about their apartness from the neighborhood than

subsequent neighborhood workers, like VISTA volunteers who moved into slum tenements in the 1960s.

Settlement residents were definitely of a different social class than their neighbors. Furthermore, this difference was deliberate. When young medical school graduate Alice Hamilton applied to live at Hull House, she found the settlement difficult to enter. What got her accepted was the fact that her socially prominent Fort Wayne, Indiana, family had impressed another Hull House resident, Florence Kelley.[11] Early settlement leaders talked about society as being "organic," by which they meant the interdependence of social classes. However, as cities increasingly split into class-stratified neighborhoods, rich and poor lost the former daily contact they had had with each other. The settlement house was designed to reestablish some of that contact. The settlement workers saw themselves as bridging class lines by interpreting the poor to the rich and using their influence among the rich to better the lives of the poor.

It is tempting to ask if the poor couldn't interpret themselves. However, around 1900 the traditional attitude that poor people had something wrong with their character was quite strong. Without better-off allies, they were unlikely to be heard. Indeed, many of the poor spoke only broken English. Furthermore, publicizing bad conditions was a major strategy of Progressive reformers. So settlement workers not only became energetic spokespersons for the poor, they were talented and prolific writers on their behalf.

Jane Addams functioned as a superb publicist. Not only was *Twenty Years at Hull House,* with its human interest stories, a classic, but she published a number of other books and articles and was in demand as a speaker. She projected a favorable public image that made her almost legendary in her own time and was an asset in drawing positive attention to the causes she advocated.[12] For example, when she allowed the organizers of the infant NAACP to add her name to their list of founders, that civil rights organization gained immediate credibility and national recognition.

Besides Jane Addams, other settlement workers published accounts of their experiences in the slums and their analyses of ghetto conditions. These included the head worker of University Settlement, Robert Hunter, whose book *Poverty: Social Conscience in the*

Progressive Era helped to establish the idea of using a minimum wage for a decent standard of living as a poverty line.[13] Earlier, Robert Woods, head of Boston's South End House, published *The City Wilderness* (1899) and *Americans in Process* (1902). Lillian Wald successfully imitated Jane Addams with her autobiographical account *The House on Henry Street* (1915). Graham Taylor, founder of Chicago Commons, and Mary K. Simkhovitch, head worker of Greenwich House, were also prolific writers.[14]

One study of fourteen well-known settlement leaders noted that they produced a total of at least forty-five books. A lesser-known settlement worker, Catheryne Cooke Gilman of Minneapolis' Northeast Neighborhood House, wrote over two hundred pamphlets and articles.[15] As publicists and "interpreters" on behalf of the poor, settlement leaders were successful in reaching a fairly wide audience and in promoting reform. In the process, they gave the early settlement movement visibility.

Settlement houses also sought to bring the poor into direct contact with those who might be influential. While a number of the early settlement house heads remained with their institutions for the rest of their lives, turnover among the residents was high. One example was Chicago Commons, which, in its first forty years, had a total of nine hundred residents, the equivalent of an average, complete annual turnover each year.[16] Most residents regarded their stay at the settlement house as temporary, but also as an experience they could take with them as they went on to other things. Among those who lived at Hull House early in their careers were the first woman appointed to the cabinet, Frances Perkins, and the first black to hold a cabinet position, Robert C. Weaver.

Settlements also recruited upper-class volunteers, bringing them into contact with the poor as club and class leaders. Young girls from New York's Lower East Side did learn some calisthenics and dances in debutante Eleanor Roosevelt's class at University Settlement, but the impact of the experience was undoubtedly greater on Eleanor. Her biographer, Joseph P. Lash, credits the settlement house with awakening her awareness of the dimensions of poverty and coupling that awareness with the possibility of social reform.[17] University Settlement chronicler Jeffrey Scheuer quotes Eleanor remembering an incident when Franklin called for her at the settlement, and the two walked a sick child back to her tenement. Inside the child's home, "Franklin looked around in surprise and horror. It was the first time [Eleanor thought], that he had ever really seen a slum and when he got back to the street he drew a deep breath of fresh air. 'My God,' he whispered, 'I didn't know people lived like that!' "[18] Other influential New Dealers with settlement house connections included Harry Hopkins (Christodora House), and Herbert Lehman, Henry Morgenthau, Jr., and Adolf Berle, all of whom had worked at Henry Street Settlement.[19] Undoubtedly some condescension on the part of the well-off toward the poor existed, but so did some real opportunities for communication.

Unfortunately, the settlement house workers often found themselves at odds with their neighbors as a result of certain conflicts in values. Progressive reform had its moralistic overtones. Jane Addams wrote a not very insightful book about prostitution called *A New Conscience and an Ancient Evil*. George Bellamy, head of Cleveland's Hiram House, put a lot of effort into reforming Cleveland's dance halls.[20] Catheryne Cooke Gilman's campaign to reduce juvenile delinquency by attacking places of "immorality" eventually offended local businessmen, such as the owners of movie theaters.[21] Many settlement workers did frequently ignore or defy local neighborhood attitudes.

Even on nonmoralistic issues, settlement workers could still find themselves in conflict with their neighbors. One such issue was housing. Because settlement workers were appalled by the wretched housing they saw in the slums, they advocated strict housing codes. What their neighbors saw resulting was either higher rents as buildings were upgraded or condemned buildings reducing the already scarce supply of housing. In response to that, settlement workers advocated "model tenements" where philanthropically minded landlords would build decent housing and limit their profits to a modest amount in order to keep rents low. It took most settlement workers several decades to realize that very few philanthropically minded landlords existed. In the meantime, their neighbors resented the settlement workers' efforts with housing regulation. Yet if the settlement workers hadn't played the controversial role of catalyst for change in their neighborhoods, would the groundwork have been laid for subsequent housing reforms? Historian Philpott criticized settlement workers for their role in housing reform in early twentieth-century Chicago, but he also spent a lot of time talking about their efforts.[22]

The early settlement house movement coincided with the Progressive Era, a period of wide-ranging reform that emphasized environmental solutions to social problems. Few social agencies, public or private, existed in the slums. Other agencies, such as the public schools, were not yet well adapted to the urban environment. When settlement workers, armed with investigative reports and firsthand knowledge of slum life, lobbied local governments for the establishment of public playgrounds, housing codes, and mothers' pensions, they often got a positive response. Settlement workers also used their own demonstration classes in English and citizenship, industrial education, and home economics plus their kindergartens and playgrounds to get these incorporated into their public school and park systems. They were instrumental in the adoption of the juvenile court and various other programs dealing with child welfare as well as working conditions. However, they almost always lacked the neighborhood-based political clout necessary to unseat the local ward boss. Jane Addams' neighbors used Hull House, but still voted for the corrupt alderman who supplied them with jobs and favors and was one of them. When Addams, a pragmatist, saw her reform candidate defeated, she went on to other issues.[23] Although not always successful, settlements were central to much of the reform of the early twentieth century.

From its beginnings, the settlement house approach to social reform has generally been a cooperative, consensus-building one that utilizes established channels. The tendency to emphasize cooperation may have been due to the fact that settlements were, historically, a mixture of well-to-do board members and contributors, middle-class staff, and lower-class clientele. Settlement house workers consciously desired to build bridges among the different urban classes that had lost touch with one another as people separated into class-stratified neighborhoods. Traditionally, part of this cooperative approach also placed the settlement worker in the role of interpreter of the poor to the well-to-do and to the larger community.

This wide-ranging concern for neighborhood needs was what set the settlement off from a purely recreational center. A good deal of recreation went on in settlements, but it wasn't merely recreation for recreation's sake. Through recreational programs, settlements maintained their neighborhood relationships. The physical facility housing these recreational activities gave the settlement an identity and an air of permanence in the neighborhood. Neighborhood-based, the settlement house focused its programs primarily on the neighborhood as well.

However, just how well settlement houses related to their immigrant neighbors through their daily activities of clubs, classes, counseling, large group activities, and child nurseries is also debatable. Some historians praise the settlement for valuing the immigrant's ethnic heritage as opposed to demanding that the immigrant give up all traces of the "Old World" in order to assimilate.[24] Other scholars suggest that institutions closer to the ethnic heritage of particular groups, such as the Catholic church, could have provided these services better.[25]

Many neighborhoods were multi-ethnic, even if they had the reputation for being Italian or Jewish neighborhoods. The settlement was about the only neighborhood institution that sought to serve all ethnic groups, overcome ethnic rivalries, and forge neighborhood unity.[26] However, not all ethnic groups responded with the same enthusiasm to the settlement. Italians were underrepresented among Hull House users in part because the Catholic church resented the settlement's successful campaign to establish another public school when the church was trying to establish a parochial one. Also, the predominantly female staff at Hull House posed a problem for patriarchal Italians until Hull House found male leaders for Italian boys' groups.[27] In spite of its limitations, settlement houses were the best means of trying to achieve social unity in diverse neighborhoods. Furthermore, it was through these daily activities that settlement houses forged their link with their neighbors.

The most praise for settlements in dealing with immigrants is in regard to their role in helping individuals "move up" economically and socially. Hiram House's outstanding success was Manuel Levine, a sixteen-year-old Russian-Jewish immigrant who could barely speak English when he asked head worker George Bellamy for help. Bellamy found Levine a tutor and helped to get him into law school. Eventually Levine became a municipal judge and a volunteer at Hiram House.[28] Such success stories were possible, in part because of the occupational structure. In Levine's time, a person could go to law school without a college degree; and in general, upward mobility was easier. The settlement house was an excellent resource for a motivated immigrant.

A question related to how well the settlement served the immigrant is the one of whether settlements were "democratic" institutions or "social control." On the "social control" side, some notorious industrialists were major funders of early settlements. Henry Clay Frick provided Pittsburgh's Kingsley House with a building in 1901 and in other ways supported the settlement.[29] Cleveland's Alta House was named after a daughter of John D. Rockefeller. George Bellamy, who started out as a reformer, became increasingly enamored of his wealthy funders, adopted their social beliefs, and aped their life-style as best he could.[30] Meanwhile, head worker Robbins Gilman of New York's University Settlement lost his job after publicly defending the IWW.[31] These pressures encouraged settlement houses to avoid controversy. Nor were they doing much to encourage grass-roots community organizing. Instead, settlement workers tended to impose their own leadership on the neighborhood, an approach partly necessitated by diversity and rivalries within their neighborhoods, but also one in keeping with the general methods of Progressive reform. But if one wants to define "democratic" as an open society of opportunity for individuals to improve themselves, the Progressive Era settlement should qualify.

The major characteristics of the Progressive Era settlements may be summarized in the settlement buildings. Some settlements started out in large houses that had been built prior to their neighborhood's deterioration. These houses continued to form the core of such flagship settlements as Hull House, Henry Street, and South End House. As the settlements prospered, they built new quarters. The original Hull mansion was surrounded by a quadrangle of new buildings done in the "old English" style. By 1908, Hull House covered a whole city block, overwhelming the neighborhood, and clashing architecturally with its surroundings. Progressive Era settlements, if they could afford it, built big buildings in their attempts to become *the* community centers of their neighborhoods. They used "old English" architecture, rather than the architecture of Italy or other countries, because they were trying to bring some American cultural refinement to the slum. Also, the sharing of the refined home life of the settlement residents was reflected in the interior decor. According to Chicago Commons head Graham Taylor: "The settlement house is really an addition to every little tenement home. Its books and pictures, the nursery and play spaces, the lobby and the living room, the music and flowers, the cheery fireplaces and lamps, the auditorium for assemblies or social occasions and dancing, are an extension of the all too scant home equipment of most of the neighbors."[32]

These buildings were a combination home for the residents, neighborhood town hall, and community center with club, class, and game rooms plus gymnasiums and an occasional theater or swimming pool. They symbolized the chief characteristics of the Progressive Era settlement—residence, "community" action for reform, and the bringing of "culture" to the immigrants. Reflecting their "*for* the neighborhood" approach, they made no attempt to fit in with their surroundings, but rather to dominate and culturally educate.

The "for" the neighborhood approach of the Progressive Era settlement leads to charges of paternalism. With the partial exception of Hudson Guild, settlement workers eschewed grass-roots organizing in favor of "interpreting" the poor to the rest of society. They were productive "interpreters," producing many publications and contributing to a variety of reforms improving life in the slums. Of course, their "improvements" reflected their middle-class values, and so they can be charged with social control. However, settlements served working-class people along with the poor; and in many ways, working-class values may not be that different from middle-class values. Low-income neighborhoods contained a number of people who aspired to middle-class status and who voluntarily took advantage of what the settlements had to offer. The settlements did help many of these people join the middle class. In that sense, they were fairly effective, democratic institutions.

THE INTERWAR PERIOD

With World War I, social conditions changed abruptly and so did settlements. The war cut the flow of immigrants into settlement neighborhoods to a trickle; and, later, quota legislation made the trickle permanent. Meanwhile, the war created job opportunities for blacks in cities, generating the first major black migration northward, which affected some settlement neighborhoods. The war also changed how settlements were funded, which in turn had implications for professionalism as well as social control.

Settlements had never done much work with blacks, in part because of the difficulty of raising money to fund operations in black neighborhoods. In fact, one reason Mary White Ovington became actively involved with the establishment of the NAACP was her failure to raise money for a settlement for blacks.[33] The few Progressive Era settlements that were established for blacks were poorly funded and short-lived. For example, in Chicago in 1930, only one house that served blacks had a full program.[34]

When blacks moved into settlement neighborhoods, the settlement workers responded in various ways. In 1919, Pittsburgh's Kingsley House abandoned its new black neighbors and moved to a new location to continue serving whites.[35] Chicago's Eli Bates House closed its doors. On the other hand, when a settlement, such as Chicago's Abraham Lincoln Centre, made a valiant effort to run an integrated program, white neighbors tended to quit using the house.[36] The end result was usually no service or segregated service. Thus, settlements tended to give in to the prejudices of their white neighbors during this period rather than impose more racially enlightened views.

On the other hand, settlements were not as responsive to the black community as they should have been. In the 1920s, some notable settlements for blacks were established. One of these, Minneapolis' Phyllis Wheatley House, had a black director active in civil rights causes, W. Gertrude Brown. In spite of Brown's success in developing the settlement over a period of thirteen years and support for her in the settlement's black neighborhood, a white-dominated board forced her resignation in 1937.[37] The settlement movement was becoming more aware of a growing black presence in its neighborhoods; but, to a larger extent, it shared the racial prejudice of the era in laying a rather poor foundation for its work with blacks that was to follow World War II.

The patriotism surrounding World War I also contributed to the rapid spread of the Community Chest. Formerly, each settlement had to raise its own funds. Some, with gifted head workers and wealthy boards, did quite well; others relied on church support and varied by how much proselytizing they did in return for that support. Still others were "shoestring" operations. The Chest eliminated reliance on church support and tended to standardize the level of funding among settlements as well as other aspects of their operation. However, it added an additional layer of bureaucracy along with social control. Should a settlement board allow a controversial program in a house, the local Community Chest, which controlled the house's budget, was likely to stop it. In practice, few settlements risked the wrath of Chest officials. Consequently, when the Great Depression hit and the unemployed had their local relief checks cut, eliminating money for rent and other necessities, it was settlements in the non-Chest cities of New York and Chicago that organized protest groups and engaged in demonstrations and other actions to get adequate relief programs.[38] Where it existed, the Community Chest had a dampening effect on action promoting labor and welfare issues.

The Community Chest also promoted professionalism, although that had limited impact on settlements during the interwar years. In the 1920s, the social work profession turned away from its earlier interest in reform to emphasize psychological approaches to problems. That fit in with the political conservatism of the 1920s, plus psychology offered a teachable technique along with less social controversy. Few settlements hired M.S.W.s during these years, but they did put more emphasis on small groups and the psychological dynamics that went on in them. They also felt pressure to specialize as social agencies began to proliferate. Finally, the traditional settlement method of residing or volunteering in the house while interacting with their clients as "neighbors" was becoming decidedly unfashionable.[39]

Meanwhile, in 1911, settlement houses had banded together to form their own national organization, the National Federation of Settlements. This organization acquired its first paid executive in 1934. The growing importance of the settlements' national organization coincided with the advent of the New Deal and the shifting of action in welfare reform to Washington. During the peak of WPA, settlement houses were given as many government-paid workers as they could supervise. One settlement with its own staff of eight took on eighty-two WPA workers.[40] The WPA workers tended to crowd out the well-to-do volunteers, most of whom did not return after WPA was abolished. Settlement workers were also involved in designing the Social Security Act, which included not only the pension program, but also unemployment compensation, aid programs based on need (Aid to Dependent Children, Old Age Assistance, and Aid to the Blind), and some minor medical programs. The twenty-three members of the Advisory Council that designed what is basically our welfare structure today included National Federation of Settlements president Helen Hall and three other settlement-connected people.[41] With welfare shifting from the local to the federal level, the National Federation of Settlements took on added importance as the organization through which settlements lobbied to better conditions in their neighborhoods.

In summary, the interwar years presented the settlement with some serious challenges. With immigrants disappearing, blacks moving into their neighborhoods, a growing emphasis on professionalism, the impact of Community Chest bureaucracy, and political conservatism followed by sudden and massive federal welfare programs, the settlement of the interwar years no longer seemed quite so relevant. Methods that had worked in the past seemed inappropriate. It was increasingly difficult for settlements to attract residents and volunteers. Those leaders such as Helen Hall, who tried their hand at writing, lacked the creative brilliance of their earlier counterparts. Jane Addams died in 1935, and no one came along in the settlement movement to replace her in the public mind. Settlements were still involved in reform, but they were hardly central to it. The advent of the Community Chest meant more pressure to function as social control agencies, while the changing ethnic and racial character of their neighborhoods raised the dilemma of how democratic in a grass-roots sense the settlements were or could be. No longer exciting, experimental agencies, settlement houses were starting to realize that they would become anachronistic if they didn't make fundamental changes.

WORLD WAR II

World War II accelerated certain national trends, such as an enlarged role for government and more concern for civil rights issues, but it also disrupted settlement houses. It delayed their profession-alization. A wartime shortage of workers meant that houses had to get by with skeleton staffs. Also, the war temporarily reordered set-tlement house priorities. Programming was skewed. Outside agen-cies, such as the Office of Civil Defense and the Red Cross, engaged in joint efforts with the settlements and, to a certain extent, sup-planted some traditional activities. Other settlement programs, such as day care, community organization, and consumer action, took on added importance. Then came the challenge to "reconvert" to peacetime work, this time with the new, professional workers.

When the United States entered the war, settlement houses quickly went from relatively stable staffs to rapid resignations and a man-power shortage. Cleveland's University Settlement illustrated the en-suing chaos. In the fall of 1941, the settlement had three full-time workers—two men and a woman. By the summer of 1942, both men were in the army. Two part-time workers replaced them. By the fall of 1943, the settlement had managed to get back up to three full-time workers when another man left, and a woman replaced him. Then half of the male student workers left. Other part-time workers tended to go into the military almost as soon as the settlement hired them. Staff supervision and training were haphazard. Somewhat sar-castically, the settlement's board commented, "Even the Director has difficulty remembering who is on the staff as of today."[42] Further-more, other war-related agencies besides the military drained settle-ment staffs. Some older men, such as Ben Stoddard, who had been at St. Paul's Neighborhood House since 1923, left to work with the Red Cross recreation programs abroad.[43] Insufficient numbers of competent male workers particularly weakened the boys' programs in settlements.

The houses also lost female workers. Some went into defense work, such as the South Orange, New Jersey, girls' worker, who claimed that her defense faculty job paid three times her settlement job.[44] The Red Cross was another major competitor for women settlement house workers. It claimed, among other women, the most prominent settlement house leader, Helen Hall. As a young woman in her twenties during World War I, Hall had organized army recreation programs in Southeast Asia.[45] In 1942, she took a leave of absence from her job as head of New York's Henry Street Settlement to be-come director of American Red Cross rest homes and clubs in the

South Pacific. Hall returned to the settlement field, but a number of others did not. Some settlements were unable to reassemble adequate-sized staffs until a couple of years after the war ended. In reassembling staffs, for the first time large numbers of settlements eagerly competed for holders of the M.S.W.

Meanwhile, volunteers became scarce. Professionalism raised questions about giving volunteers major responsibilities. Also, the extensive use of low-income WPA and National Youth Administration (NYA) workers in settlement houses lowered the status of volunteers. During the peak of WPA and NYA, these government-sponsored workers had increased the staffs of some settlement houses tenfold. By 1940, only small numbers of WPA and NYA workers remained.[46] They were completely gone by 1943,[47] and few volunteers were available to take their places as wartime employment and other activities cut into their time. At Chicago's Benton House after several leaderless teenage boys' groups got out of control, breaking windows and furniture, two male board members were forced to volunteer. Because of the shortage of club leadership, Benton House ran at 56 percent capacity.[48] The old, free-spirited volunteering on the part of the well-to-do that had been at the heart of Progressive Era settlements came largely to an end.

In addition to staff shortages, the war affected programming in a number of ways. The effects of the draft and the boom in employment caused a particularly severe membership decline in the age range sixteen to twenty-five. To compensate, settlements placed more emphasis on work with youngsters under age sixteen and the elderly.

The war also meant that youngsters had more money and less supervision. In Cleveland, the juvenile delinquency rate increased 41 percent. Since younger teens like to ape the behavior of older ones, some settlements began modeling programs on the USO canteens.[49] For example, Cleveland's University Settlement remodeled its recreation hall into a "Soda Bar."[50] The teenage canteen, a place where youngsters could dance to records and drink Coca Cola, became a fixture of some settlements and lasted in popularity well into the 1950s.

Programs for adults also took on a wartime flavor. These activities included forming a Service Wives Club, holding regular meetings for parents of servicemen, helping immigrants write letters to their sons in service, sending a newsletter to boys from the neighborhood in service, and helping war-motivated immigrants achieve citizenship. After the war, the influx of displaced persons would temporarily increase the settlements' work with immigrants.

Wartime programming also involved coordinating with war-related agencies. Several settlements operated like a USO. They put on dances and offered sports and ethnic dinners to servicemen stationed nearby. At least one house, Alexander on Maui in Hawaii, actually became an operating agency of the USO.[51] Cooperative projects with the Red Cross were common. Settlements offered first aid classes along with sewing and knitting groups.[52] Settlement houses also helped Civil Defense build patriotism through informational meetings. The shock of Pearl Harbor triggered quite an interest in air raid precautions, even in the continental United States. Pails of water, sand, shovels, and pumps began appearing in the halls of some settlement houses, along with the necessity to hold meetings to explain the need for air raid precautions, rationing, price controls, and just to build up civilian morale.[53]

The war did have implications for settlement houses as agencies of grass-roots democracy. From their participation in Civil Defense, not from Stanton Coit, settlement workers learned the block approach to community organizing. Settlements organized neighbors living on given blocks into groups which elected block captains (called "captains" in an attempt to avoid the inevitable "blockheads" joke). Settlements then called the block captains together into block councils, which sponsored well-attended community meetings and rallies.[54] Some block councils got involved in community planning. The one at St. Martha's House in Philadelphia fought the establishment of a slaughterhouse in the neighborhood and ran a Job Opportunities Program for teenagers. With settlement house help, at least twenty-four of St. Martha's block clubs survived into the War on Poverty, when block organizing saw a revival.[55] However, St. Martha's prolonged success with block clubs was unusual.

Another settlement activity which gained added emphasis because of the war was day care. Day care had long been a staple settlement function. The first activity Jane Addams began at Hull House was a kindergarten for children whose mothers worked.[56] Settlements had continued to run nursery schools. With World War II, working mothers, many of whom were employed in defense industries, demanded more day care. Settlements helped campaign for federal day care subsidies by publicizing the long waiting lists for their own day care facilities, doing studies to document the need, and stressing adequate day care standards. Their efforts paid off with the inclusion of federal day care subsidies in the Lanham, or Community Assistance, Act. Under this law, local public agencies, usually boards of education, received federal funds to run day care centers. These agencies varied in their willingness to subsidize settlement house facilities. In Cleveland, twelve day care centers located in social agencies received funding, and Karamu House also got Lanham Act funds to cover two-thirds of the construction cost of a new combination theater and nursery building.[57] On the other hand, only two Chicago settlements received Lanham Act funds.[58] WPA had provided a direct federal-city relationship. The Lanham Act was one more step on the road to a direct federal government/private agency relationship. This enlarged role of the federal government would benefit private agencies, such as settlement houses, but it would also make them more vulnerable to shifting federal policies. The grants would not always be there for settlements.

In making funds available for day care, the federal government was more interested in furthering the war than in promoting day care. After the war, settlements joined in the campaign to continue federal day care subsidies, but the federal program ended in 1946. In spite of growing numbers of working mothers, popular support for day care waned. New York settlements appear to have been unique in getting state and local funds to take the place of federal day care subsidies. These funds supported day care centers in thirty-nine New York settlements through 1947. Then the state withdrew support because the "Horan Report" charged that day care actually contributed to juvenile delinquency and was not widely accepted.[59] Stanley Isaacs, president of United Neighborhood Houses and a Manhattan politician, took issue with the attitude that working mothers who couldn't afford day care on their own should quit work and go on relief. Isaacs said that that would lower family living standards and morale.[60] Settlements led the way in organizing the Day Care Council, composed of fifty-eight private agencies running ninety-two day care centers. The best the council was able to do was to maintain the level of funding coming through the city. To their credit, settlements never adopted the prevailing, negative attitude toward day care.

Part of the settlement's purpose in being was to work for basic reforms—for better housing, better race relations, better welfare and social insurance programs. When the war began, settlements realized that social progress would be retarded by huge war expenditures. They willingly set these social issues aside as they geared their programming to the war effort. As the war drew to a close, settlements faced reconversion to peacetime with enthusiasm. To them, World War II had been an idealistic crusade. They sought to transfer some of this idealism, especially the feeling that our men should not have fought and died in vain, to an assault on domestic social problems.

In looking at the heritage that settlement houses brought to post–World War II social problems, paternalism seems to be a key element. As well-to-do residents in the slums, settlement workers sought to bridge class lines and promote reform by "interpreting" the poor to the rest of society. The method was effective in the Progressive Era when settlement houses were central to a wide variety of reforms. Through their clubs, classes, and personal contacts, they also helped upwardly mobile immigrants take advantage of opportunity in America. The conservative 1920s brought their reform successes to a halt. When reform resurfaced in the 1930s, settlements outside New York and Chicago found the Community Chest a new barrier to controversial activity. Nevertheless, an expanded professional organization, the National Federation of Settlements, and selected leaders carried on the reform tradition in the New Deal. However, as residents in the slums rather than professionals in possession of the M.S.W., they increasingly lacked prestige. Furthermore, as their slum neighborhoods changed, the settlement residents would be increasingly charged with being agents of social control. By 1945, their original method of well-to-do people residing in the settlement house had become more of a liability than an asset.

CHAPTER 2

THE TRADITIONAL SETTLEMENT
HOUSE PROFESSIONALIZES:
AN OVERVIEW OF
CHANGING METHODS

A FUNDAMENTAL CONFLICT EXISTED BETWEEN THE original settlement house idea and the growing trend toward professionalism in social work. The original settlement idea was that well-to-do people would "settle" in a slum neighborhood, gain added insights into poverty by residing there, and help the poor around them on the basis that they were their neighbors. On the other hand, the professional idea was that people with a desire to help others would first go to a social work school where they would learn theories and techniques. The schools would certify their graduates as competent by awarding them master of social work degrees (the M.S.W.). These M.S.W. degree holders would then acquire professional jobs, which were separate from their personal lives. On the job, an M.S.W. helped people on the basis of professional expertise through a professional, not a personal or neighborly, relationship. The separation of the professional from the personal could not be reconciled with the traditional settlement house idea. Something had to give, and it was residence in the settlement house.

In place of residents, the post–World War II settlement house hired increasing numbers of M.S.W.s, changed its methods and image, enlarged its professional organizations, and attracted different kinds of people as settlement house workers. Professionalization was the underlying cause of these changes, and its impact on settlements raises a number of questions. What was the nature of the new "professional" settlement house or neighborhood center? How did professionalization affect who became settlement workers, and what were the workers' career patterns? What role did professional organizations play in the settlement house movement? Did professionalization make the settlement house more democratic or more an agency of social control?

THE CHANGING NATURE OF
THE SETTLEMENT HOUSE: NEIGHBORHOOD FOCUS

In spite of professionalization and the accompanying disappearance of settlement residents, the settlement house's goals, orientation, and methods continued to focus on the neighborhood. However, professionalization brought with it greater emphasis on working with people in smaller groups. Furthermore, since the Progressive Era, a multitude of public and private agencies and recreational facilities became available to slum residents. No longer the only major place for wholesome recreation in their neighborhoods, many settlements came to regard their large, old buildings as "white elephants." Settlement workers were also tending to perceive their neighborhoods as smaller units. Thus, after World War II, many settlements eagerly unloaded their large buildings and moved into new, smaller, and more cost-efficient ones. The shrinking size of their buildings reflected less of a tendency to try to function as the focal point of their neighborhood.

Post–World War II settlement workers also took a more professional approach to the interior design of their buildings. Jane Addams and other early settlement workers had deliberately aimed to create a homelike atmosphere of good taste. The early settlement house parlors were to give "immigrant women a glimpse of middle-class luxury and refinement,"[1] which settlement workers hoped would encourage their immigrant neighbors to adopt middle-class values. However, after World War II, settlement workers were more concerned about ease of maintenance and supervision along with protection against vandalism. While their attempts to provide a tasteful, homelike atmosphere did not completely disappear, post–World War II settlement buildings have a more functional, efficient, institutional character about them. Thus, the design and decoration of recent settlement house buildings reflects the emphasis on professional, as opposed to personal or neighborly, relationships.

Traditionally, most settlement workers had cultivated neighborly relationships largely by working with people in recreational groups and interacting with them on a normal basis. In writing my history of the 1930s settlement house movement, I was critical of settlements for emphasizing recreation and not devoting more resources to social change. Recreational programs usually required costly facilities and staff to maintain and so seemed to be a drain on settlement resources. However, in looking at settlements over a longer time span, these nonsocial action activities take on added significance. They become the key to maintaining a continuous relationship with the neighborhood, even in periods unfriendly to social change. Providing recreation and, to a lesser extent, individual services has given settlements stability over time. Also, recreational programs have given settlement workers a relationship with their neighborhoods on which to build more serious social reform efforts. In a settlement house, recreation is more than an end in itself.

However, with professionalization has come more of a tendency for settlement workers to interact with their neighbors on the basis of the neighbors' personal problems. From their earlier days, settlements had always offered some individual counseling. Larger settlement houses often had a full-time staff position devoted to "friendly visiting." By the 1920s, social work schools were well on their way toward transforming the "friendly visitors" into caseworkers. The schools gave casework major emphasis in part because they could draw on the subject matter and techniques of psychology for curriculum. Reform techniques were not considered a fitting subject for social work schools until the 1960s. Consequently, the increasing dominance of the social work schools diverted the profession away from its early interests in reform. After World War II, some settlements showed the effects of social work's high regard for psychology by developing psychological and psychiatric services and by adding more caseworkers as well as psychiatric consultants to their staffs.[2] Social action activity in settlements correspondingly suffered.

Just how far settlements should go in the casework and mental hygiene direction was a subject settlement workers debated in the 1950s. Mental hygiene programs were especially strong in New York settlements because of state funding as well as the prestige the social work profession accorded them. Bill Brueckner, head of Chicago Commons, worried that the "uniqueness" of the settlement would be lost if too many houses added mental hygiene clinics while departing from their traditional pattern of interacting with their neighbors on a normal, as opposed to a psychological problem, basis. He thought that mental health clinics belonged in either public agencies or private family service agencies. While a settlement might sponsor one as a demonstration project or for research purposes, it should not become an ongoing service of major proportions.[3] Nevertheless, a number of New York settlements added mental hygiene clinics, including Henry Street and Hudson Guild. The National Federation was also concerned that Mattie Rhodes Settlement in Kansas City would cease to function as a settlement and evolve into a group therapy institution.[4] Too much activity of this kind could undermine the willingness of people who saw themselves as normal to make use of regular settlement services, and the settlement house's relationship with the neighborhood as a whole would suffer.

Within social work, even group work reflected the influence of psychology through its emphasis on individual adjustment. Settlement workers with the M.S.W. were most likely to have specialized in group work. Thus, they became more concerned with the therapeutic value of recreation. A typical group was the Wednesday morning coffee hour for seventeen mothers of multiproblem families at Philadelphia's Germantown Settlement. Group activities ranged from a Christmas party for their total of eighty-nine children to meeting with the local public housing manager. The women discussed their personal problems, which included missing husbands, alcoholic husbands, illegitimate children, and even hunger. They were supportive in helping one another face these problems, better utilize community facilities, and increase their self-esteem.[5] Occasionally, other settlements organized groups for the physically handicapped, particularly the mentally retarded. In the tension over whether settlement houses should interact with their neighbors on a "normal" or a "problem" basis, professionalism tended to add weight to the problem orientation. The effect was probably to weaken the settlement's neighborhood ties.

THE DECLINE OF RESIDENCE AND VOLUNTEERING IN THE SETTLEMENT HOUSE

If psychological applications were very much in tune with professionalism, the practice of settlement workers living in the settlement house was at odds with it. In the early days, some of the settlement residents were on the house staff; and others, who worked elsewhere, did volunteer work for the settlement in return for the privilege of living in the house. After World War I, residence in a settlement lost much of its initial vatality; but it continued into the post–World War II period, getting a brief, but temporary, boost from the postwar housing shortage.

The ideal resident group included people from a variety of professions and backgrounds. Residing together in the settlement, they had the opportunity to exchange ideas and make wider contacts in the community. Albert J. Kennedy, head of New York's University Settlement in the 1930s and 1940s, noted, "Much of the best social action in settlements has come out of the work of residents and volunteers who have used their settlement experience to influence the thinking of associates in their own professions, such as law, education, medicine, etc."[6] One might also add that volunteers and residents not on the house payroll were freer to act in controversial matters than were employed professionals. Thus, a concerned corps of residents and volunteers could add an additional dimension to the house's social action efforts.

Unfortunately, the ideal resident group was becoming harder to find. Reasons why include professionalization, a growing trend on the part of young people to prefer the independence of their own apartments, and the feeling that living as well as working in a neighborhood was "too large an investment of one's self and one's family."[7] Hull House continued to attract some prominent people, such as Robert C. Weaver, who lived there after World War II and in

1965 became the first black to hold a cabinet post. However, other would-be residents may have been put off by the routine sort of volunteer service typically demanded of residents. At Hull House, that ranged from directing clubs to operating the switchboard.[8] In 1947, the head of Hull House, Russell Ballard, tried to get out of residing there for family reasons. The board unanimously voted to fire him if he did, but then softened the blow by giving him his Hull House apartment free of charge.[9] Hull House did not abandon residence until its original buildings were torn down in 1963. By then, the typical resident group at Hull House and elsewhere was composed of settlement staff plus students from nearby colleges.

For a number of settlements, the debate over the value of residing in the house culminated when urban renewal or freeway construction dictated a move to a new neighborhood, when residents interested in the settlement program became hard to find, or when the residents' rooms were needed for some other aspect of the program. In the mid-1950s, when Chicago Commons was planning a new building, head William Brueckner sought the advice of several leaders in the settlement field. One danger of residence in the house was that the resident group would turn in on itself. John McDowell, executive director of the National Federation of Settlements in the 1950s, believed that the main purpose of residence was for the settlement workers to identify with the neighborhood, something that could be better accomplished by living in a neighborhood dwelling rather than the settlement house. To preserve resident group interaction, McDowell suggested that a house's settlement workers gather weekly for lunch or dinner. McDowell noted the trend away from residence in the house and summarized the complaints most workers had against it. Residence interfered with family life (most of the new male professional workers were married), it was an excuse to pay a low salary, and the space could be better utilized in the regular program.[10] When the Commons did move into a new building in 1958, living space for the director and one to three residents only was provided.[11] However, the Commons continued to serve lunch and dinner for staff and volunteers.[12] As for McDowell's comments about residing in the neighborhood, that was something settlements never required.

Criteria for admission to the National Federation of Settlements reflected this trend away from residence. All that the national organization required of its member settlements in this respect by 1969 was that the professional staff show some evidence of identifying with the concerns of the neighborhoods they served.[13] In England, where the settlement house movement began, some settlements had also developed without residents. The English response was to have two national organizations, one for those with residence and one for those without.[14] If that had been done in the United States, the organization with residents would have had only four member houses in 1970. By 1986, probably the only United States settlement to still have residents was Henry Street, where executive director Daniel Kronenfeld and some students lived.

During March 1970, I had the pleasure of living at Henry Street. The resident group of about a dozen or so consisted mainly of social work students at Columbia and some undergraduates from a Southern black college on a work/study assignment in New York. In addition, some settlement staff lived in apartments that Henry Street owned in neighboring cooperatives, and Henry Street head Bert Beck lived with his wife and young twins in the apartment formerly occupied by the previous director, Helen Hall, and her predecessor, Lillian Wald. Understandably, Mrs. Beck was concerned about such aspects as family privacy and drug traffic on the adjacent playground. On the surface, I saw little "social action" taking place. None of the residents did any volunteer work, and the only meeting we had to protest the quality of the food coming out of the kitchen.

Yet the resident group made the dining room possible. In the bright, yellow dining room overlooking Henry Street with brass objects given to Lillian Wald on the sideboard and coffee passed around in demitasse cups after dinner, one met some very interesting people. It was there that I first discovered the significance of Mobilization for Youth. The dining room helped Henry Street unify a decentralized staff, and it attracted outsiders to the settlement. Some, like me, would treasure the experience and publicize the settlement. While we residents did almost nothing directly for the neighborhood, we ourselves benefited and, hopefully, so did Henry Street by reaching out to us. However, as residence facilities virtually came to an end, settlement houses lost their most visibly unique and identifiable feature.

Given the impact of professionalism, volunteering tended to go the same way as residence in the settlement. Professionalism stressed the importance of training and possession of an expert body of knowledge in order for the worker to be effective. An untrained, uneducated amateur could do a great deal of damage in certain situations. Thus, social agencies were reluctant to give much responsibility to volunteers. Also, settlements occasionally found volunteers to be undependable, incompetent, or inexperienced. The bad neighborhoods in which settlements were located discouraged other would-be volunteers.

With the drop in volunteers from traditional sources, such as well-to-do housewives and professionals, settlements turned increasingly to using volunteers from their own neighborhoods. Neighborhood volunteers gave the settlement more contact with the surrounding area, and some developed into indigenous leaders. However, with fewer volunteers from outside the neighborhood, less opportunity existed for the settlement to bridge class lines and extend its influence throughout the city. Thus, this avenue of settlement houses influence beyond the neighborhood narrowed.

However, through volunteering, the university tie has remained. From the beginning of settlement houses, universities regarded them as laboratories for their students. In connection with course work in education, sociology, and psychology, undergraduates continued to be coerced or required to "volunteer" several hours a week. Of greater value to the settlements were the graduate fieldwork students, who often amounted to half-time professionals. To get these students, settlements had to offer trained supervision, which was a major factor in their hiring of M.S.W.s on their regular staffs. Thus, the schools were kept busy filling the demand for M.S.W.s, which they were also creating. Besides influencing settlement house staffing, the schools' faculties played a major role as grant evaluators and program reviewers when settlements sought funds. Thus, it was increasingly important for settlements to have a strongly professional image.

THE NEW PROFESSIONAL
SETTLEMENT HOUSE WORKERS

In 1939, virtually no settlement house workers possessed the M.S.W. During the ensuing decade, most of the remaining people who had headed settlement houses first in the Progressive Era retired. Robbins Gilman had counted around ten "pioneers" at the 1940 National Federation of Settlements convention.[15] Gilman himself retired from Minneapolis' Northeast Neighborhood House in 1948. George Bellamy retired from Cleveland's Hiram House about the same time, a position he had held since 1896.[16] Mary Simkhovitch, an important figure in the history of public housing, retired from New York's Greenwich House around 1946. As these people left, the trend toward hiring M.S.W.s gathered momentum.

During World War II, Albert J. Kennedy, the "elder statesman" of the settlement movement, called for the "wholesale hiring of workers with professional training *to revive the influence of the settlements*" (Italics added).[17] By 1947, the National Federation estimated that one in eight workers in professional positions had an M.S.W.[18] The trend seems to have reached a peak in the early 1960s. At that time, Chicago Commons reported that out of its ten professional workers, eight had master's degrees.[19] (The average settlement house staff included over four workers, with the largest number of houses having five to nine full-time workers plus part-time staff.)[20] By 1970, the M.S.W. had become the prerequisite not only for head workers (the term now was usually "executive director"), but also for a variety of subordinate positions, such as program director.

The new professionals saw themselves and their work differently. They usually declined to live in the settlement house. They tended to think of the house's neighbors as clients, in effect telling them, "We're helping you because we have M.S.W.s, not because we are your neighbors." In place of spontaneity and being available around the clock, they made appointments and "treatment plans." Instead of seeking to do *with* the neighborhood, they sought to do *for* the neighborhood. Their "professional" detachment from the neighborhood was not only physical, it was psychological.

In addition to certifying expertise, the M.S.W. literally paid dividends. If a board member objected to an M.S.W.'s style or beliefs, possession of the degree was one line of defense. The degree also conferred a certain amount of status. When Robert Armstrong joined the staff of Erie Neighborhood House in 1959, he was the first to be hired with professional training. The Erie board tended to regard the staff as servants, a role the staff literally filled when they served the board members dinner at their monthly meetings. That stopped with Armstrong. When the staff was upgraded, the board/staff relationship became more equal. Along with added respect, contributions to the settlement from the sponsoring suburban churches also increased.[21] For most other settlements, Community Chest pressure was a major factor in deciding to hire M.S.W.s.

The new professional workers showed different career patterns, particularly in their tendency to switch agencies as their careers progressed. In the early days, the settlement movement attracted a number of women and some men just out of college who remained with their chosen settlement house throughout their careers. Even when a socially ambitious man like George Bellamy was offered a post in 1910 as head of a national organization, the Playground Association, he turned it down to remain as head of the settlement he founded, Hiram House.[22] Bellamy had studied for the ministry, as had several other leading male settlement workers. They may have remained with their settlement houses out of humanitarian motives. In addition, women may have found agency-hopping up the social work career ladder difficult due to sex discrimination. However, the major reason why both men and women settlement house workers tended to stay with one house in the early days may well have been a reluctance to leave the network of personal relationships constructed over the years. Bellamy valued his friendships with his board members. When Helen Hall left Philadelphia's University Settlement in 1933 for Henry Street Settlement, the loneliness of being in a neighborhood of strangers bothered her. She quickly reached out to Henry Street's neighbors, asking them for their friendship,[23] and didn't leave until she retired thirty-four years later. Personal relationships built up over a long period of time were at the heart of the original settlement house concept.

On the other hand, the new, professional settlement house workers were far more mobile. One of the earliest M.S.W.s to run a settlement, W. T. McCullough graduated in 1933 with a specialty in group work from the School of Applied Social Science, Western Reserve University. While heading Alta House, he began working part-time for Cleveland's Welfare Federation. After several years, he was full-time with the federation, and he spent the rest of his career in federation and Community Chest positions. Several holders of the M.S.W. eventually left the settlement field for academia. In 1958,

Clyde Murray resigned as head of Manhattanville Community Centers to become the assistant dean of the University of Chicago School of Social Work. That same year, John McDowell left the executive directorship of the National Federation of Settlements to become the dean of Boston University's School of Social Work. Other settlement workers left the field to take teaching positions. Still others moved back and forth between various private and public social agencies.

As they professionalized, settlements themselves developed a tendency to go outside their field for top executives. For example, prior to assuming the head of Henry Street Settlement in 1967, Bert Beck had worked for the Children's Bureau, the National Association of Social Workers, and Mobilization for Youth, but had no settlement house experience. He stayed with Henry Street for ten years until moving on to a research and family service agency, the Community Service Society. About the only settlement experience Walter Smart had before becoming associate director of the National Federation of Settlements in 1970 was his fieldwork placement as a graduate student. Most of his professional career had been with public housing. With settlements placing less emphasis on neighborly relationships, professionals, who were more receptive to the career ladder concept, were freer to move.

Mobility seems to be even more popular in the 1980s. In a recent discussion with five male Minneapolis settlement directors, the middle-aged ones, rather than the elderly ones, began to speculate on who would replace them. One holder of the M.S.W. said he originally planned to say with his agency for only five years, had been there for eight, and had some interest in eventually moving into a job related to education. He and another talked about burnout. The third had come to his agency from the low-income housing field; and the fourth, who had an M.S.W., had moved on to United Way after spending twenty-three years with Pillsbury-Waite House. The fifth had entered the settlement field in 1950 with only a B.S. in education, stayed with East Side Settlement in Minneapolis for fifteen years, directed another settlement for seven years, then returned to East Side where he is still the director. While this sample was small, relative youth and the M.S.W. appear to be factors coinciding with a pattern in which a settlement house or community center has become only one rung on a career ladder.[24]

Another major difference between the early settlement leaders and their successors was social stature. When social work was developing, society valued the settlement worker's role as interpreter of the poor. However, with the development of mass communications, the poor today often speak more effectively for themselves. Also, settlement workers lost social status as more specialized organizations emerged to deal with problems of social welfare and reform.[25] Still another aspect of their changed status was the settlement workers' own social class background.

By the time of World War II, settlements had been around for a couple of generations; and immigrant youngsters who had once patronized the settlement houses had, in some cases, managed to go to college. Some returned to settlement houses, this time as staff, volunteers, and board members. They were difficult to spot because they didn't usually call attention to their immigrant background. In at least one case, a settlement worker changed his name from a Polish one to Anderson. The settlement, which had a Polish constituency, hired him only after being sure that he was not ashamed of his Polish heritage.[26] Until the 1960s, few settlement workers called attention to a lower-class or ethnic background.

One of the more prominent settlement workers, Lillie Peck, was the daughter of an Austrian immigrant. Her father migrated first to New York City, then eventually became the public librarian in a small town in New York. I went through the National Federation of Settlements records for the 1930s (Peck was the federation's executive secretary), plus additional records, obituaries, a memorial pamphlet, and so on without realizing how close Peck herself was to immigrant life. About the only clue was that she had a remarkable fluency in German for someone born in the United States. A chance inquiry to the Gloversville Free Library, which her father once headed, yielded the immigrant background information. In Gloversville, the Peck family belonged to the Congregational Church, but their origins may have been Jewish.[27] Thus, it is difficult to gauge the impact at this time of settlement workers coming from an ethnic background when they themselves did not make an issue of their ethnicity.

Occasionally, someone from an ethnic background headed a settlement. Guido Tardi was one. He grew up in the neighborhood around Hull House, quite self-conscious of his modest Italian background, and was very ambitious. He worked part-time as a group worker at Hull House,[28] eventually earned a master's degree in social work, and moved on to increasingly responsible settlement positions until 1961, when he became head of Mary McDowell Settlement.[29] That settlement, which was losing community and contributor support, did not fare well under Tardi, perhaps because Tardi was "too ethnic." On the other hand, Michael Rachwalski grew up on Chicago's Near Northwest Side,[30] became director of Northwestern University Settlement in 1947,[31] and remained in that position for decades. And of course Bill Brueckner of Chicago Commons, one of the outstanding settlement leaders during the postwar period, was an immigrant who left Nazi Germany for the United States when he was around thirty-nine. Referring to someone as "too ethnic" may be more of a social-class comment than an actual reference to immigrant status. Whether or not an immigrant did well as a settlement director seems more related to personal factors, including social-class background and individual style, rather than ethnic background. Because post–World War II settlements were working less with immigrants, the ethnic background of settlement workers does not seem to be of very much significance, but social-class background was.

Since the late 1960s, a large number of blacks from inner city backgrounds have moved into settlement executive positions. Atkins Preston was an example. Born in Texas in 1930, Preston dropped out of school before he was fifteen to help support his family. Later, while serving in the army, he earned a high school diploma. At the age of twenty-seven, he entered Columbia, earning a B.S. in 1962 and an M.S.W. in 1963. Preston's fieldwork was in mental hygiene and public welfare. Prior to becoming associate director in 1967 of Henry Street Settlement, he worked as a caseworker and administrator for a family service agency.[32] Preston may not have had difficulty relating to well-to-do board members and other "establishment" persons, but many professionals who came from low-income backgrounds did have problems. On the other hand, a background like Preston's was very valuable in helping a social agency relate more effectively to its clientele.

During the 1960s, the War on Poverty promoted the idea that the poor themselves could be more effective in working with poverty than middle- and upper-class outsiders. As a result, poor people moved onto agency boards and staffs. Professionals, if they had a modest background, became quite open in talking about it. This trend has survived. For example, in a 1984 group interview with five Minneapolis community center workers, four traced their interest in settlement work to growing up in low-income, black, or ethnic neighborhoods. Three shared memories of youthful participation in settlement house activities, with good-natured comments like, "Where's your trophies?" and "I didn't say I was any good."[33] The fourth grew up in an ethnic neighborhood without a settlement, but felt he was attracted to the movement by having experienced a close-knit neighborhood.[34] Two earned M.S.W.s and two had only bachelor's degrees but with considerable professional social service experience. Their degrees and experience transformed them into middle-class professionals, giving them a useful dual-class status. They could relate as professionals to wealthy donors, but they didn't share a common social-class identification with them in the sense that Jane Addams did.

Whether they retained an identification with their low-income neighbors was problematic. Tony Wagner recalled how, growing up in a low-income neighborhood, he was asked as a young man to be a "neighborhood" representative on a social agency board and then to serve as a "neighborhood" representative on United Way's board. However, after Wagner earned the M.S.W., United Way told him he no longer qualified as a "neighborhood" representative. He was still poor and still living in the same neighborhood. All that had happened was that he had received an M.S.W.

Social welfare historians have tended to see professionalism in social work deflecting attention away from reform and instead focusing attention on individual adjustment and provision of social services. While the settlement house didn't hire M.S.W.s in significant numbers until after World War II, it did reflect what was happening by becoming less a center for reform and more a center for social services.[35] The new professional settlement worker was quite conscious of his role as a professional administrator of a complex organization. An interest in reform persisted, but it was to be carried on in "professional" ways, by supporting "scientific study of social problems" and by playing the social "expert."[36]

The inclusion of a reform commitment in a settlement worker's professional identity was facilitated first by the fact that group work emphasized not only human relationships but also democratic decision making. One-fourth of group graduates in the 1950s went into settlement house work. In the 1960s, when the community organization curriculum in social work schools began dealing with pressure tactics and other less genteel ways of achieving social change, the professional had a heightened awareness of the role of reform in social work. Full-time settlement workers with the M.S.W. in 1965 numbered 42 percent.[37] The 1960s were the peak period for employment of M.S.W.s in settlements, and the M.S.W. did pave the way for a major change in the nature of settlement workers. However, the reform commitment of these dual-class professionals may lessen as they get locked into administrative jobs with good salaries, and they may be less inclined to run the risks of the financially independent volunteers in the preprofessional era.

SETTLEMENT HOUSE PROFESSIONAL ORGANIZATIONS

The settlement house professional organizations were important in transforming the individual houses into a movement by giving them visibility and a sense of shared identity and in emphasizing and coordinating their social reform efforts. Although graduate social work education was relatively late in making an impact on the settlements, settlement workers formed a professional organization, the National Federation of Settlements, in 1911. Until the 1970s, most settlement houses belonged. After World War II, the National Federation broadened the definition of eligible agencies to include neighborhood centers. A neighborhood center may be defined as a settlement without residents. Neighborhood centers are distinguished from community centers in that neighborhood centers are almost always located in the slums, are open more days for longer hours, have more small group activities, provide more help with individual problems, have larger staffs and more diverse programs, and get their basic funding from private sources. The National Federation's growth also relfects the movement of settlements into public housing facilities and additional slum neighborhoods as more urban social service money became available.

When the National Federation of Settlements began to grow, so did its budget and staff. Until 1944, Lillie Peck was the only full-time, paid, regular employee. When the staff expanded to four in 1947, Peck stepped aside for John McDowell. The federation financed this staff expansion by raising member house dues first to .5 percent and then around 1950 to 1 percent of their respective agency budgets. In return for their dues, the federation offered consultation and field services, ran training seminars and a job placement service, and facilitated communication among settlements through a newsletter and national and regional conferences. It represented the movement with other national organizations and the federal government, including testimony before congressional committees, and occasionally published special reports. More than any other element, the national organization gave focus and direction to the reform efforts of the settlement movement. (See chapter 6.)

Among the National Federation's special projects was a training center established in 1960 to develop the skills of settlement house workers. Under the direction of Roosevelt University sociology professor Arthur Hillman, the center offered conferences on topics such as neighborhood organization, and numerous one-week courses such as "Administration of Neighborhood Centers," designed for new settlement directors.[38] It did a lot to promote the settlement philosophy and a sense of common identity among settlement workers. However, because of a National Federation budget deficit, the federation closed the center in 1971.

Until 1950, the National Federation was an organization of settlement house workers, and each federation president was the director of a house. That practice changed with David Rosenstein's election to the presidency. Rosenstein is yet another example of immigrant success. The son of an Orthodox Jewish "contractor" in the garment industry, Rosenstein went to University Settlement while growing up on New York's Lower East Side. The settlement encouraged his ambitions. When elected president of the National Federation in 1950, he was also president of the Ideal Toy Corporation, a large toy and industrial plastics manufacturing concern.[39]

The new policy of including settlement board members did not appreciably affect the role of women. Roughly half the board's presidents, other officers, and members were female. The inclusion of local board members on the federation's board, however, did weaken the liberal tone of some of the resolutions the board passed. (See chapter 6.) Because the local board members during the 1950s and much of the 1960s were often well-to-do supporters of the establishment, they had a generally conservative effect on the organization. However, when the composition of local boards shifted in the late 1960s to include large numbers of settlement neighbors, that too had a major effect on the National Federation, which took on some of the characteristics of a grass-roots organization (see chapter 10). The overall impact of broadening board representation in the long run was to make the National Federation more unstable.

Unlike other national social service organizations, such as the Boy Scouts and the YWCA, the National Federation of Settlements is not a "franchise" operation. With the Scouts and the Y, the local groups have to belong, or they can't use the name. With the National Federation of Settlements, membership is voluntary, which results in a much weaker, less generously financed, national office. On the other hand, the National Federation is probably more liberal and more responsive to what is going on at the local level than other national organizations. With a national staff of six and a half in 1969, Margaret Berry reminded the member houses, "The real manpower of the settlement movement is the 8,000 local board members; 4,000 full-time staff members; 12,000 volunteers; and 250 members of the national board and committees."[40]

City federations are another aspect of the professional association configuration. In 1939, the only one with a paid staff was United Neighborhood Houses of New York. However, after World War II, city federations expanded and took on new roles. In the non–Community Chest cities of New York and Chicago, the local settlements' federations moved into joint fund-raising for their member agencies. Elsewhere, local federations helped settlements combine their grant requests to increase their chances of funding and exerted increasing leverage on the Community Chests as well as the National Federation. Whereas in the 1930s city federations of settlements

functioned largely to coordinate basketball tournaments, by the end
of the 1960s a couple were powerful administrative and financial
agencies.

   Thus, in a number of ways, the new professional settlement house
that emerged in the two decades after World War II differed from
the earlier settlement house. The professional approach meant an
end to residence in the house. Whereas settlements had almost no
M.S.W.s on their staffs in 1940, by the end of the 1950s, M.S.W.s
occupied the majority of professional positions. These M.S.W.s practiced a more detached, more efficient, more treatment-oriented approach to the neighborhood. They tended to define the neighborhood itself as a smaller, more treatable unit, a tendency that the
smaller, more institutionally functional settlement buildings symbolized. Gone was much of the former bridging of class lines as well-to-
do volunteers and board members tended to disappear. However,
another kind of bridging occurred as some former settlement neighbors earned M.S.W.s, thus acquiring a useful dual-class status, and
returned to the settlement houses as professional staff. Meanwhile,
professional organizations expanded. The National Federation of
Settlements gave increased direction and visibility to settlement house
reform efforts. At the same time, in the 1960s its professional functions of job placement and training peaked. Thus, the professional
settlement house of the postwar decades became more bureaucra-
tized and institutionalized.
   Symbolizing the changing nature of settlement houses were two
name changes in its national organization. In 1949, the National
Federation of Settlements voted to add "and Neighborhood Centers" to its name. Thirty years later, the national organization completely dispensed with the word "Settlements" to become simply
"United Neighborhood Centers of America." Professionalism had not
only operated internally on the settlements to change their nature,
but certain external professional forces made settlement workers
eventually regard the word "settlement" as a liability.

CHAPTER 3

FROM FEMALE TO MALE
SETTLEMENT HOUSE WORKERS

———•—•———

THE TREND TOWARD THE HIRING OF M.S.W.s COIN-
cided not only with a shift in the ethnic/racial and social-class
backgrounds of settlement house workers, but also a shift from a
female-dominated to a male-dominated movement. Two things about
this shift are important. First is understanding why it occurred. Second is what the implications were for the nature of the settlement
house movement. How would the settlement house method, programs, and commitment to reform be affected? The settlement house
was one of the few institutions women controlled. Thus, their loss of
this institutional base is of major significance.

Using the directories of the National Federation of Settlements
(NFS), one can count the number of female, as opposed to male,
settlement heads. The result is a steadily declining number of female
executives. Historically, women had dominated the leadership positions. In 1910, women accounted for two-thirds of the head workers,
and they increased to 76 percent by 1930. In 1946, they were still in
the majority with 59 percent of the settlement head positions. Seven
years later, the tables had turned. Women in 1953 headed only 43
percent of the settlements. The percentage of female executive directors continued to shrink. In 1960, it was 40 percent, in 1967, it
was 33 percent, and in 1973, the percentage of women heads sank
to 29 percent.[1] During these years, some settlements, such as Pitts-

burgh's Kingsley House, were quite open in their preference for a male director, although the NFS personnel referral service followed a policy of submitting the names of all qualified people.[2] Also, at least as late as 1958, women accounted for a majority of all settlement employees, even though they had lost their dominance of the top executive positions.[3]

The trend toward male executive directors was not only in terms of numbers, but also in terms of who held key leadership positions within the movement. At Hull House, Russell Ballard replaced Charlotte Carr in 1943; at Chicago Commons, William Brueckner replaced Lea Taylor in 1948; and when Helen Hall retired from Henry Street in 1967, Bert Beck replaced her. In 1970, the largest city federation of settlements, United Neighborhood Houses of New York, went from Helen Harris' direction to Tom McKenna's. The following year at the National Federation of Settlements, Walter Smart replaced Margaret Berry. Thus, the transition from female to male leadership was both numerical and qualitative. It is my thesis that the trend toward professionalism along with the absence of an active feminist movement underlay this change from female to male leadership.

One cornerstone of professionalism is social work education. During the 1950s, the Council on Social Work Education switched from female to male leadership. While the majority of social workers were female, social work administration was a male specialty. The sexist graphics used in the Council on Social Work Education's recruiting literature in the 1950s reflect this prejudice. In this literature, designed to encourage people to go into social work, administrators were pictured as men. Caseworkers were pictured as women.[4] The council influenced settlement houses, since the NFS was a constituent member of the council and United Neighborhood Houses of New York was an associate member.[5]

Social work schools added to the bias against female leadership. In transforming their students into "professionals," the schools conveyed knowledge, techniques, and values. Supposedly, one of these values was equality. Yet in the area of equal opportunity for women, the schools delivered a double message. The top social work school administrators were almost invariably men. Although women accounted for roughly two-thirds of the membership of the National

Association of Social Workers, women headed only a handful of social work schools in the United States.[6] In time, the social work profession along with settlements mirrored the schools—administration was a male specialty.

Settlements were pressured into going along with the schools and their corresponding male bias in order to maintain their flagging prestige. M.S.W.s on a house's staff added to its prestige, and male M.S.W.s usually carried more prestige than female ones.[7] Also, most settlements were dependent on their local Community Chests for funding, and the Chests did pressure settlements to add M.S.W.s to their staffs. Since one part of a settlement director's job was to deal with Chest officials, who were usually male, settlements may have felt male M.S.W.s would be more effective in securing funds. However, professional pressures of various kinds were only part of the reason for switching to male leadership.

A second major reason was that during the 1940s, 1950s, and early 1960s, being a feminist was "old-fashioned." The cultural ideal discredited feminism. Women who aggressively sought leadership positions were regarded as overbearing or unfeminine. Instead, the cultural ideal encouraged women to seek fulfillment through marriage and family life. If they worked, it was not to promote their own career, but to put their husband through college or help with the down payment on a house in the suburbs. Should a woman criticize what was happening, for example, should she point to the trend toward men replacing women as settlement house directors, no active feminist movement existed to give significance and validity to such concerns. Betty Friedan did not publish her criticism of the postwar ideal life-style for women, *The Feminine Mystique,* thus inaugurating Women's Liberation, until 1963. It wasn't until 1970 that many people became aware of Women's Liberation. In the meantime, women lost control of the settlement house movement.

The stories of two settlement leaders representing different generations illustrate the importance of reaching professional maturity in a feminist context. Helen Hall represents the transitional generation of settlement workers, the one that joined the movement after the first generation of settlement house pioneers founded the leading houses. Margaret Berry is indicative of the next generation, the first generation of settlement house workers to hold M.S.W.s in significant numbers. Hall's generation came of age as the feminist movement neared victory in achieving suffrage; Berry's generation came of age as the feminist movement was being disparaged as "old-fashioned." Their stories show how important a feminist context was in shaping the attitudes, perceptions, and experiences of leading women throughout their careers. Thus, these two women help to explain why women in general lost leadership of the movement.

As a twenty-eight-year-old woman with a budding career when women got the vote in 1920, Hall seems to have taken a feminist life-style and commitment for granted. The daughter of a small manufacturer, she recalled that both her parents believed that women along with men should lead purposeful lives. Hall also grew up with a sense of social class. When her father's factory with its new and hard-to-come-by machinery burned, a crowd gathered to cheer the spectacle. To her family standing apart from the crowd, the cheers was cruel. Hall rationalized that the crowd lacked awareness of what the fire meant to her family. Later, as an adult, Hall saw the settlement's job as overcoming this lack of awareness by acting as an interpreter between the haves and the have-nots.[8] In other words, she saw the settlement worker as bridging the chasm between the rich and the poor.

Hall used the settlement house as a base for a long, devoted, and energetic career on behalf of liberal social legislation. Her professional training was meager, though good for her generation. In 1915, she attended the New York School of Social Work, but she never received the M.S.W. (At this time Mary Richmond was the key figure in social work education. Indeed, social work is unique among female-dominated professions because women took the lead in defining the profession.) Hall was active in many organizations, including professional ones, and presided over the National Federation of Settlements in the late 1930s and early 1940s. From 1922 to 1933, she ran University Settlement in Philadelphia, then took over the leadership of Henry Street Settlement. Two years later, in 1935, she married Paul U. Kellogg, editor of the popular social welfare journal Survey. At this time, Hall was forty-three and Kellogg fifty-six. It was Hall's first marriage and Kellogg's second. Like her contemporary, Secretary of Labor Frances Perkins, Hall chose to retain her single name professionally.

Sue Steinwall, the processor of the Helen Hall and Henry Street records, thought that Hall and Kellogg must have had a very dynamic relationship, that there must have been a certain electricity between them. They were both involved in many of the same causes. For example, both served on the Advisory Council that put together the Social Security Act, where both signed a minority report arguing for more income redistribution within the framework of Social Security. Kellogg had been a settlement resident in his youth. On marrying Hall, he joined her in living at Henry Street Settlement. The couple also shared a love for an old colonial house they acquired in Cornwall for weekend and vacation use. High on a hill, the house had a lovely view of the Hudson River valley and rambling flower gardens. Hall added gardening to her hobbies of sculpturing and cats. She and her husband had complementary personalities. Hall was stately in her bearing, outgoing, and had a quick wit and good sense of humor. Kellogg's nature was more subdued. Both were strongly devoted to their careers as well as to each other. Their marriage was not only a personal partnership but an indirect career partnership.

Hall and her husband had twenty-three years together, the last several marred by Kellogg's poor health. In 1958, as her husband approached death, Hall found compensation in her work, which she described as "increasingly absorbing and stimulating." At this time, she was playing a crucial role in launching what became the prototype program for the War on Poverty, Mobilization for Youth (see chapter 8), only to see her leadership of this program repelled a couple of years later by the social work profession. While the major reasons for rejecting her leadership relate to the profession's low opinion of settlements, one wonders if the profession's bias against female leadership wasn't a factor.

As a reformer, Hall's interests were wide-ranging and included consumer issues, child welfare, and the War on Poverty. Throughout her career, Hall periodically testified in Washington on behalf of liberal legislation.[9] As an administrator, she not only took the leadership in allocating tasks and provided the driving force, but she also knew when to withdraw and how to lose with graciousness. Largely unbothered by feminist issues, Hall was the most influential settlement house leader from the 1930s until her retirement as head of Henry Street Settlement in 1967 at the age of seventy-five.

Nevertheless, Hall was no Jane Addams. Neither Hall nor any of the other settlement workers following Jane Addams possessed Addams' genius as a publicist nor her ability to project a strong public image of herself. A comparison between Addams' *Twenty Years at Hull House* and Hall's *Unfinished Business* illustrates the difference. In her autobiography, Addams occasionally altered facts to heighten the dramatic quality of the narrative and to evoke in her readers a strong and very positive response toward herself. Hall's autobiography is a far more straightforward, administrative account. Instead of sustaining a human interest narrative, Hall falls into the trap of giving credit by name to her associates; and once begun, the names multiply for fear of offending anyone missed. Hall also lacked Addams' outspoken feminism; but then, for most of her career, Hall lacked an active feminist movement that might have made speaking out practical politics. She was more of an administrator than a publicist, and neither she nor any other settlement worker was able to fill the void Addams left behind.[10]

Some of Hall's feminist views on what women should do with their lives were expressed privately in correspondence with Frances Edwards Brueckner after Women's Liberation surfaced as a movement. Helen Hall and Frances Edwards were two settlement house directors who both married successful men thirteen or fourteen years older than themselves, who were also in the same or similar fields. However, Frances Edwards was a generation younger than Hall. Edwards had earned an M.S.W. from the New York School of Social Work,[11] and had shown considerable promise during the 1940s while working on the National Federation of Settlements staff as director of Social Education and Action. Then Bill Brueckner hired her to run a branch house of Chicago Commons, Emerson House. The two subsequently courted and married. At this time, Frances was in her late thirties, and Bill Brueckner was around fifty-one. When Frances became pregnant, she resigned as head of Emerson to devote herself to marriage and bringing up their only child, Pamela. While she did take occasional part-time, temporary research assignments, she abandoned her career.

Meanwhile, husband Bill Brueckner, who lacked the M.S.W. but did have master's degrees in education and sociology,[12] was having exciting experiences being in the vanguard experimenting with the detached worker and storefront center approaches to juvenile delinquency. In the early 1960s, he was a key government consultant and grant reviewer for projects that paved the way for the War on Poverty (see chapter 8). Eventually daughter Pamela grew up, married, and then divorced. In their life-styles and values, Hall and Frances Brueckner represented two different generations.

In the late 1960s, Hall admonished Frances for having "no drive," a charge Frances repeatedly denied.[13] At the age of sixty-three and with an ailing seventy-seven-year-old husband, Frances decided to reenter the job market full-time.[14] After considerable job-hunting, she landed a position with Juvenile Court. She bitterly complained to Hall that her supervisor was a twenty-nine-year-old "deprived, under-educated black squirt," who had been a delinquent at the age of nine.[15] The sense of regret at having missed a career that Frances conveyed to Hall underscores the generational differences between the two women.

Frances Edwards matured professionally at a time when the cultural ideal frowned on career-oriented women. Her decision to abandon her career for family reasons may have typified her generation of women settlement workers. About the same time that Frances resigned her position at Emerson, another National Federation staff member, Lois Corke, resigned her job as head of personnel to marry Minneapolis settlement worker Camillo DeSantis. The couple adopted children when adoption agencies ruled out working mothers for child placements. Lois did work part-time for a settlement, taught temporarily at the local university, and spent about half a dozen years as executive secretary of NASW's Minnesota chapter. She maintained her interest in social action, serving on the Metropolitan Council's Committee on Aging and participating in the League of Women Voters. Her husband described her as a feminist "with balance"—she's "not strident," but expects women to get their rights. As a practical politician, she "knows what's do-able." [16] Given the sharp drop in the number of women settlement leaders after World War II, one wonders if there weren't a number of women like Lois Corke and Frances Edwards who set aside their careers for family reasons, and who may have had some mixed feelings about it once the cultural ideal changed with Women's Liberation.

One woman of the "feminine mystique" generation who did become a leader was Margaret Berry. However, even though she may be regarded as an exception for her generation, her story also illustrates the pervasiveness of a nonfeminist cultural ideal. In 1937, Berry, who has never married, received an M.S.W. with a specialty in group work. After working four years with the YWCA, she joined the staff of Soho Community House in Pittsburgh, rose to be executive director, then moved on to the staff of the National Federation of Settlements in 1952 and became head of that organization in 1959. Given the turmoil resulting from the black male takeover of the settlement movement, she resigned this position in 1971 to become the executive director of the National Conference on Social Welfare. In spite of her 1971 forced resignation from the NFS, throughout her 1982 memoir runs the theme of not being conscious of discrimination against herself as a woman.[17]

In recalling her youth, Berry wrote that the possibility that men and women might have "antagonistic roles" was never a factor of her family's thinking. Her minister father and schoolteacher mother migrated from England in 1912, making Margaret Berry a first-generation American. Her mother was active in the suffrage campaign in both England and the United States. Berry grew up assuming she would attend college and probably become some kind of professional. Because the stock market crash wiped out money set aside for college, Berry had to rely largely on a combination of domestic service jobs and scholarships to get her bachelor's degree from Albion College. She studied what interested her, majored in sociology, and recalled that throughout college being female was neither an obstacle nor an asset. It was simply irrelevant in making choices. An undergraduate project organizing a club of black women led her to attend the School of Applied Social Sciences at Western Reserve University in Cleveland. The stipend she received for her fieldwork there was another consideration.

Likewise, Berry did not recall sex roles being an issue in graduate school or in her field placement in a Cleveland settlement house. Prior to the mid-1940s, if their staffs were large enough, settlement houses usually employed a "boys' worker" and a "girls' worker." Most settlement house educational/recreational activities had always been sex segregated. Although early settlement workers were often feminists, they made no attempt to promote feminism among their neighbors. Instead, their objective was to recognize and respect the

existing neighborhood values. Thus, the early feminist leaders had
bowed to the fact that historically the feminist movement has been a
strongly middle-class movement, with little or no working- or lower-
class support. However, feminism was important to the early settlement leaders in another way. They could speak out on feminism
from an occupational base that women controlled. In that way, they
were almost unique. However, that uniqueness was lost during Berry's generation.

While Berry did not see being a woman an issue in Cleveland, she
did while working summers in West Virginia. For example, one female colleague ended her usefulness as a volunteer social worker by
shocking the spectators at an impromptu baseball game when she
removed her skirt and ran the bases wearing perfectly proper shorts
which matched the rest of her outfit. Berry also noted that women
hitchhikers in rural West Virginia were often presumed to be asking
for rape. As a volunteer social worker, she promoted a birth control
clinic. Her sympathy was equally divided between the desperate
women and their ashamed, unemployed, and desperate husbands.

In 1937, Berry attended the Bryn Mawr Summer School for Women
Workers. There she met Esther Peterson, who became head of the
Women's Bureau under President Kennedy and who induced him
to form a Commission on the Status of Women, which helped pave
the way for the Women's Liberation movement. The purpose of the
School for Women Workers was to help women become more effective union members. However, Peterson's subsequent feminism, if
present in the late 1930s, had no effect on Berry. Berry recalled no
specific sense of discrimination against women. Instead, the assumption of the school was that women came late to the labor movement
and needed an opportunity to catch-up.

At Soho Community Center, Berry brought certain feminine qualities to her work. Albert J. Kennedy believed that women should
head settlements because they had "a nurturing approach." The
nurturing was what Berry enjoyed about Soho. She remembered life
at Soho in family terms. Along with daily realism were a lot of hilar-
ious happenings and human vitality. She felt obliged to care for each
of the family's elements—neighbors, staff and board—and to assist
each in loving and appreciating each other. She had to "pet along"
so many things—the dilapidated buildings, relationships with public

housing managers and the Community Chest's budget committee, plus cooperation among different groups in her neighborhood.

However, she didn't see this nurturing quality as basically female. To her, both women and men had patience and a nurturing approach. At this point, settlement house work may have become more than a career for Berry. Many of her personal friends were people in the settlement house movement. Like a number of single career women, Berry's professional and personal lives tended to merge.

Being a white female social worker in an agency reaching out to blacks presented special problems. (Soho's neighborhood included a public housing project that was in the vanguard of 1940s integration with " 'checkerboard' occupancy"—all-black buildings alternated with all-white ones.) Soho worked to defuse racial hostility, while blacks tested the sincerity of white workers. At settlement dances, if a black youth asked Berry to dance, her policy was to dance only one dance. That way she demonstrated her support for equality without making the black girls jealous. Black male social workers in other agencies also socially tested the sincerity of her beliefs in equality. She treated these personal overtures as a game to be lightly handled. As a person, she was gracious, charming, outgoing, and very controlled. The processor of the National Federation records, Brian Mulhern, saw her as "always trying to do the right thing."

Margaret Berry had a kind of mentoring relationship with Soho's director in the early 1940s, John McDowell, that facilitated her move up the settlement career ladder. A number of parallels existed between McDowell and Berry. McDowell was an ordained Presbyterian minister; Berry was a minister's daughter. McDowell headed Soho when Berry joined the staff. In 1944, McDowell left to become assistant executive secretary of the National Federation. In 1947, the year McDowell became head of the national organization, Berry became director of Soho. McDowell then recruited Berry for the National Federation staff in 1952. When he left to become dean of Boston University's School of Social Work, she took his place as head of the National Federation. Both believed in working for related welfare organizations. The year before McDowell left the National Federation, he served as president-elect of the National Association of Social Workers. Berry served as president of the National Conference on Social Welfare just prior to her resignation as head of the Na-

tional Federation of Settlements. A warm, personal regard and understanding support for each other characterized their professional
relationship. However, feminists have criticized the "mentor" approach to upward career mobility as too much like "If you marry the
right man, everything will work," but the mentor approach was what
worked for Berry.

Berry didn't perceive any problems because she was a woman executive. Male staff accepted her supervision, and she never felt that
they questioned her authority. Berry's style was that of the quiet fa-
cilitator, who didn't push her own ideas but unobtrusively moder-
ated a forum for others. The National Federation was really committed to equality and that made it possible for Berry to correct certain
practices, such as not reimbursing moving expenses for women staff
but doing so for men. The NFS meticulously observed the practice
of "equal pay for equal work." What difficulties Berry encountered,
such as having to use the ladies' entrance at the Harvard Club, she
regarded as minor. As for male settlement workers in the field, Berry
felt that they had no difficulty accepting support or help from women
on the NFS staff. She did, however, complain about male settlement
executives and job candidates who made passes at a woman staff
member doing job interviews in a conference hotel room. Moving
the interviews to a more public place ended the harassment. She did
not see sexual harassment at the National Federation in general as a
problem, since no women were under male authority. Grace and
good humor were enough to dispose of most sexual overtures. Since
women were being treated with equality at both Soho and the National Federation, they did not need to organize as women. Thus,
she personally rejected the concepts of sisterhood and a female support network so important to feminists.

Berry was aware of the shift from female to male settlement heads.
She thought the early women settlement leaders had a variety of
personal motives that attracted them to settlement house work. Some
were quietly revolting against a stultifying life. They deeply identified with their neighbors in their search for better lives. Others enjoyed the battle for social reform; some relished their dramatic role
as reformers with the slum as a backdrop; some could flaunt their
versatility with many skills; and finally some were profoundly involved in the life of the resident group. Berry noted that the settle-

ment took on more of a family aspect in the United States, with having dinner together possessing strong family overtones. She blamed the shift to male leadership on the decline of the major family aspect of settlement work—residence in the house. She might also have added the corresponding emphasis on professionalism as a cause.

In addition, Berry offered a number of other reasons why women were losing their favored position in the settlement movement by the early 1960s. As a result of the G.I. Bill of Rights, the number of men with the M.S.W. was increasing. More men than women went into community organization. Even more important, settlement neighborhoods were tougher. Berry claimed that in the 1940s she was never afraid to walk the streets of her settlement neighborhood at night, since she knew all the rough kids. However, neighborhoods changed. Urban renewal robbed them of their former stability, and the increasing prevalence of drugs made them more dangerous. Given tougher neighborhoods, settlement boards felt that physical force was necessary to buttress the worker's authority. Thus, women were at a disadvantage.

A related factor was the strong concern settlements had with juvenile delinquency in the 1950s. Most delinquents or predelinquents were male, and it was thought desirable to hire men as "detached workers" and in other work with delinquents. Not only would men have better rapport, but they could also serve as male role models in a delinquent subculture characterized by absent fathers. Berry regretted the trend toward male workers and tried, where possible, to encourage hiring settlements to be more open-minded regarding the sex of applicants. However, throughout most of her tenure as head of the National Federation, she lacked a vocal Women's Liberation movement to give emphasis to her equal employment pleas.

Along with Albert J. Kennedy, Berry believed that women settlement house leaders had a different style from men. Looking back to the early days of the movement, Kennedy observed that the male settlement leaders had access to important men in professions, politics, religion, education, business, and labor. The women leaders, however, had a special sensitivity toward the problems of poor women and children. For example, Kennedy describes Jane Addams leaving a Board of Education meeting and noticing a kneeling scrubwoman. Milk from the scrubwoman's breasts was dripping onto the wet floor.

Addams realized that the scrubwoman would have no milk for her screaming infant when she returned home. What the women brought to the settlement movement was an outraged sense that something should be done to help the poor. They were influential in changing national attitudes. Their first success was the creation of the Children's Bureau, a landmark because it was the first time the federal government got involved in social services as such.[18] Berry also recalled that Kennedy felt that women had more to give to a small agency. They would nurture it along, accepting inadequate salaries. Men tended "to be realistic and move on if the agency cannot meet their demands." Berry saw herself as having the kind of feminine, self-sacrificing commitment Kennedy admired in women.

Consequently, she must have felt especially shortchanged when growing numbers of black male settlement leaders repudiated her leadership in 1971. She recalled that confrontation was then in vogue. Many of her male opponents presented a strong, "macho" image and used the National Federation of Settlements to try out roles they were reluctant to try in their individual settlement houses. Since the value system of the National Federation supported the civil rights movement, the NFS wasn't in a position to resist. Berry indirectly indicted the black men for sexism when she commented that black women suffered doubly. Both the white community and black men repudiated black women's leadership. Her resignation was part of an entire shake-up in the National Federation that included wholesale turnover on the board. Afterward, even more black men assumed leadership positions in the settlement movement. (See chapter 10.) However, even with the passage of time, it was difficult for Berry to admit the roles sexism and reverse racism played in her resignation.

Although Berry refused to directly acknowledge major sex discrimination against herself personally, she did express concern over several aspects of sexism in social work. For example, she mentioned the double message conveyed by the administrators of her alma mater, the School of Applied Social Science at Case Western Reserve University. At the same time that they were voting to keep the National Conference on Social Welfare from meeting in states that hadn't ratified the Equal Rights Amendment, they were also paying women less than comparable men. Another of Berry's concerns was how the "old boy" network limited women's ability to get government grants. In spite of these concerns, she maintained that being female was not a hindrance to her in her forty-two years in the social work profession. While she could acknowledge the Women's Liberation movement and relate it in general to social work, she could not personally use it to resolve her own problems.

Berry continually had difficulty identifying with Women's Liberation. She recalled receiving a National Association of Social Workers questionnaire around 1978 asking how she, as a woman, had managed to "get ahead." Berry couldn't relate to the questionnaire's assumption that those women who succeeded were competitive and had the ambition to get to the top. She never consciously mapped out a career plan with top executive positions as goals. To her, only two factors were operating. First, she was competent, and second, she was available for the job when asked. Modesty may have kept her from adding that she had a strong reputation for integrity.

In explaining why she didn't personally identify with the women's movement, Berry cited the generation gap. She came to professional maturity during the years of the so-called "feminine mystique." After World War II, for a woman to be aggressive, career-oriented, and feminist was old-fashioned. In denying her career ambitions as she moved upward and in refusing to recognize sexism where it existed, she reflected the cultural ideals of her time. When Women's Liberation gathered momentum in the 1960s and 1970s, Berry could appreciate and understand its ideas, but she couldn't change how she saw herself or how she functioned as a woman.

One can speculate further as to why Berry did not personally identify more closely with the women's movement. Denial of the problem is one way of "coping" with sex discrimination. Furthermore, Berry was responsible for leading organizations with both males and females. To make an issue out of being female could have had a divisive effect on organizations she had the responsibility to hold together. Her attitudes and perceptions were quite characteristic of the generation of women who lost control of the settlement movement.

In reviewing these life stories, what stands out is Hall's commitment to a feminist life-style and Berry's inability to internalize feminism and relate it to herself. The values of an early feminist environment were something Hall carried with her throughout her life. Unfortunately, she didn't see the need to publicly defend that feminist perspective. Thus, women like Berry were without a supportive feminist environment as well as firsthand feminist experience.

The presence of a feminist movement may be essential for women to maintain their position within a profession. Without that movement male replaced female leadership in the settlement house movement and elsewhere in the social work profession. Hall's year at the New York School of Philanthropy in 1915 when she was twenty-three must have conveyed a more optimistic message of women's potential place in the social work profession than Berry's Great Depression stint at Western Reserve. A feminist movement out of favor did nothing to check male-oriented professional trends. In this sense, the social work profession simply reflected the larger context of society. But doesn't a profession have an obligation to lead, to set standards and support certain ethics, including equity for women? If so, that question was very far from the minds of professional social workers and M.S.W.s in settlement houses after World War II. It is to Hall's credit that she personally retained her early feminist orientation; and Berry's lack of feminist commitment is understandable in view of a society and a profession that failed to provide her with a supportive feminist environment.

Once we have analyzed why men replaced women in the leadership of the settlement house movement, the next question is how the male leadership changed the movement. In what ways did male settlement workers differ from female ones? What impact did women have?

Because women dominated the settlement movement in its formative stages, settlement houses developed in certain ways. A group of men in England initiated the idea of residence in the settlement house, modeling it on the college dormitory. However, settlement residence was a life-style best suited to single women. In the Progressive Era, society did not think it proper for single women to live by themselves. Likewise, to go out into the neighborhood as Stanton Coit envisioned and organize the men into block clubs was too aggressive for most early settlement house women. They preferred to passively invite the neighbors into the settlement house instead. This passive approach leads to a self-selected clientele using the settlement house. It worked at a time when social services in the slums were scarce.

An alternative to the consensus, passive, "utilize the established channels" method of the settlement house is the conflict-oriented, pressure group method of Saul Alinsky. When Alinsky tried to organize the neighborhood around Hudson Guild in the 1950s, he was appalled when project director Dan Carpenter hired as his assistant a female organizer. Alinsky doubted whether a woman could do his "rough and tumble kind of street organizing in Chelsea's tenements and in its waterfront bars."[19] As the Alinsky style of organizing gained professional credibility, women faced another handicap.

Likewise, the early settlement women tended to blend their personal lives with their work. The settlement house was a kind of family substitute, an alternative life-style, and a lifetime commitment. Traditionally, much settlement house work tended to be with neighborhood women and children. Women settlement house workers related more easily to children and other women, but correspondingly had difficulty relating to men. Sociologist Herbert Gans described most female settlement workers as single and saw them relating to the neighborhood women and children in a "pseudofamilial" manner. He claimed some settlement workers actually referred to their young clients as "their children."[20]

It is worth speculating on what impact the early female dominance had on the goals of the settlement movement. Were women settlement house workers more reform-oriented? Kenneth Boulding, a University of Michigan economist, observed that a number of the most prominent early settlement house workers were not only women, but feminists. He described women's motivation for reform as growing out of a sense of alienation from power that caused them to identify with other alienated groups, such as the poor. The settlement house became a vehicle whereby women could work for social change. In so doing, they "might rise to positions of influence in the community where the existing framework of institutions denied them."[21] (This analysis could also apply to blacks, who have been among the most consistently social reform–oriented in the movement.) Being less career-oriented, women may have been more willing to take risks on behalf of social change than men.

Another question is, Do men and women tend to function differently or be effective in different ways as social reformers? In comparing the purposes of men as opposed to women, psychologist Anne Schaef talks about the male goal of winning versus the female goal of bridging, understanding, and being understood.[22] Bridging was at the very heart of the original settlement idea. From its beginning, the settlement house method has stressed consensus and cooperation across class lines and working through established channels to achieve social change. Women were inclined to favor consensus over conflict. They worried that if they became too aggressive, they would be labeled "strident" or unladylike. In the 1960s, however, the conflict approach associated with Saul Alinsky came into vogue. A 1969 study showed that three times as many men as women social workers were in community organization. In explaining why so many men, a male professor of social work suggested, "Community organization requires behavior more typically identified as male: activism, aggression, self-assertion, and organizing more frequently associated with the 'managerial sex.' "[23] It is important to note the changing concept of social activism, with women generally being considered more suited to the earlier, consensus style, and men to 1960s aggressive activism. Boulding summed up the differences between men and women social workers with the following "doodle":

> *Man vs. Woman*
> Man is always on the move
> Woman does not quite approve
> Man is on adventure bent. . . .
> Woman likes a settlement.[24]

Men did increasingly displace women in executive positions within the settlement movement, but the settlement method remained basically one of consensus into the 1960s. Then, the conflict-oriented community organizer usually sought another base for his activities than the settlement house. However, after the 1960s, settlements, largely under black male leadership, lost some of their former ability to "bridge" and create consensus.

Women also brought to settlement house reform efforts a certain idealism and sensitivity. In her day, Jane Addams projected a strongly moral image and was among those suffrage advocates arguing that women were the morally superior sex and so would have an uplifting influence on society. Since then, this morally superior image has been modified, but women are still often conceded to be in general more sensitive. A parallel may be drawn with librarianship. In her study of the library profession, Dee Garrison claims that many traits associated with librarianship today resulted from the fact that most early librarians were women. For example, librarians frequently castigate themselves for being overly cautious, too self-sacrificing, and too willing to subordinate themselves. These are feminine traits. What is most striking to Garrison about women's contribution to librarianship, however, is their "traditional feminine concern for altruism and high-mindedness."[25] Also, the former head of the national settlement organization, Walter Smart, observed that compared with women, men have a greater tendency to ask, "What's in it for me?"[26] In addition, longtime settlement worker Camillo DeSantis thought women operated out of a deeper sense of conviction, leading to the charge that they're more emotional or excitable. He thought women paid more attention to values, how one does things, courtesies, and doing things right. Even more than men, women were demanding about what was right and wrong.[27]

Women's style of leadership differed in other ways as well. DeSantis noted that women had a greater tendency to hire other women, perhaps because they were more comfortable with women. As part of their attention to doing things right, they tended to keep their settlement houses cleaner than the men. Also, according to DeSantis, women settlement leaders could be just as authoritarian as the men and just as influential in relating to outsiders like aldermen. However, as authoritarian, a woman tends to stand out from the rest of women. An authoritarian male is regarded as more typical of his sex.

In summary, then, professionalism and the absence of an active feminist movement brought men into the dominant position; and men did bring a different style to the settlement movement along with certain changes in program and methods. With a preponderance of male head workers, settlement house work ceased to be a personal life-style. Residence in the building was lost. Settlements placed less emphasis on recreation with children and more on specific social services (see chapter 10). The male M.S.W.s were more career-oriented. Few were content to stay thirty-four years with one settlement, as Helen Hall did at Henry Street. However, women's idealism and tendency to be less career-oriented may be a reflection of fewer career opportunities open to them. For example, had Mrs. Brueckner remained in the settlement house movement after her daughter's birth, one can question if she would have had the same opportunities that Mr. Brueckner did. Perhaps what Hall called Mrs. Brueckner's lack of drive was really her realistic perception of her lack of career options. Women and men may not be fundamentally so different, but society has handed them different opportunities; and so, women brought certain characteristics to the settlement movement that have since been lost or diminished. Whether it's the loss of these female characteristics or other reasons, perhaps related, such as professionalization, the settlement movement has a lessened commitment to reform, less idealism, less self-sacrifice, and less emphasis on "bridging" among conflicting groups.

CHAPTER 4

CHANGING NEIGHBORHOODS

——•—

FOLLOWING WORLD WAR II, MANY INNER CITY NEIGH-
borhoods experienced a major changeover in population along
with overcrowding and deterioration of buildings. Federal programs, such as FHA home mortgage insurance and the G.I. Bill,
helped finance the move of better-off inner city whites to the burgeoning suburban tract developments. To help those left behind and
to counteract inner city deterioration, Congress passed the 1949
Housing Act, which inaugurated a major program of urban renewal
and public housing projects to house the displaced slum dwellers.
The projects tended to reinforce the ghetto and brought with them
their own set of social problems. Yet housing reformers at the time
welcomed them in view of the tremendous housing shortage for low-
income people. The overall effect of these developments was to draw
a sharper line between the inner city and more affluent urban neighborhoods.

Settlement houses both campaigned for and were buffeted by these
changes. Cohesive, ethnic settlement neighborhoods shrank and
sometimes disappeared entirely. Working-class neighbors who were
unionized prospered and headed for the suburbs . In many cases,
blacks and Hispanics took their places. A settlement worker who had
spent years in a neighborhood only to see within a short time urban
renewal leveling tenements and a whole new racial or ethnic group
move into rapidly constructed public housing projects might easily
wonder what value existed in his long-term association with the

neighborhood. That neighborhood was now, physically and socially, quite new to him. The disrupted neighborhood sundered the former stable settlement/neighborhood relationship while exposing certain social control tendencies of the settlement house.

WORKING-CLASS PEOPLE AND ETHNICS LEAVE

Historically, settlements had achieved their major successes helping immigrants and working-class people move up in American society. During World War II, labor unions were fairly well established, but organized labor hadn't yet made major strides in wages. Many unionized workers lived in settlement house neighborhoods. Consequently, unions still identified with low-income people and supported public welfare programs and settlement houses. For example, in December 1939, the AFL and CIO indirectly asked Cleveland's University Settlement to conduct a study of the relief situation.[1] Two years later, a representative from the Laundry Workers' Union spelled out the kind of cooperation between settlements and labor that could be mutually beneficial. She said that settlements could help labor in "interpreting" union aims, "teaching people not to fear the unions," and encouraging pride in union membership.[2] In return, settlements would benefit through union support.

The settlement response to the overtures of organized labor was mixed. Several times during the 1940s, the National Federation endorsed labor positions. These included enforcement of child labor laws,[3] an increase in the minimum wage,[4] and an attack on the Taft-Hartley Act's restrictions.[5] Also in the 1940s, the Chicago Federation of Settlements twice supported strikes of packinghouse workers.[6] The University of Chicago Settlement was especially active in making its facilities available to strikers, running a soup kitchen,[7] and participating in an emergency aid committee to help strikers' families.[8] But when it was all over, the University of Chicago Settlement head found himself having to defend his settlement's participation to potential contributors.[9] The need to raise funds made prolabor activity difficult for settlement houses.

At the prodding of organized labor, some settlements appointed labor representatives to their boards. However, in 1945, Lucy Carner, head of the Education and Recreation Division of Chicago's Council of Social Agencies, lamented "the widespread failure of many settlements to make connections with organized labor, even in a day when organized labor is going more than half way to meet social work."[10] She continued to criticize settlements for not appointing more union members to their boards.[11] Likewise, settlements showed considerable reluctance in letting unions use their facilities. By the 1950s, settlements and organized labor had virtually no relationship with each other.

A sidelight on the union issue was unionization of settlement workers themselves. The National Federation decided that if the majority of the workers in a settlement house wanted to form a union, the house should recognize that union.[12] The University of Chicago Settlement was one of several houses that did so in the 1940s. The entire University of Chicago Settlement staff joined the CIO's Union of Social Workers and negotiated with the settlement board over hours and holidays.[13] I discovered only two strikes against settlement houses, although others may have occurred. In 1965, with many government-funded antipoverty workers on its staff, Henry Street Settlement workers struck over the definition of their bargaining unit. Arbitration settled the strike in management's favor.[14] The second strike occurred in 1982, when two hundred members of the Hull House Employees Union, affiliated with the United Auto Workers, struck for higher wages. The highest paid worker in the union, which included some professional social workers along with cooks and janitors, made $19,500 a year. Most earned an hourly rate of $3.75–$5.50. Even though management was proposing a wage freeze, most strikers went back after nine days, saying they could hold out no longer.[15] Settlement house unions failed as vital organizations because professional social workers were more inclined to identify with professional organizations and also because funding realities made strikes and bargaining largely ineffective.

As social advocates on behalf of their neighbors, settlements lost interest in labor issues for several reasons. Labor matured, and no longer needed the settlements. Also, settlements were never very comfortable with the conflict style of American labor unions. Finally, as organized labor prospered, many working-class people left settlement neighborhoods for more affluent ones.

Perhaps settlements continue to deserve some credit for the upward mobility of those who moved out of their neighborhoods. A Minneapolis settlement director recently recalled the annual reunions of three hundred former members of Pillsbury House. They still meet once a year "to drink and bullshit about the old days." One reason for their get-togethers is their leadership. Their number includes a district court judge and the vice president of an insurance company in addition to "a lot of guys who are just making it." [16]

Along with unionized workers, immigrants were disappearing from settlement neighborhoods. Their numbers dwindled after the quota laws went into effect in the 1920s. Following World War II, the arrival of large numbers of displaced persons temporarily revived the settlement mission of helping immigrants adjust. As they prospered and moved on, their places were taken by poor whites, blacks, and Hispanics.

Settlements provided their immigrant neighbors with a variety of social and cultural services. During World War II, the federal government bowed to hysterical prejudice and interned Japanese-Americans in relocation camps. Several settlements reached out to the Japanese as they left the camps, and at least one, Philadelphia's House of Industry, provided a few Japanese-Americans with residence in the settlement house until they found jobs so they could leave the camps early. [17] With the influx of displaced persons, settlement English and citizenship classes revived, usually in cooperation with the local board of education. Some settlements also hired foreign-speaking staff to help new arrivals find jobs, learn English, and achieve citizenship.

Besides English and citizenship classes, settlements helped immigrants assimilate in a variety of less formal ways. Chicago Commons housed the New Americans Club, which consisted of around thirty recent immigrants from Italy who had met in settlement English classes. They wanted to become like other "social" clubs at the Commons, but they didn't speak English very well, didn't know how to dance, and weren't familiar with American ways. The settlement worker assigned to the club commented, "Their efforts to be like American boys and girls were almost pitiful at times." The group started out holding meetings in Italian and spent most of its time

learning how to dance. Within a year, the group voted to speak English at its meetings and began to include non-Italians in club affairs.[18] Chicago Commons was concerned with, but not necessarily
successful in, avoiding what it called "a cheap assimilation of American ways."[19]

Settlement workers in the post–World War II era differed from
their Progressive Era counterparts in that they placed more emphasis on preserving the immigrants' ethnic heritage. One way was to
form groups along nationality lines. In Cleveland in the late 1950s,
East End Neighborhood House organized separate Italian and Hungarian Golden Age Clubs and Hungarian Boy Scout troops. At one
cultural event featuring Hungarian music and dancing, East End
workers tried to get everyone present to do the czardas.[20] Recent
immigrants especially enriched ethnic dance groups. Finally, some
settlements responded to the desire of second-generation immigrants to learn their native languages by offering courses in such
languages a Lithuanian, Polish, and Italian. Even though these efforts at the preservation of ethnic culture tended to be sporadic and
superficial, they also show settlement house workers going along with
the cultural trend of people identifying with each other on the basis
of common ethnicity or race rather than a shared geographic area
or neighborhood. It was a trend that made mixed neighborhoods
less cohesive.

The changing composition of neighborhoods meant that sometimes an agency intended originally for one ethnic group found itself surrounded by another ethnic group. Philadelphia's Federation
of Jewish Charities supported Neighborhood House; and although
Jews accounted for only 10 percent of the surrounding neighborhood, most of the people using that settlement were Jewish. Jews
actually lived closer to St. Martha's House, but avoided that settlement, perhaps because of its name.[21] Eventually, St. Martha's changed
its name to Houston Center in order to attract a wider clientele.[22]
As for Neighborhood House, it continued to reflect the tendency of
settlements supported by Jewish charities to limit, if possible, their
work to Jews.

After World War II, Hispanics moved into a number of settlement
neighborhoods. Some were Mexicans who scattered throughout the

Southwest, but who dominated an occasional settlement neighborhood in the Midwest. Puerto Ricans concentrated primarily in New
York and Chicago.

Hispanics were more resistant to assimilation than other groups
with which the settlements had dealt in the past. Because of the language barrier, settlements deliberately sought Spanish-speaking staff.
When they hired them from among their Spanish-speaking neighbors, that was a way of letting Hispanic newcomers know the house
wanted them. Furthermore, through these workers, the settlement
gained a better understanding of its new neighbors. Occasionally, a
settlement was able to hire a Hispanic with an M.S.W. Workers such
as Manuel Diaz, who grew up in Harlem, earned an M.S.W. at the
New York School of Social Work, became group work director at
the Bronx Union Settlement, and then in 1960 assistant director of
Rochester's Baden Street Settlement, had a foot in two worlds—that
of the disadvantaged Hispanic and that of professional social work.[23]

Local prejudice against Hispanics could be quite strong. To counteract this prejudice in the Southwest, churches and individuals established a number of small settlement houses. Settlement workers
dealt with neighborhood schools that were unsympathetic to, or
sometimes alarmed with, a sudden Hispanic influx. They provided
translators Hispanics often needed in applying for a job, going to a
clinic, or dealing with the American legal system. Settlements also
encountered prejudice that resulted in occasional acts of violence.
For example, a part-time, Spanish-speaking settlement worker was
stabbed as he was helping a Hispanic family move into a neighborhood apartment.[24] In trying to counteract local prejudice in the 1940s,
settlements sometimes concentrated on developing the Hispanic individual's abilities.[25]

One of the most difficult aspects of working with immigrant groups
was the rivalry, prejudice, and occasional violence one group exhibited toward another. For example, a fifteen-year-old Polish girl
charged five Mexican boys who regularly used the University of Chicago Settlement with rape. After the boys were released on bond, a
relative of the girl shot at one of the accused Mexicans as he left the
settlement house. The bullet missed the boy and struck the front
entrance instead. The settlement continued to allow the accused boys
use of the building but refused to support them in court. Mean-

while, Polish gangs were attempting to eject Mexicans from certain neighborhood dances, restaurants, and other spots. To keep from getting caught in this kind of fight for urban turf, settlements cracked down on loitering in their buildings and temporarily expelled the worst offenders.[26]

In turn, ethnic groups often displayed considerable prejudice against blacks. Puerto Rican parents would keep their children out of mixed-racial settlement groups where their children might have learned English because they didn't want them associating with blacks. Verbal expressions of prejudice could be very strong. Settlement workers tried to counteract prejudiced statements by attempting to get the youngsters into sensible discussion.[27]

Counteracting prejudice was even more difficult when ethnic groups felt themselves personally victimized by the minority group. This happened when the black migration northward accelerated. As blacks encroached on certain ethnic neighborhoods, the younger and more prosperous ethnics fled to the suburbs. Those remaining saw the breakup of their ethnic community and took their resentment out on blacks. The fact that settlement workers could not condone such strongly prejudiced attitudes marked them as outsiders.

URBAN RENEWAL AND PUBLIC HOUSING

Also marking settlement workers as outsiders in inner city neighborhoods was their advocacy for housing reform, at times in defiance of their neighbors' wishes. From their beginning, settlements worked to improve housing for low-income people. Their early approaches stressed housing codes and "limited dividend" or "model housing" projects built by private owners who agreed to limit their profits. Not until the 1930s did settlement workers in general come to the conclusion that some form of government subsidy would be necessary if low-income people were to have adequate housing. In 1937, with settlement house support, the landmark Wagner-Steagall Public Housing Act became law. However, the war soon intervened, so that massive construction of public housing had to wait until the 1950s. Then, many settlements not only saw cataclysmic change in their neighborhoods; but some, on losing their buildings to the urban renewal bulldozer, physically moved their facilities into the projects themselves. Meanwhile, some settlement workers sensed the need for better neighborhood planning. Settlement house activities in fostering citizen participation in urban renewal were significant in view of the emphasis to come on "maximum feasible participation of the poor" in making local policy in the War on Poverty.

To generate support for housing reform, settlements actively publicized bad housing conditions. For example, about the time of the outbreak of World War II, a three-month-old baby in the Chicago Commons neighborhood died of a rat bite. The coroner's jury included a settlement staff member who helped convince the WPA to renew its rat extermination project.[28] About ten years later, rats fatally bit a little girl whose family belonged to a Chicago settlement. Reasoning that all the Chicago settlements united would have more effect than the protests of one lone settlement, the Chicago Federation of Settlements put additional effort into its campaign to improve housing.[29] Even more effective were the efforts of the National Federation of Settlements.

The National Federation asked member settlements to send it graphic descriptions of a particular problem, such as bad housing. It used these descriptions to illustrate statistics and abstract arguments in reports designed to encourage national action. A 1948 report described a New York City dwelling whose walls were so damp that they caused clothes to mildew. A California settlement described a family of four living in a San Pedro residential hotel. The family lived in one room crowded with three beds and a two-burner stove. The hotel provided one community bathroom for thirteen or fourteen families, and the plumbing was bad. A Chicago settlement relayed an account by a neighborhood resident of what rats mean. The slum-dweller said that they have to use disinfectants to counteract bad odors associated with the rats. Also, youngsters were afraid to go alone into the bathroom because of the rats. Even a ten-year-old was scared.[30] Through this kind of data, gathered nationally, the National Federation of Settlements tried to make the postwar housing problem specific and immediate to those who might be influential in changing conditions.

The oldest type of government intervention in bringing about better housing was through regulatory laws or housing codes. Many of these codes did not reflect higher contemporary standards for health and safety, nor were they systematically enforced. In 1940, the Chicago Commons board wrote to the mayor, reminding him that two neighborhood children had died in tenement fires and urging him to bring about more efficient housing inspection.[31] Two years later, the Commons' head, Lea Taylor, complained publicly about inadequate housing inspection. She recommended that the Health Department increase the number of housing inspectors from thirteen to one hundred. Taylor's voice carried added weight because she was then chair of the private Metropolitan Housing Council's minimum standards committee.[32] Nothing much happened. Then, in 1947, a major disaster occurred. Three hundred people were crammed into a tenement building with only one exit to the outside, sharing four kitchens and four toilets. When a fire broke out, nine died. Taylor stressed that the tragedy illustrated the need for housing inspection on a regular basis. The following year, Taylor again served on a coroner's jury investigating the deaths of six people who had been living in a converted stable.[33] Still nothing happened. Settlement workers lacked the political clout to be effective with code enforcement.

The regulatory problem could be approached from the bottom up as well as the top down. Settlements at various times staged campaigns to get their neighbors to report code violations. They occasionally met with resistance from tenants who feared that if the owners of their buildings were forced to make expensive improvements, their rent would be increased accordingly.[34] The basic problem with code enforcement was that if the landlord recovered his costs to upgrade by raising rents, could the poor afford to pay? Many couldn't, and so they opposed settlement workers' efforts.

Strict code enforcement would have compounded the already severe housing shortage. Thus, a better solution to substandard housing was subsidized construction of public housing for low-income people. Having urged states to pass enabling legislation to put the Wagner-Steagall Housing Act of 1937 into effect, settlement workers began to consider the quality and the kind of public housing being built. The early projects, even in Manhattan, were no higher than six stories and didn't require elevators. With foresight, in 1940 the United Neighborhood Houses board warned that the probable fu-

ture construction of high-rise buildings containing self-service elevators "may not be sound." The board also expressed its concern
with the lack of local input in project planning.[35] By 1945, some
settlement leaders were already apprehensive over the concentration
of public housing projects into what one called "a poor man's town."[36]
In spite of these concerns, the settlement movement continued to be
a strong supporter of public housing.

The war was barely over before settlements resumed the fight for
more public housing. At a United Neighborhood Houses workshop
in New York in October 1945, participants reviewed the strategy that
had been successful in getting state housing legislation in the 1930s.
First came the decision on the part of an organization such as United
Neighborhood Houses to sponsor the cause. The next step was to
recruit politicians in both major parties, if possible, to lead the fight.
Settlement workers then utilized a variety of tactics to get neighborhood support. These included "meetings and discussions to educate
the neighborhood," publicity, the formation of a committee, and the
gathering of endorsements from suitable organizations. (Unfortunately the aggressive leadership and dominance the settlement workers exerted in gathering support subsequently hurt them.) Having
gathered this grass-roots support, the final steps involved seeing the
bill through the legislative process and into law.[37]

Settlement workers essentially followed the above steps in the late
1940s to get Congress to inaugurate a major public housing program. In 1947, the Chicago Federation sent Bert Boerner as its delegate to the "Rally on Housing." Afterward, Boerner's group visited
with congressional leaders Robert Taft and Joe Martin.[38] In 1948,
Lea Taylor was among those personally testifying at the congressional housing hearings.[39] These efforts finally resulted in the passage of the 1949 Housing Act and the biggest public housing construction program that the United States has seen.

A 1953 survey showed that half the settlements had public housing projects in their neighborhoods,[40] and that the number would
increase. Because of their involvement with public housing, settlement workers were among the first to become aware of developing
problems. They began calling attention to such issues as public housing site selection, tenant selection, income ceilings for tenants that
resulted in the eviction of the more stable ones, the need for units

for single people and the aged, discrimination against blacks, and inadequate recreational facilities for project dwellers.

Settlement workers also began to discover neighborhood opposition of a different kind to proposed projects. During a neighborhood meeting at Chicago's Benton House, the local alderman denounced public housing for reducing the property tax base and disrupting neighborhoods. He wanted private enterprise to improve local housing, a hope which Benton's head worker, Isabel Pifer, said was unrealistic.[41] In the Chicago Commons area, retail merchants strongly opposed public housing. One of their reasons was that blacks might move into a future project.[42] Public housing was an issue that often pitted the settlement workers against their neighbors.

Further complicating site selection was an economic dilemma. If a project was of the row house or low-density type, it was often built in an outlying area with little or no public transportation, something on which low-income families depended. If the project was located near the city's center, high land costs dictated high-rise construction. In either case, the project look of the architecture set the housing apart. National Federation of Settlement leaders warned that concentrating together thousands of families of the same low-income level was promoting economic ghettoes for which society would eventually pay.[43]

Tenant selection resulted in a negative homogeneity among project residents. Elizabeth Wood, a former executive secretary of the Chicago Housing Authority, claimed that project tenants before 1949 were different from those who came later. Before 1949, "projects blossomed with all kinds of committees to create health programs, play schools, and all kinds of recreational activities." The social environment had a positive effect on children. That was because the more successful families avoided eviction as their income passed the maximum allowed because of the wartime moratorium on over-income evictions and the lack of income-ceiling enforcement after the war. That changed when the 1949 Housing Act gave priority for admission to public housing to those displaced by urban renewal. More and more, projects were home to female-headed families on welfare.[44] Initially, public housing projects also lacked units for single people and the aged. In 1953, the National Federation of Settlements recommended that units for the elderly be integrated into regular projects rather than segregating the aged. The federation also recommended more flexibility on income ceilings.[45] Instead, what occurred in the 1960s was separate middle-income projects and projects for the aged. The institutional desire to sort out and categorize was overwhelming.

Until the 1950s, most local public housing authorities also sorted out tenants by race, unofficially designating certain projects white and others black. The National Federation formally attacked that practice in 1949 with a resolution condemning the federal government. At first settlements had more success getting open occupancy policies on the local level. For example, in 1953, United Neighborhood Houses of New York contributed to the passage of a state bill outlawing discrimination in future public housing projects.[46] The following year, the settlements induced the New York City Council to pass the Brown-Isaacs bill ending discrimination in all projects, existing as well as future.[47] One of the bill's sponsors on the city council, Stanley Isaacs, was president of the board of United Neighborhood Houses. The federal law the settlements wanted finally came in the form of an executive order in 1962.[48] In effect, open occupancy in projects in cities with large black populations tended to make public housing synonymous with black housing, since whites fled projects once a certain percentage of blacks moved in. White neighborhoods also became even more resistant to the construction of additional projects. As Johnson's Secretary of Housing and Urban Development and former Hull House resident, Robert Weaver, ironically observed, "Had there been an open-occupancy policy at the time the affected projects were constructed, many of the developments now subject to integration would never have been built."[49]

Congress attempted to correct some of the worst abuses associated with public housing and urban renewal with the Housing Act of 1954, which contained the "Workable Program." Settlements particularly supported the parts of the Workable Program that called for the involvement of the poor in planning for their neighborhoods and the establishment of services to relocate the slum dwellers that urban renewal displaced.[50] Not only had settlements campaigned for relocation services as part of the 1954 Workable Program, but they actively assisted relocation services. Boston's United South End Settlements actually ran a relocation service under contract from the local Redevelopment Authority. In return for $72,000, the settlement agreed to survey relocation needs, contact each site occupant at least once a week, trace those who moved, run an information program, aid people in filling out applications for moving expenses and property losses, maintain files of available housing, and inform and screen prospective house buyers for the FHA.[51] South End helped 644 families relocate, 90 percent of whom had been living in substandard housing. In addition, the relocation workers often put a family with health and/or welfare problems in touch with agencies that could help them. When it was all over, United South End Settlements felt that the project was worthwhile.[52] The settlement signed another contract in 1966 to relocate 3,550 families.[53]

Thus, in the area of public housing, settlements saw the problems that would be forthcoming with the projects, but they still gave priority to the construction of public housing. They had two fundamental reasons for doing so. One was that settlement workers knew first-hand how incredibly bad much of the private housing was in their neighborhoods. Second, having gotten public housing projects approved, they could then work to improve them by advocating open housing policies and citizen participation in planning, plus they could actually provide relocation services under government contracts. In spite of their disappointment over the federal government's lack of enforcement of citizen participation in planning in the 1950s, the controversy the projects caused with their neighbors, and the need for additional improvements, settlements remained constant in their support for the continued construction of public housing.[54]

In turn, public housing projects had an impact on settlement house programming. In 1939, some neighborhood project residents induced Philadelphia's Wharton Centre to establish a workshop to renovate old furniture.[55] Some other settlements conceived the idea of combining a consumer education program with similar workshops. They warned their neighbors about costly installment purchases and gave advice on judging quality in furniture materials. Several housing projects loaned settlements model apartments to be furnished to stimulate ideas among the tenants. At least one settlement had its members furnish the demonstration apartment.[56] Thus, for early tenants, moving into a housing project was often an exciting step up that stimulated the desire for further improvement, a feeling settlement houses encouraged.

By the late 1950s, settlement programming shifted to teaching good housekeeping. That was the purpose of Germantown Settlement's model apartment.[57] Another Philadelphia settlement, Friends Neighborhood Guild, developed a program of teaching housekeeping to tenants threatened with eviction for poor housekeeping habits. It was easier for settlement workers to do this task than Housing Authority workers because the settlement workers were less of a threat to the tenants.[58] Even so, efforts to improve housekeeping rarely produced lasting results, primarily because poor housekeeping was symptomatic of deeper, underlying social problems.[59]

Settlements repeatedly urged housing projects to utilize more social workers and other professionals to work with their problem tenants. A number of settlements negotiated agreements with local housing authorities under which they actually provided some of these services. Settlement leader Helen Hall used her position as consultant to New York City's Housing Authority to recommend that instead of evicting problem families, authorities hire social workers to deal with them.[60]

Project dwellers lacked a sense of neighborhood cohesiveness, which made them vulnerable to robberies, other crimes, and social problems. Since the day-to-day program of most settlements revolved around recreation and creating a sense of neighborhood, housing authorities were eager to have settlements operate in or near the projects. Also, settlements were persistent campaigners to get recreational facilities incorporated into the design of the projects themselves.[61] That space then required staffing, either by the local housing authority, a settlement, or some combination of the two.

From the earliest days of public housing, settlements provided recreation for tenants, although no one pattern appears dominant. Some houses simply assigned workers to do programming in project facilities. New York settlements made the most extensive use of public housing facilities, beginning with Henry Street's Home Workshop in the basement of Vladeck Houses. By 1942, United Neighborhood Houses of New York was seeking public funding for the settlement workers staffing public housing community facilities.[62] Eventually, the New York Housing Authority paid for one settlement worker in each federally funded project served by settlements and two settlement workers in each state-funded one, plus it furnished supplies and equipment. Facilities also improved. After starting out in project basements, following 1949, settlements often got ground floor space. Some even managed to influence the design and allocation of the space they would occupy.[63] For those settlements that lost their buildings to urban renewal, the alternative was often to totally move their operation into public housing facilities. By 1959, settlements, along with Y's, the Children's Aid Society, and the school board, operated sixty-nine community centers in New York City's public housing projects.[64]

If the project's community facility was not a separate building, and it usually wasn't, the settlement in the public housing project suffered some loss of identity. The old, free-standing settlement house was a symbol of permanence and independence that was lost with the move into a project. Settlements also faced the possibility of having their participation in controversial activities curbed. H. Daniel Carpenter, whose Hudson Guild moved completely into project facilities, noted another settlement that was barred form having meetings on controversial topics. Hudson Guild sought to protect itself through a clause in its lease permitting the guild to continue with its past policies and philosophy.[65] The underlying problem, however, was the quasi-public evolution of these settlement houses. A settlement worker paid with public funds, and working in a public facility was coming close to being a settlement worker in name only. The motivation for this transformation grew out of a desire to serve the neighborhood, and in some cases, was dictated by financial necessity.

A Minneapolis settlement experienced another side to the loss of independence when it was evicted from community center space in a predominantly black project. The project residents charged that the settlement in the project was a dangerous place to go. It was a setting for drugs, fights, and alcohol. Settlement staff exerted no control. While the facilities included a gymnasium and equipment, the staff provided no programming and lacked skills. None had an M.S.W. One was from the project itself, another was a friend of the board president, and the third was a longtime settlement employee. The project residents felt they had no say in the operation of the project's community center and that the settlement board was too middle class and was ignoring their demands. A minister worked with the project residents against the settlement, which got terrible publicity in the local newspaper. Eventually, the Housing Authority asked the settlement to leave, and a church-sponsored community center replaced it.[66] The evicted settlement concentrated on its operations in other locations. While some merit probably existed to the charges, lack of its own building and the settlement's confrontation with grass-roots democracy contributed to the instability of that house's public housing operation.

The crime and disorder problems mentioned in the above example added another dilemma to a house's relationship to its neighborhood, whether it was in a project or not. The settlement house building was a symbol. However, because of increasing crime problems, some settlements had to take measures to protect themselves, such as bars on the windows. But these features could also symbolize the barrier between the house and the neighborhood. It could appear to be an alien fortress. The building may give visible evidence that the neighborhood does not choose to protect it. As neighborhoods became more disorganized and crime-ridden, these problems became more frequent for settlement houses.

Michael Harrington in his indictment of poverty, *The Other America*, claimed that the only effect high-rise public housing projects had on their occupants was that their housing was no longer dilapidated; the projects did not alleviate social problems. Harrington pointed to Hudson Guild in New York's racially and income-mixed Chelsea district as one of the best programs of settlement-project cooperation. Hudson Guild, "an old, established community center" operating out of a project-owned building, tried to serve as a bridge between project residents and the rest of the neighborhood. The guild ran a nursery available both to project residents and middle-class people in the area. However, few project children used it. They lacked enough aspiration to take advantage of an opportunity clearly offered. Harrington perceived that the problem was not one of housing or even the availability of services, but of "slum psychology."[67] Neither the settlement house nor the public housing facility had broken through that psychological barrier.

The impact of settlement houses on their host public housing projects was often minor because of the sheer scale and subsequent problems of some of the projects. The construction of 1950s public housing in major cities coincided with the vogue for high-rise projects that would remove tenants from street noise and air pollution. Built without air conditioning, the buildings were technologically obsolete when new. The architects failed to anticipate or confront behavior control problems. Unmonitored elevators made notorious crime sites. Sometimes the design worsened the situation, such as one infamous project in St. Louis that included a large public laundromat/play space on each floor that turned out to be indoor crime space. Had prospective tenants had some control over the design, some of the worst in public housing might have been avoided.

The most extreme example of a settlement dwarfed by such a project was Firman House in Chicago's Robert Taylor Homes. Ironically, the project was named after the man who had been forced out of the chairmanship of the Chicago Housing Authority in the 1940s because he opposed large-scale projects. He then suffered the added indignity of having the United States' largest project named after him. Robert Taylor Homes in Chicago consists of around two dozen identical high rises aligned in repetitious U formations and is inhabited by over 25,000 people, of whom 90 percent are women and children and virtually all are poor and black. Serving this "neighborhood" is a little Presbyterian-sponsored settlement, Firman House. The author of a book on low-income housing in Chicago called Firman House a positive factor "but of so little consequence in the overall situation as to be insignificant."[68] As for other Chicago settlements, they were busy serving other housing projects and other slums.

In reaction to projects like Robert Taylor Homes, housing advocates in the 1960s tried different kinds of projects and public subsidies. Settlement workers helped to lay the groundwork for these innovations. As early as 1945, the National Federation of Settlements went on record favoring an increase in the supply of middle-income housing,[69] and settlement workers intermittently contacted Congressmen and testified before committees. In 1961, Congress passed the Mitchell-Lama Bill, establishing middle-income public housing projects. Settlement workers then supported more government funds for these projects.[70]

Settlements also advocated other innovative housing programs that sought to break down the project concept of public housing. In 1960, Lea Taylor helped promote the Conference on Housing the Disadvantaged, from which emerged a plan for federal rent subsidies that would help nonprofit private groups sponsor housing projects.[71] Charles Liddell, head of United South End Settlements in Boston, represented the National Federation of Settlements in testimony before the Senate Banking and Currency Committee on behalf of rent subsidies. He had the honor of witnessing the signing of the law in ceremonies in the White House Rose Garden.[72] Legislation also provided for rent supplements, which meant that the poor would locate their own housing and pay 25 percent of their income toward rent, and the government would supplement the rest. Rent subsidies and supplements are ways of trying to disperse the poor over a wider area, thus loosening up the ghetto.

Besides working for better government programs, settlement houses also became directly involved in the low-income housing business. In the 1950s, several settlements undertook neighborhood self-help and rehabilitation efforts. For example, Friends Neighborhood Guild in Philadelphia purchased a block in a redevelopment area, rehabilitated most of the housing, and constructed a new apartment building. Its project was organized as a cooperative, and the occupant-owners could reduce their down payments by doing interior painting and other tasks.[73] Beginning in 1959, Congress sought to encourage nonprofit organizations to build more low-income housing by making available federal loans specifically for that purpose.[74] The first organization the government selected under this program was Hudson Guild, which borrowed $495,000 for fifty years at 3.5 percent interest to construct an apartment for the elderly.[75] Other settlements took advantage of subsequent legislation that allowed them to borrow government funds at favorable rates to construct low- and middle-income projects.

Low-income housing was tied to urban renewal and city planning. For example, Pittsburgh is known for the low quality of its housing. Historically, the city government's answer to the fact that many dwellings lacked showers or bathtubs was to partially subsidize public bath houses, several of which were operated in conjunction with settlement houses. As late as 1954, Woods Run Settlement was still running "public shower baths for men."[76] The baths and showers at

Woods Run were used 20,250 times in 1946 at a charge to nonsettlement members of five cents a time and two cents for settlement
members.[77] Yet Pittsburgh chose to concentrate on an outstanding
program of downtown redevelopment at the expense of housing. A
key factor in evaluating the priorities of urban renewal was whether
or not poor people had significant participation in making renewal
plans.

Settlements encouraged citizen participation in planning long before it was mandated by federal law in 1954 and enforced in the
1960s. During the Great Depression, Boston settlements had a program organizing neighbors into planning groups. However, when
the Ford Foundation organized its "gray area" projects, it tried to
avoid using settlements because it thought they were too directive of
their groups.[78] In the Boston "gray area" project, ABCD (Action for
Boston Community Development), South End House was already active in urban renewal because South End's depression-born neighborhood planning council survived into the 1950s. Also, during 1961,
South End loaned its director, Charles Liddell, to ABCD.[79] For two
years the settlement contracted with ABCD to run a Youth Training
and Employment Program and in other ways benefited from ABCD
and the subsequent antipoverty program. However, United South
End Settlements never served directly as the coordinating agency for
ABCD or the local War on Poverty.

Without the participation of the poor in planning, the politically
powerless often found themselves in the path of demolition, and that
path included a number of settlement houses. In Detroit, urban renewal took three settlement buildings,[80] and in Minneapolis six out
of eight settlements were forced to relocate.[81] Chicago Commons
voluntarily chose to vacate the building it had occupied for sixty-
three years because most of the neighborhood was demolished for a
freeway.[82] In the postwar metropolis, freeways are among the most
effective barriers defining or redefining neighborhoods. Even if their
path didn't take the settlement house, they could cut it off from
most of its neighborhood or otherwise isolate it.

The most publicized settlement house loss was the original Hull
House. Without consulting the neighborhood, Chicago offered the
Hull House site to the University of Illinois as the location for its
Chicago Circle campus. The city chose that site in part because Hull

House was unlikely to block the action, considering the deteriorated state of its buildings. However, area residents fought the site selection and bitterly charged that the Hull House board had sold them out. Their fight was futile. On March 5, 1963, the city paid Hull House $875,000 for its buildings. By March 31, all the settlement house furnishings were either sold or taken to a new location, and the historic buildings abandoned.[83] Eventually, the University of Illinois bowed to public pressure and reconstructed the first Hull House building minus its third story so as not to disturb the street-level view of the roof line of the modernistic campus building behind it. Meanwhile, the settlement went to a decentralized operation at a number of locations around the city. In losing the original Hull House buildings, the settlement movement lost its most famous house. The very bad museum reconstruction at Chicago Circle hardly illustrates what the settlement house was like. Furthermore, the publicity surrounding its neighbors' efforts to stop the most famous settlement house in the United States from selling out reinforced the "social control" image of settlements elsewhere.

When Hull House went to a decentralized operation, it reflected a growing trend among settlements to view their neighborhoods as smaller units. Thus, settlements unloaded many of their big, old buildings and replaced them with smaller ones (the National Federation of Settlements specified 10,000 square feet as minimal)[84] or did away with building ownership by moving programs into public housing, schools, and other free or low-rent facilities. Settlements set up these smaller, decentralized operations in part to get closer to their neighbors and in part to reduce building costs. However, in doing so, they may have contributed to the fragmenting of the larger neighborhood. They virtually eliminated large group interaction. Gone were Hull House's open houses for the neighborhood and Hiram House's outdoor movies on summer nights. The smaller settlement buildings competed with a multiplicity of other slum-based social agencies. No longer were they able to function as the coordinator of neighborhood action or be the neighborhood focal point or crossroads.

As individual settlement house facilities got smaller, the houses began administrative mergers. Initially, in the 1950s, the National Federation of Settlements promoted settlement mergers as a way for the houses not only to operate more efficiently, but to expand their influence. One little neighborhood by itself didn't have much influence, but several neighborhoods combined would be more influential. Community Chests also pressured settlements to merge as a way of achieving an agency of optimum size for administrative efficiency. In 1968, the Chests considered a $150,000 budget minimal for this purpose.[85] Later, little pretense was made for mergers other than financial necessity. Few settlements would go completely out of business. Instead, they would merge.

However, the mergers further undercut the settlement's special neighborhood relationship and its traditional role as the neighborhood advocate. A number of early mergers were between settlements in adjacent neighborhoods. Administratively, they probably worked the most smoothly, especially if individual staff members worked in more than one neighborhood. However, that undercut staff identity with and loyalty to a particular neighborhood. Where the merger was in the form of a loose association of settlement operations each with their own staff and board in scattered neighborhoods, administrative tension was high, and houses frequently dropped out of the merged organization. At the heart of the settlement concept was the worker's relationship with the neighborhood. A desire to see one's own neighborhood be well endowed with resources worked against the success of mergers.

Often, much settlement energy was channeled into the administrative politics of the merged agency. In fact, one settlement worker who saw his agency through two mergers thought that settlement workers were so drained by their own agency's politics that they had little energy to give to city or national settlement federations. He blamed mergers for the tendency of settlement workers to turn inward on their own agency with the corresponding decline in the 1970s and 1980s of the city and national federations.[86]

Mergers also called into question the settlements' identity or function. In 1977, Hull House was a federation of ten organizations scattered around Chicago, and some of these ten had as many as three branches.[87] A merged settlement lost its role as an advocate of a particular neighborhood. It no longer focused on a specific neighborhood nor did its branches tend to serve *entire* neighborhoods. In fact it was difficult to say how the merged settlement's relationship to its neighborhood differed from that of other social agencies operating in the neighborhood.

Given the decline in funding for social programs, mergers have increased in the 1970s and early 1980s. Rather than two agencies competing for a smaller amount of funds, they merge. Tony Wagner, head of Pillsbury United Neighborhood Services, remarked that merged agencies are likely to have a "schizophrenic structure." His own agency was the result of a 1984 merger between Northside Settlement Services, with three branches in north Minneapolis, and Pillsbury House, with three branches in south Minneapolis. The staff numbered 110 (about 75 full-time-equivalent positions). Only five had M.S.W.s. Many were neighborhood people, but they didn't necessarily work in the branch of their home neighborhoods. Of the six physical facilities, one is a new 30,000-square-foot, concrete and glass building that houses a day care center, a theater, a game room, conference and meeting rooms, a dance floor and health club, a kitchen, and art and other activity rooms. It was built in 1980 with money raised by United Way to replace other property. The largest of Pillsbury's facilities is a former 50,000-square-foot public school. Another is a building owned and constructed by the Park Board, which Pillsbury operates under a forty-year lease. In managing this merged operation, Wagner must decide if the agency employees are going to be organized by geographic area or by service function.[88] For example, will a specialist in work with seniors work in several branches, thus not developing loyalty to one neighborhood over another, or will that specialist remain in one center where work with seniors will be the substance of the program and the rest of the neighborhood be ignored? Thus, mergers have continued to undercut the settlement house's traditional role as the focal point of the neighborhood.

The physical and social changes settlement neighborhoods went through altered the relationship of settlement house workers to their neighbors. When urban renewal obliterated many of the old settlement house buildings, some settlement houses literally followed their neighbors into public housing facilities. Thus, what had formerly been a completely private agency was now a quasi-public, institutional one. The move into the housing projects often removed the settlement house buildings as a permanent, identifiable symbol or focal point for the neighborhood. Settlement mergers further undercut neighborhood ties. Shifting ethnic and racial groups also eliminated the advantage of long-term residence in the neighborhood. If few of the neighbors had lived for long in that location, it made little difference if the settlement workers did. In addition, social trends saw more emphasis on ethnic pride as opposed to assimilation. The settlement house relationship to its neighborhood had become fragmented.

While settlement workers' professional training told them to respect the mores of the neighborhood, their professional values told them urban renewal and public housing were right and prejudice was wrong. Not only did they clash with their neighbors over housing code enforcement, but settlement houses can also be accused of some self-interest in connection with their support of urban renewal and public housing. Following World War II, many houses found themselves strapped for cash and with antiquated buildings on their hands. Through urban renewal, they found buyers for their buildings, and through public housing, they obtained their new space for free plus, sometimes, money for staff. The spectacle of Hull House's neighbors urging that famous settlement not to sell out was the best-publicized example of a house turning its back on its neighborhood. While settlements did support citizen participation in urban renewal and did occasionally engage in projects along those lines, they were better known for a social control rather than a grass-roots democracy approach to housing reform. Thus, they were in a more institutional, less stable, and occasionally at odds relationship with their new post–World War II neighbors. At the same time, with fewer working-class whites and immigrants to serve, pressure increased on settlement houses to find a new clientele.

CHAPTER 5

BLACKS, EQUAL RIGHTS, AND INTEGRATION

————— •‒• —————

ALONG WITH PROFESSIONALISM AND REFORM, RACE IS a major theme of this study. The 1940s saw the beginning of the second major wave of black migration northward. Settlement neighborhoods were changing, and settlement houses would have to reassess their policies and practices regarding black participation. Meanwhile, many of their white neighbors adamantly opposed accepting the blacks. Would settlements integrate their playgrounds, their clubs, their dances, their staffs? Would they defend the rights of their new black neighbors to have equal opportunities in recreation, education, and housing? Few settlements ducked these issues by moving to another neighborhood. Instead, by the 1950s, most who found increasing numbers of blacks in their neighborhoods moved to accommodate them.

Work with and on behalf of civil rights had been a minor part of the settlement house commitment to social action since the Progressive Era. The three founders of the NAACP in 1909, Mary White Ovington, William English Walling, and Henry Moskowitz, were all connected in varying ways with settlements; and another settlement worker, Jane Addams, lent her prestige to the establishment of the infant NAACP. However, even as late as the 1930s, most settlement workers still thought of their movement as being primarily for whites. In fact, historian Thomas Lee Philpott actually sees the settlements prior to the Great Depression as racist.[1] Before World War II, only a handful of settlements were established for blacks, and hardly any of the other settlements made more than a token attempt at integration. A couple even closed their doors rather than serve blacks.

The reasons why the settlement movement had done so little for blacks prior to the 1940s are varied. First, fund-raising for agencies to serve blacks was difficult. Second, the civil rights movement lacked widespread support until after World War II. Many reformers, including settlement house workers, were liberal on a variety of issues, but they had a blind spot on civil rights. Consequently, few early settlement houses reached out to blacks. Those that did sometimes established black branches. Another pattern that emerged was for one settlement house in a city such as Minneapolis to serve blacks and other houses to refer blacks to that settlement house. Third, while some settlement workers were forward-looking on racial matters, they ran in to resistance from both their white neighbors and donors. Without a civil rights movement to give momentum to their efforts, racial liberals within the settlement movement accomplished little. Belatedly, the settlement houses came to the recognition that their former clientele, largely European immigrants, was disappearing; and increasingly, blacks were taking the immigrants' places in the urban slums.[2] Because settlements had done relatively little for blacks prior to the 1940s, meeting the needs and winning the trust and respect of their new black neighbors was to be that much more difficult.

The first step for many settlements was to adopt the values and goals of the civil rights movement. That movement was gathering momentum, and equal rights and integration became its major themes. To head off a threatened march on Washington during the war, Roosevelt created a Fair Employment Practices Commission. Blacks, who had switched their allegiance to the Democratic party, were finding a successful political strategy. They were also in the vanguard of mid-twentieth-century social change techniques. Their court cases, boycotts, and sit-ins pointed the way for other protest groups. Blacks were also benefiting from the public's abhorrence of the excesses of prejudice displayed by Nazi Germany and by growing U.S. sensitivity to how its racial policies appeared to the rest of the world. Also, black aspirations rose as they migrated out of the South. Mainly what blacks accomplished in the 1940s and 1950s was to expand their foothold in the so-called "Promised Land," There, some encountered settlement houses, which would make a major shift in the direction of serving blacks. In doing so, a number of settlement houses found themselves in severe conflict with their white neighbors while also experiencing difficulty winning the acceptance of their black neighbors.

THE SETTLEMENT HOUSE COMMITMENT TO CIVIL RIGHTS

Social work schools and professional organizations took the lead in stressing the importance of civil rights to the individual settlement houses. In the summer of 1944 at the School of Applied Social Sciences at Western Reserve University, one of the courses designed with settlement house workers in mind was "Inter-Racial and Inter-Cultural Problems in Group Activities."[3] Also, the settlements' own national organization, the National Federation of Settlements, had long been interested in better race relations. In the 1940s, it accelerated its activities in this area. In 1944, its president, Clyde Murray, explicitly urged member houses to be outspoken on behalf of civil rights and to visibly demonstrate racial equality in their programs.[4] Through resolutions, reports, and discussion, the national organization pointed the way for member houses. Among other activities, in 1943 its Committee on Intercultural and Interracial Relations recommended that those houses with a substantial black clientele include blacks on their boards and professional staffs.[5]

By the mid to late 1940s, some settlements serving mixed neighborhoods had at least token blacks on their boards.[6] Unfortunately, this decade also saw some reactionary boards that acted to exclude or limit black participation in the house. The neighborhood surrounding Kingsley House in Pittsburgh was 30 to 40 percent black, but the board refused to allow blacks to become members of the settlement. When the head worker, Mrs. Charles C. Cooper, raised the issue with her board, she was met with such responses as "Do your Italian parents want you to bring in these colored children?" and "If they don't want them, what right have you to force it?" The board ignored Mrs. Cooper's arguments about the need for recreational opportunities for the neighborhood's black youngsters.[7] Sometimes a director was able to bend discriminatory board policy a bit. The board of Community Settlement House in Corpus Christi, Texas, told its new director, Mrs. Clara L. Plevinsky, not to allow blacks and Latin Americans to meet in the house at the same time. Mrs. Plevinsky did anyway, but she carefully assigned them to different parts of the building.[8] What were needed were more black board members.

The number of black board members continued to increase. By 1964, blacks probably accounted for around 12 percent of settlement board members. In part, this increase reflected a trend toward appointing more members from the settlements' neighborhoods. For example, Henry Booth House operated out of a Chicago public housing high rise. The board was half white, half black and contained three people who lived in the project. Board members, including project dwellers, occasionally hosted board meetings in their own homes.[9] Members of such a board were in a good position to learn from each other.

However, in spite of the presence of some blacks and a growing commitment to civil rights that often took the form of specific agency actions, most boards were reluctant to publicly state these policies or endorse the National Federation of Settlements statements on civil rights and social action.[10] Serving on white-dominated boards, blacks experienced a certain amount of powerlessness. For example, a settlement director noticed how a white lawyer on his board squelched discussion with the result that blacks were unable to talk frankly and felt frustrated.[11] However, the "general picture of 'reactionary boards' being prodded by 'liberal social workers' " is exaggerated, and occasionally a board was "ahead of the staff."[12] While the boards were the key to making policy, the staff was crucial in carrying it out.

The 1940s saw a rapid increase in the number of black staff members.[13] The following incident from the interracial Five Towns Community House illustrated the need for them. A white worker replaced a black who had left the agency. Initially, the black mothers' club ignored the white worker. Eventually, the white worker broke down their resistance by involving them in emphasizing black accomplishments during Negro History Week.[14] However, she then ran into trouble with some black youngsters who thought her effort on behalf of Negro History Week "was making fun of them. . . . They said, 'We don't want a Negro History Week. Why don't you have a Guinea Wop week? Why don't you have a white week?' "[15] Had the worker been black, she probably would have met with a very different reaction. She might also have taken a different approach.

Milton Brown, head of United Neighbors Association in Philadelphia, decided that the renewed emphasis on integration could best be achieved if the settlement staff reflected "somewhat the racial patterns of the community."[16] Therefore, around 1950, United Neighbors hired Goldie Gibson Edwards to be the first black on the staff of Southward House. She met with initial hostility in the neighborhood. Many whites looked the other way when she passed, and others made racist comments. Patiently, she found opportunities to explore the subject of prejudice with whites, to remind whites of the lack of recreational services for blacks, and most of all, to simply get to know the neighbors and give them an opportunity to know a black person. After about a year, she felt that she had caused settlement members to question their prejudice. She had shaken racial stereotypes. Black members were somewhat more comfortable, and the local neighborhood was seeing itself in a broader context of national racial and religious concerns.[17] Edwards thought she could be more effective modifying people's prejudices by acting like a program director and not like a reformer.

In keeping with the 1950s emphasis on integration, settlements used black leaders not only to reinforce the pride of blacks, but also to break down the prejudice of whites. That meant that in a settlement with a mixed staff and clientele, blacks occasionally worked with white neighbors and whites with black neighbors. In both situations, the worker often met with hostility. A skillful leader could use the hostility as a wedge to get the group to explore the nature of prejudice and bring about change. However, not all groups could be so handled. Where the prejudice was too great, settlements like Hamilton-Madison assigned leaders to groups of their own race.[18]

How a house approached integration of board and staff varied greatly, depending on the nature of its neighborhood and whether it was located in the North or the South. Cleveland's Little Italy was an all-white neighborhood separated by a cemetery from East Cleveland, which was rapidly becoming all black. Little Italy was fanatically determined to remain white and had a well-known reputation for hostility to blacks. At one time, black mailmen delivering neighborhood mail were physically attacked, until the post office threatened to cut off the area's mail service.[19] In 1963, however, the area seemed quiet; and Alta House's director, Al Alissi, decided the time had come to hire the first regular black staff member. He chose Ben Gibson, a part-time ceramics and art teacher, whom the children liked. Meanwhile, a school board plan to bus black students from overcrowded ghetto schools into Little Italy triggered a riot, demonstrations, and violence. Gibson picketed on behalf of an integrated school and was present and photographed by the news media when a tractor crushed to death another civil rights demonstrator. With neighborhood hostility now turning toward Gibson, Alissi fired him, claiming that he did so for Gibson's own safety. However, the local social work community criticized Alissi for this response.[20]

About the same time, Alta House had better luck when it appointed its first black board member, John Turner of the School of Applied Social Science at Case Western Reserve University. Alissi was very apprehensive about how the neighborhood would treat Turner when he came for board meetings. Therefore, Alissi took the precaution of taking Turner to lunch at one of the neighborhood's Italian restaurants so that he would be recognized as being associated with Alta House. Alissi also saw Turner had a parking space near the settlement so that he wouldn't have to walk through half the neighborhood to get to the board meetings. As time passed, Turner, who was a specialist in community organization, made significant contributions to the settlement.[21] While Alta House's attempts at integration were relatively feeble, the house did enough to risk losing neighborhood support.

Still another way of incorporating blacks into a primarily white institution was as residents. During the late 1940s, Hull House served as the home of Robert C. Weaver, then director of Community Services in Chicago for the American Council on Race Relations.[22] It is unclear just how involved in Hull House activities Weaver was, but in later years Hull House could claim among its residents not only the first woman to serve in a presidential cabinet (Frances Perkins) but also the first black.

Most blacks who worked in settlements worked with an all-black clientele; and while some of these blacks rose to become head workers of black settlements, a number of black settlements had white directors. In the South, where the Methodist Church established a string of settlements to serve blacks known as Bethlehem Houses, these settlements had in the 1940s mixed staffs with white head workers.[23] Elsewhere, in some neighborhoods which changed very rapidly, the white head worker of a black settlement was simply a holdover from the days of white clientele. The experience of Neighborhood Association in St. Louis illustrates the extreme disorganization that could result from rapid neighborhood turnover. The settlement decided to serve blacks entirely in 1943, and began replacing white staff members as they left with blacks so that by 1945 the only white left was the director, J. A. Wolf. In the meantime, the settlement had gone through four heads of boys' work and three directors of girls' work. The program had little continuity. Wolf estimated that if the staff in 1945 remained, it would take another two or three years before the program could be productive.[24] The head resident at Henry Booth House in Chicago, which had a mixed staff, justified the presence of whites by saying, "We are doing everything possible to teach Negro children not to be afraid of white people."[25] Undoubtedly, black neighbors would have preferred to see more black staff in top positions, but militant demands along these lines lay largely in the middle and late 1960s.

Meanwhile, as more blacks moved into settlement neighborhoods, black settlement workers found increasing opportunities. In a 1964 sample of thirty-eight agencies serving neighborhoods ranging from all black to all white and in-between, blacks accounted for slightly more than one-third of the staff members.[26] The variation ranged from two-thirds of the staff in all-black neighborhoods in the South to one-third in mixed neighborhoods of the Midwest to none in a Southern white settlement.[27] The survey also showed 27 percent of settlement executives to be black.[28] Subsequently, agency demand for black settlement workers accelerated. In 1968, the head of the National Federation, Margaret Berry, noted that their placement office could not begin to fill the demand for qualified black applicants. She commented that if any discrimination were operating, it was the "reverse" kind.[29] The movement of black social workers into the settlement house field was a major development that would have important future ramifications for the settlement movement.

SETTLEMENTS ACCOMMODATE THE BLACK INFLUX

In the 1940s, blacks were more concerned about denial of settlement facilities to black neighbors or the offering of facilities on a segregated basis. A Detroit settlement was willing to allow blacks to attend a music class but not to become full members of the house.[30] Columbus' Godman Guild served both Southern white migrants to the city and an increasing number of blacks, but on different days of the week. When blacks first became a substantial minority at the house, their groups were all scheduled on a certain day of the week. As the black population increased around the settlement, black clubs were assigned two days per week and, later, three days. The rest of the days were for whites only. The settlement also ran separate camps for blacks and whites.[31] In 1956–57, Godman Guild finally dropped its segregated policies, but only after pressure from the NAACP and the National Federation of Settlements.[32] Another settlement in Columbus and two in Toledo also followed the special days for blacks pattern.[33]

Occasionally, a settlement would refuse to serve blacks at all, even when becoming surrounded by blacks in the neighborhood. At Richmond's William Byrd Community House, whites had to pass through a black area to reach the house. As a result, nighttime attendance among teenage girls dropped. Whites were asking, "When can we move our Community House?" At the same time, neighborhood blacks had no year-round recreational facilities. They would gather on the porch of William Byrd to watch the whites dancing and having fun inside. The resulting envy created "ill feeling and some hostility." Eventually, William Byrd Community House decided to abandon its building to blacks and move its program for whites elsewhere.[34] Sophie Wright Settlement in Detroit also did just that.[35] For some settlements faced with a changing neighborhood, their decision was to follow their white clientele out of the black neighborhood.

Fortunately, most settlements faced with an influx of blacks in the 1940s sought to make as orderly a transition as possible to serving their new clientele without losing their white members. Chicago Commons made special efforts in this regard, but one of the problems faced in building an interracial program was that as black attendance became substantial, whites began to withdraw. Lea Taylor, head worker at the Commons, was particularly concerned because she saw these whites as "the prejudiced group that we need to work with."[36] The Commons found that to get girls of both races to attend necessitated numerous home visits and often a guarantee of the safety of both races by a promise on the worker's part to walk the girls home from the settlement at night. Within the settlement house, workers seized opportunities for informal conversations with youngsters lounging around the game room, at dances, and elsewhere to draw out their feelings about the racial situation. The Commons also found it necessary to accept social groupings within the house along racial lines, but it did try to promote activities between the black and the white groups.[37]

The staff was also nervous about the possibility of racial violence occurring in the Commons. The head of girls' work described an incident that occurred during January 1946. The front hall was filled, mostly with newly returned G.I.s from the neighborhood, when a club of eleven black youngsters passed through. After they left, a very emotional, rabidly anti-Negro young man began yelling that blacks "did not have a right to a square deal, they were not human, they were just animal." Twice later on that night, groups of younger boys demanded to know where the blacks were meeting, the implication being that they wanted to disrupt the black group. When the blacks left the house, the white boys were waiting for them outside. They grabbed one black boy, then ordered, "Come on jitterbug, dance." The black managed to slip out of their grasp just as his friends started to turn on the white group. Fortunately, two social workers were present. One urged the black group quickly across the street "in no uncertain terms" while the other projected an "everyday manner" that broke the tension. Chicago Commons stood firm on its policy of integration, and a milestone was passed.[38] Yet in spite of the Commons efforts, attendance declined.

Settlements which made the decision to integrate often did so in stages, usually starting with the playground. In Pittsburgh, when blacks first moved into the Irene Kaufmann neighborhood, they were excluded from the settlement. Then Kaufmann decided to integrate in stages. The announcement that on a certain date blacks would be admitted to the settlement's playground evoked hostility on the part of some neighbors. Internally, all comments and expressions of hostility on the part of members were recorded and analyzed in staff meetings and conferences. Various board members also helped by interviewing neighborhood people regarding their attitudes and explaining the settlement's racial policy to them. The settlement remained committed to its decision and proceeded to integrate.[39]

Especially among older youngsters and adults, settlement athletic teams and clubs usually were either all black or all white, in spite of staff efforts at club integration. In a club consisting of a dozen little girls at Five Towns Community House, the staff noticed a certain "restlessness" on the part of the whites when the percentage of blacks approached one-third. When it reached one-half, the whites suddenly stopped coming, thus leaving the club all black. Staff attempts to insist that all groups be open to both races didn't work. They found that to keep whites in Boy Scouts, they had to organize a separate white troop because blacks overran the existing troop. The settlement also had all-black and all-white mothers' clubs. The white mothers criticized the settlement for making the house available to blacks and strongly resented having to share facilities, such as the kitchen. Apparently so much segregation existed among the groups and activities at Five Towns that one black woman protested, "It's like the toilets in the South."[40] Toward the end of the 1940s, Five Towns staff began assigning the younger children to achieve a roughly fifty-fifty interracial balance in each group. However, as soon as the youngsters were given the opportunity of free choice, they immediately segregated themselves.[41] The best that settlements could do with single-race clubs was to get them to occasionally participate in joint activities.

It was much easier for the settlements to achieve integration in interest groups as opposed to social clubs. In Philadelphia, Friends' Neighborhood Guild boasted that with one exception its ninety-five group activities were interracial. An analysis of the activities shows that they all fell under the interest group category—airplane modeling, sculpturing, children's theater—and the one segregated activity was social dancing for teenagers.[42] Another settlement, Irene

Kaufmann, was unusually successful with its Forum, a series of programs revolving around social issues such as housing, police protection, and sanitation. The Forum usually attracted around 250, of which most were black but about 20 percent were white. The Forum spawned a Social Action Committee which tried to follow up on Forum discussions. For example, it acted as a medium to convey housing complaints to the local officials.[43] The settlement goal of integrated activity was one reason why socially liberal settlements pushed interest groups at the expense of social clubs.

Following World War II, these more liberal settlements began using their camps to promote interracial experiences. In 1947, an affiliate of Chicago Commons, Emerson House, joined black Parkway Community Center at Camp Reinberg. They made a film to publicize the interracial camping experiment.[44] The next winter, the Chicago Federation of Settlements decided to protest the discriminatory policies of those camps that had them. A group from the federation met with the boards of the offending camps to explain their position on integration and to announce that they would boycott those camps that persisted in discriminating.[45] Camping offered the ideal opportunity for settlements to involve their neighbors in interracial experiences because reluctant parents faced with a choice of integration or no camp would usually send their youngsters to camp, and admission was easily controlled to achieve racial balance.

The most difficult part of the settlement program to integrate was social dancing. In Pittsburgh, Soho Community House had a phonograph in its game room, and one of the informal activities was social dancing. When black youngsters began to use the room, whites protested, saying that blacks would overrun it. The settlement insisted on the right of blacks to be there, but decided to limit use of the room to members of clubs at Soho. Nevertheless, the game room situation got out of hand with some very rowdy sessions; in one, the lights were shut off, the water in the boys' rest room overflowed, and the settlement worker was locked out of the game room. That worker recommended no more house-sponsored dances or large group activities.[46]

What bothered some even more than the mayhem was that in some people's minds, only a short step existed between interracial dancing and intermarriage, where many racially liberal people drew the line.

In the 1940s, a worker from Five Towns Community House related the following incident:

> One of our colored clubs gave a dance, and the membership was automatically all colored. Two white girls happened to be in the gym, and they stood around, looked in, and of course they both were very good jitterbugs and wanted to dance. And after about an hour's hanging around, some of the colored boys asked them to dance. They danced two or three times, and then walked out of the room in a state that just about bordered on mental collapse. . . . If their parents had seen them looking that way, there would have been—something in the neighborhood. So, our director of activities . . . took them into his office and sat and talked with them for an hour or so, until they calmed down sufficiently to be able to leave the building and go home.[47]

In the 1950s, forward-looking settlements insisted that house dances had to be open to both blacks and whites. However, that did not by any means imply that blacks were to dance with white partners. When a young black man happened to attend a Chicago Commons dance on a night when no black girls were present and made the mistake of dancing with a white girl, the staff took him aside and suggested he leave. They even got him a cab. In justifying their actions, the staff mentioned the black had been drinking, and said he was carrying a gun and they feared whites would accost him. Nothing had happened. When, in a subsequent staff meeting, a woman raised the question "Should a Negro, in a crowd of whites, be allowed to dance or not?"[48] the rest of the staff sidestepped the question. Nevertheless, a great deal of effort went into a rather timid and artificial integration.

One of the most extreme examples of controlled activity was Hyde Park Neighborhood Club. Early attempts at integration resulted in having to station police in the lounge–game room to maintain order. The settlement brought in a new director who decided to drop any activity that did not promote integration. He began by closing the lounge–game room and discontinuing all nonmember mass activities. While some segregated social clubs continued, the new emphasis was on interest groups such as wood shop, modern dancing, dramatics, and basketball. Teens registered at the settlement were finally allowed to once again have dances, but only on the condition that they be integrated. To control racial hostilities at these dances, the house went to extraordinary lengths. The dances were heavily staffed, with twelve workers to every fifty or more participants. Coca Cola was sold "in paper cups so bottles were not available as weapons." Records were previously tape-recorded so the actual records would not be available for throwing and breaking. Staff kept a strict eye on attendance and escorted youngsters home after the dances. No wonder the director concluded, "Integration works, but . . . it is a hard, tough job."[49]

Besides carefully controlling or eliminating activities that could not be successfully integrated, some settlements tried imposing racial quotas on membership. By the end of the 1950s, the public housing project that provided facilities to Hamilton-Madison House was 5 percent Chinese, 21 percent black, 22 percent Puerto Rican, and 52 percent white. At the same time, a new public school community center opened in the neighborhood. Italian youngsters flocked to the school center in hopes that it would be all white. Meanwhile, Hamilton-Madison reserved a certain number of staff workers and rooms for each minority. When whites failed to come to Hamilton-Madison for fall registration, the settlement refused to accept additional Puerto Rican applicants for membership while aggressively recruiting whites. Once it became apparent that the school center was also to be integrated, whites began to drift back to Hamilton-Madison. In addition, another neighboring settlement, Henry Street, occasionally rejected youngsters to achieve a racial balance.[50] Thus, Lower East Side settlements worked together to achieve integrated memberships reflective of the neighborhood.

The reluctance of many settlement neighbors to participate in integrated programs was based on racial prejudice combined with a desire to avoid a potentially violent situation. Where interracial gang fights and other forms of violence occurred, they were usually outside the settlement house, but they sometimes involved settlement members and staff. For example, a gang of white teenagers attacked and stabbed a male worker at Hull House who was escorting some black youngsters to their homes.[51]

However, other incidents occurred in which skillful settlement programming helped alleviate a volatile situation. To ease racial tensions in a housing project that was 60 percent black, the Boston Housing Authority in 1961 invited South End House to set up a Community Services Center in the project. The settlement workers gave the project residents opportunities to become better acquainted through an open house, informal coffee hours, the formation of social groups, and athletic teams. When open fighting broke out between black and white teenagers in the project, the settlement workers acted to calm feelings and track down rumors. They also set up a meeting where black and white teenage leaders were able to express their feelings and where facts dispelled some of the rumors. As a result, both blacks and whites agreed to a truce; and no more trouble occurred that summer.[52]

Sometimes a crisis in the neighborhood was the catalyst for bringing blacks and whites together. Philadelphia's United Neighbors Association was unable to get the two racial groups together to create a neighborhood tot lot, or associate much in any other way. Then a neighborhood child had a near accident, and both blacks and whites went together in a combined delegation to city authorities that quickly brought about the designation of a one-way street. That interracial group went on to create the tot lot.[53]

Even in those settlements that did have some success with integration, the feeling existed that this success was tenuous. Also, the settlement workers who pushed so hard for integration in the 1950s didn't seem to be aware that perhaps an element of condescension existed in this goal. Integration implied that it was good for blacks to associate with whites. Furthermore, integration appealed more to middle-class blacks than to the hard-core poor. Thus, promoting integration may have been more in the "social control" than in the grass-roots democracy tradition. Nevertheless, in the 1950s, settlement workers could feel progressive when purging their movement of the last vestiges of formal segregation.

The National Federation of Settlements got tougher in promoting integration. It developed the category of "provisional membership" to pressure houses that excluded or segregated blacks into integrating. Not all these Jim Crow settlements were in the South. Union Settlement in Springfield, Ohio, was one that the National Federation threatened to drop from membership if it continued to refuse to admit blacks to its program.[54] Thus, settlement liberals used their national professional organization to strengthen their efforts to achieve integration within their movement.

By the early 1960s, according to a National Federation survey of twenty-two responding agencies, about half the Southern houses were practicing integration to some degree. Specifically, twelve had integrated their program, though only six of those had done so completely. Half the agencies also had integrated boards and staffs. The survey revealed that most of the houses desegregated their programs between 1954 and 1960.[55] Thus, Southern settlement houses made major changes toward integration.

The Methodist church sponsored a number of the Southern settlements. Historically, its agencies for blacks were called Bethlehem Centers. The white ones were Wesley Houses.[56] In 1966, the Methodists had sixteen Bethlehem Centers scattered across the South, but did not plan to establish any more because they were embarrassed by the racial stereotyping.[57] Meanwhile, they were trying to draw blacks into the Wesley Houses. In Oklahoma City, the local Bethlehem Center and Wesley House merged their boards and staffs.[58] Bethlehem Center in Atlanta had an integrated board, but one that tended to avoid public controversy. The board was reluctant to take a public stand in favor of open housing or to ask Mrs. Martin Luther King to join the board because she was "too controversial." However, when a staff member was jailed for two days for participating in a sit-in, the board paid him his regular salary for the jail time.[59] As part of its commitment to integration, the ultimate goal of the Methodist church was that the distinction between Wesley Houses and Bethlehem Centers disappear.[60]

Settlements that chose to make a positive stand on behalf of civil rights had to work to retain white neighborhood support. In the 1940s, an anonymous letter sent to the treasurer of the board of Chicago's House of Happiness said: "While people living in the immediate vicinity of this organization walk around with holes in their shoes, the colored people living out of the destrict [sic], and who have their own charities, seem to have a better standing at the House of Happiness than the white race. This is all due to the Communistic mind and attitude of the head resident."[61] The operator of a neighborhood wading pool who was also a community leader told the mild and fair-minded Lea Taylor, head of Chicago Commons: "You know the folks talk about you. They say they're boycotting the Commons," and that the Commons was responsible for a tenement house arson fire that killed a number of blacks. "Now they know who owns the building. They [say] you did."[62] Such charges were outlandish, but they were also warnings to the settlement workers to go slow or lose even more white support.

At Chicago Commons in the 1950s, the staff made special efforts with a local Polish priest, who had grown up in the neighborhood and attended the Commons as a youngster. The priest was normally friendly with the settlement, but he considered most blacks undesirable as residents of the neighborhood. He refused the settlement's invitation to meet with the Catholic Interracial Council on the issue. In fact, the priest was quite anxious that the neighborhood not find out that he'd even discussed the subject at Chicago Commons.[63]

Chicago Commons' reputation favoring civil rights nearly killed its efforts to get a zoning variance which would allow it to extend its work into an adjacent Polish neighborhood. The Commons needed the variance to convert a former dairy building into a recreation center. The local alderman resented Chicago Commons' efforts to get blacks to vote, the fact that the Commons had occasionally by-passed him in complaints to city departments, and the Commons' defense of blacks moving into the community. Fortunately, the Commons was able to get the alderman's support by working through one of his protégés and by getting the seller of the dairy building to apply pressure.[64] Several years earlier, the Commons blamed "the political machine and the police force" as the main reasons why blacks had not moved into certain parts of the neighborhood.[65] Partly because of their support of civil rights, the settlements had an uneasy relationship at best with Chicago's powerful machine politicians and their neighborhoods. Ironically, the machines, in some ways, were closer to grass-roots democracy than the settlements.

White neighbors' protest continued into the 1960s. When Philadelphia's University Settlement took one black and three white children swimming in a pool previously used by whites only, the swimming occurred without incident. However, in protest, the mothers of seventeen youngsters pulled their children out of the settlement's play school.[66] For settlements promoting integrated programs, the basic problem continued to be how much could they do for blacks and still have reasonable working relationships with their white neighbors.

By 1944, at least twenty-five houses served primarily black neighborhoods. A few were established prior to the Great Depression to serve blacks. Others had originally served a white or mixed neighborhood, but as the black population expanded, they found themselves with an all-black clientele. Finally, a couple were newly established in the 1940s expressly to meet the increased demand for black services.

One of the new settlements established in the 1940s to serve blacks was Chicago's Parkway Community Center. The Congregational Church of the Good Shepherd started the settlement in 1940.[67] At that time the staff consisted of two people, one of whom was Horace Cayton. By 1948, Cayton had built the settlement staff up to thirty-one workers, of which only four were part-time.[68] As the director of one of the few black settlements in Chicago, Cayton frequently addressed civic groups and served on a variety of committees. For example, in 1943, he was a regional chairman of the Community Fund, on the Executive Committee of the group work section of the Council of Social Agencies, chairman of the Public Relations Committee of the Urban League, and a member of the NAACP's Interracial Committee, the Mayor's Interracial Committee, the Governor's Race Commission, and other organizations.[69] Cayton also found time to collaborate with St. Clair Drake on *Black Metropolis,* a two-volume study of race relations and black ghetto life in Chicago, first published in 1945.[70] Black leaders of black settlements seem to have had a much stronger sense of social mission than the average settlement director.

In its early days, the Urban League operated out of community centers similar to settlements, except they usually did not have residents.[71] Among the Urban League projects in the 1940s was Brooklyn's Lincoln Settlement. In spite of the close affinity between the settlement method and those of the Urban League, the league was reluctant to identify itself with the settlement movement. In 1947, Lincoln Settlement dropped its membership in United Neighborhood Houses of New York.

Previously, the New York Urban League denied its support to a proposal that Union Settlement develop a center for blacks. The executive director of the Urban League commented that if the proposed center's program was to be "just 'tiddeley winks' [and] recreational activities for children," he was definitely "not interested, since the real need was to help the adults work for better housing."[72] Besides the suspicion of a frivolous program, there was a Jim Crow aspect to a center established specially for blacks near a predominantly white agency. Union Settlement did not establish the center, and New York blacks remained a major group largely unserved by settlement houses.

Another black settlement, Ada S. McKinley House, had an uncanny ability to spring back to life in spite of several inept directors almost killing it. The settlement was originally founded during World War I to work with blacks on Chicago's South Side. After the war, the settlement, then known as South Side Community House, fell under the direction of a black woman, Mrs. Ada S. McKinley. Unfortunately, the agency was never able to meet the standards for membership in the Welfare Council, which would have helped it raise funds. By the late 1940s, Mrs. McKinley was the only one on the staff, the settlement had no program of which to speak, and the board was inactive.[73] However, several key people and institutions became interested in reviving the moribund agency. These included the Illinois Institute of Technology, which was expanding its campus in the neighborhood; the Chicago Urban League; the Welfare Council; Clara Langston, a black who worked to reactivate the board; and Lea Taylor and William Brueckner, leaders in the Chicago settlement movement.[74]

Ada S. McKinley House was reorganized.[75] A new administrator was hired, who had settlement experience and a master's degree from Western Reserve University.[76] Unfortunately, he couldn't keep the books straight or do much to develop the program, perhaps because he was spending too much time playing politics. He ran unsuccessfully for alderman, then harassed the winning candidate into giving him a full-time job on the city payroll. He held the city job concurrently with his full-time settlement position, all without informing the board. The settlement also neglected to pay withholding taxes on its employees during this period. The board eventually had to close the house.

In 1958, under a new director, Ada S. McKinley House reopened again.[77] Problems with financial records continued, with the result that the Ada McKinley board's Executive Committee voted to recommend dissolution of the agency.[78] It looked like the end, but the settlement was still going strong two years later.[79] Such an up and down history was partially due to the fact that Chicago's Welfare Council lacked the budgetary controls over member agencies that Community Chests elsewhere possessed. Also, the repeated attempts to make a going concern out of McKinley are a reflection of the growing concern for civil rights and recognition of the need to provide more social services to blacks.

These settlements that were established primarily to serve blacks were in a very different position when it came to civil rights issues from those houses with a basically white clientele. The black houses were, without question, committed to the civil rights movement. However, even in the 1950s, they placed less emphasis on integration as a goal and more emphasis on black pride and the provision of services to blacks. White liberals sometimes had difficulty understanding the black position. For example, the National Federation of Settlements turned down Hester House in Houston for membership because the settlement listed as its purpose to benefit blacks in Houston. To the National Federation, that was a violation of their belief in integration.[80] Also, as early as the mid-1950s, whites were having to deal with the fact that black leaders were coming to resent the white presence on integrated boards of agencies with a predominantly black clientele.[81] Finally, the civil rights movement suddenly caused more money to be available to black agencies.

SETTLEMENT ACTIVISM ON HOUSING AND CIVIL RIGHTS

The accelerating civil rights movement and the wartime housing shortage contributed to the major racial confrontation of the 1940s—the Detroit riot of 1943. Shortly after the riot began, black and white staff workers and neighbors gathered at Franklin Settlement to prepare a statement urging the surrounding neighborhood to respect the privileges and rights of fellow Americans. The settlement groups then distributed the statement to four hundred families.[82] Also following the riot, the Detroit Federation of Settlements proposed a plan for interracial cooperation, which city authorities accepted.[83]

Around 1944, black families began moving into the Chicago Commons–Emerson House neighborhood. With the wartime housing shortage and the extreme demand for housing on the part of blacks, realtors discovered that they could make a good deal of money converting buildings from white occupancy to black by raising rents and cutting up apartments into smaller units. When that first began to happen on Chicago's Northwest Side, a group of Italian neighbors bought a newly converted building and, without warning, evicted all fifteen black families. Ten managed to find shelter elsewhere, but eighteen others were left on the street. Emerson House took them in, housing them over the weekend. Given the temper of the neighborhood, it was a courageous thing for the settlement to do.[84]

The settlement houses watched as more buildings on the near Northwest Side were subdivided into smaller apartments, rents were raised, and whites who could find better housing for less left to make way for blacks. In the reconversion of these buildings, numerous housing code violations occurred. The living conditions that resulted were incredibly bad. One of the worst examples unearthed by a Chicago Commons survey was the illegal conversion of a basement into a series of "apartments." One apartment consisted of two rooms newly walled off by plasterboard and no larger than ten or twelve square feet. A double bed, gas kitchen stove, and a table occupied most of the space in one room. Two double beds took up the space in the second room. The apartment had no toilet, sink, or running water. Tenants poured waste water through an open tile. The contents of a pipe coming down from the first floor also emptied into this tile. The three families occupying the basement apartments used the first-floor toilet, which was also shared by those renting apartments on the first floor. As one of them said, "We use it when we can get to it."

The family living in the two-room basement apartment described above consisted of a mother and father (employed and earning seventy-five cents an hour) and ten children. They had been in Chicago two months, having left a life as sharecroppers in Mississippi. Because of their large family, decent housing was impossible to find. A second family of seven occupied a ten-by-twenty-foot room in the same basement. The Commons workers noticed that a thirteen-year-old girl was trying to do her homework sitting on the floor and using the bed for a table. The girl had been in the eighth grade in the South, but in Chicago was put back into the fifth. A third family and a single, self-styled minister occupied the rest of the basement. For a basement to be used for dwelling purposes in Chicago, half of it was supposed to be above ground. Since that was clearly not the case, Chicago Commons reported the illegal remodeling to the Metropolitan Housing Council.[85]

In the mid-1940s, the Commons reported a number of other housing violations to various government agencies. For example, Taylor called to the attention of the Rental Division of the Office of Price Administration a building in which an Italian family was paying eleven dollars a month for a four-room apartment with toilet. A similar apartment in the same building was rented to *two* black families at nine dollars *per family per week*. The two families shared toilet and kitchen facilities.[86] In other words, an apartment rented to whites for eleven dollars a month could, if rented to blacks, yield at least seventy-two dollars a month. Such an example was not unusual.

The situation emphasized the need for more low-income housing as well as the need to reduce racial tensions. Lea Taylor had some input into government policy as a member of the Mayor's Committee on Race Relations, an appointment she accepted in 1946.[87] In addition to dealing with racial tensions when blacks moved into all-white areas, the committee dealt with such matters as where future public housing should be located. By the late 1940s, public housing was coming to mean housing for blacks in Chicago, with the result that white areas strongly and effectively opposed public housing construction in their neighborhoods. Beginning in 1948, Taylor also served as chair of the Housing Committee of the Commission on Human Relations and continued in that capacity through the selection of major public housing sites in the early 1950s.[88] Since then, public housing projects in places like Chicago have come in for strong criticism on the grounds that they tend to reinforce the ghetto. Yet knowing the conditions that public housing replaced, one can better understand why a socially conscious person like Lea Taylor would give public housing her support.

Housing was tied to the most typical form of racial violence in the

1940s—arson. Neighborhood burnings of buildings newly occupied by blacks were a problem in the Chicago Commons neighborhood. Lea Taylor recalled the following, fairly typical, incident:

> A frightened Italian neighbor telephoned. . . . The new landlord, a white man, was showing a succession of Negro men and women some vacant apartments in the building. . . . What should she do? We called immediately and tried to reassure her that these were people needing apartments, that they probably had children too, and that they had no intention of harming her. . . . But she was frightened by the many myths that bring on tensions. The next day we heard that she had moved in with relatives. Within a few days the entire house was occupied by at least a dozen Negro families transplanted from other seriously overcrowded sections of the city.
>
> The following morning two Negro men, fathers of families of young children, came and said: ". . . Last night a can of gasoline was set on fire at the foot of the stairway leading to the apartments we have just occupied on the second floor. We got the children out through the windows, and the fire department put out the fire before it gained headway. But what we want to know is, will the neighborhood ever like us and will we be able to sleep nights and feel that our children are safe?"
>
> They went on to tell us that they had lived long in one or two rooms in a crowded dark tenement on the South Side, looking daily for more healthful quarters. They saw an advertisement in a South Side paper which read, "Nice light rooms for rent." When they applied at the real estate office they were told if they were interested they would have to put up two months rent in advance on a furnished room basis. They asked the location and were told that they would not be given that information until the apartment was ready for them. They decided to take a chance. . . . So one day they were told they could move that night. They did so, and went to work the next day. When they returned home they found the family very fearful, because as they said, "It seems to be a white neighborhood, and the store people are unfriendly." And that night came the fire.
>
> Through the city's commission on human relations, police protection was guaranteed to that house on a day-and-night basis, and was maintained for months, while other houses suddenly changed hands and needed police protection until the neighborhood became less fearful.[89]

The worst incident of arson in the Chicago Commons neighborhood occurred in October 1947. A midnight fire broke out in a tenement occupied by blacks and with no rear exit or back stairs. Ten people were trapped in the building and perished. Another sixty were left homeless, and Chicago Commons housed them overnight. Lea Taylor was among those requesting "a thorough investigation and a special coroner's jury."[90] The director of Parkway Community House, Horace Cayton, was foreman of that jury. The hearings before the jury served to publicize the housing plight of blacks in Chicago. Lea Taylor also testified before the coroner's jury, in spite of the fact that her action set her white neighbors that much more against her settlement house. The jury's verdict was arson, but the arsonist was never found.[91]

In the 1950s, as more blacks arrived, settlements continued to be active in trying to counteract realtors' exploitation of the situation and to promote housing code enforcement. Germantown Settlement in Philadelphia waged a campaign against panic selling. It distributed signs, which it asked its neighbors to place in their windows, saying, "This house is not for sale."[92] Other settlements increased pressure on the city authorities to enforce the housing code. Sometimes threatened whites broadened their concern with the housing code to include neighborhood planning in general and put together a local community organization. In spite of the fact that part of the stimulus to form these groups was the desire to hold the color line in the neighborhood, settlement leaders such as Eleanor Bonham, head of University Settlement in Cleveland, found it prudent to join them.[93]

More routine were the efforts of settlement houses to assure blacks equal access to public housing, recreational facilities, and schools. In Philadelphia, settlement workers protested when the local Housing Authority threatened to turn a newly completed public housing project, which had replaced a black slum and been promised to blacks, into housing for war workers who were mostly white. The protest was effective and blacks, who badly needed housing, moved into the project.[94] In Pittsburgh, Rankin Christian Center actively campaigned for a public housing project and was effective in getting a number of units assigned to blacks in spite of white protests.[95] However, Chicago Commons was unable to convince the operator of a neighborhood wading pool to allow black youngsters to use it. No white force in the neighborhood would support the Commons on this issue.[96]

Integration continued to be the goal of the settlement movement into the 1960s. As the racial situation became more volatile, the National Federation of Settlements saw the need for a major survey of member houses' involvement with blacks and black issues. Therefore, it secured grants from the New World Foundation, the Stern Family Fund, and Board of Missions of the Methodist Church.[97] St. Clair Drake headed a team of eight interviewers and wrote *Race Relations in a Time of Rapid Social Change,* published by the National Federation in 1966. Out of 261 National Federation agencies, 142 actively participated in the project.[98]

The choice of St. Clair Drake for this problem-solving assessment was unfortunate. As late as 1966, Drake had a strong tendency to see integration as the all-encompassing issue. He had little sympathy for black power. As a black, middle-class sociology professor at Roosevelt University, Drake's attitudes were also compatible with a settlement movement that whites dominated and which emphasized consensus as opposed to conflict methods of social change. Symbolically, throughout the study, Drake used the word "Negro" rather than "black." He praised settlement attempts at interracial programming and promoted interracial staffs and boards, even for settlements in all-black neighborhoods. Correspondingly, he deplored the all-black settlement houses. His study, while not as vivid as its supporting interviews with settlement workers and related professionals,[99] was the largest on the subject of race relations that the National Federation of Settlements attempted. However, it failed to help the settlement movement adjust to rapidly changing conditions.

Nevertheless, by 1963, some fundamental conflict between the settlement house movement and civil rights was starting to become apparent. The settlement house was rooted in the idea that it was to serve an entire neighborhood, not just one ethnic or racial group, which may partially explain the appeal of integration as a goal. The emphasis on integration also underscored the "social control" nature of the settlement. Integration antagonized some remaining white neighbors and didn't always show much sensitivity to the needs and perspectives of black neighbors either. However, the settlement method stressed the peaceful bridging of class lines throughout the larger community. Finally, while settlements were serving more blacks with more black staff and black board members and were more committed to civil rights than ever before, the settlement movement on the eve of the War on Poverty was still basically a white movement burdened by a past that had often ignored black needs. These factors portended trouble for settlements as the civil rights movement entered its "black power" phase, neighborhoods continued to change from white to black, and even more blacks joined settlement staffs.

CHAPTER 6

PROFESSIONAL REFORM— SETTLEMENT HOUSE STYLE

———•◦•———

PROFESSIONALISM AND CHANGING NEIGHBORHOODS were important factors affecting the settlement house. A third important factor was the nature of social reform. This chapter analyzes the standard settlement method of achieving reform by focusing on settlement efforts on behalf of welfare issues. Just as the settlement shift toward being more responsive to its growing black constituency was slow, settlement efforts in other areas like welfare reflected a philosophy of incremental change achieved by working patiently through established channels.

The relatively mild settlement house efforts in the health and welfare field reflect certain forces minimizing the movement's impact. First, the burgeoning federal welfare bureaucracy made private agencies, including settlements, seem increasingly minor. Also, the settlement house goal of bridging class lines dictated a low-key, traditional consensus approach—an approach hardly likely to make headlines. Furthermore, except for the Great Society years, welfare reformers have lacked the sympathetic, widespread support needed for major accomplishments. McCarthyism intimidated many liberals during this period, not just settlement workers guarding their respectability. Also, the impact of conservative, well-to-do board members on the National Federation had a dampening effect on the organization's social welfare leadership. Finally, for some individual settlements to take a liberal stand on a controversial issue like birth control could cost them neighborhood support. Nevertheless, what is significant about the settlement workers is that in spite of all these obstacles, they persisted in campaigning for better welfare programs. Prior to the mid-1960s, in the mix of board members, settlement staff, and neighbors, it was the settlement workers themselves who provided the major impetus for social change. As one settlement house worker saw his job, "There was no sense in working with kids from 3:30 to 5:30 if we knew they were going home to a table with no food."[1]

The post–World War II years weren't the first time that settlements had tried to carry on reform in a conservative period. In the 1920s, they had persisted through the Red Scare, political conservatism, and the growing influence of a social work profession that recommended adjusting an individual to society rather than trying to change society. In the course of their efforts, settlement workers by the end of the 1920s had become less sentimental, more career-oriented, and less mission-oriented. Nevertheless, they still helped to provide continuity between the reforms of the Progressive Era and those of the New Deal.[2] If, during the 1950s, settlement workers were again going through the motions of advocating welfare reform with the hope that another reform period would arrive, they had past experience to bolster their optimism. A look at how settlements campaigned on behalf of welfare issues in the decades following the Great Depression not only reveals the settlement method at work, but also shows the effects of certain conservative social control forces operating to limit settlement efforts.

THE ROLE OF THE NATIONAL FEDERATION OF SETTLEMENTS

One of the major changes in settlement advocacy of better welfare programs was the increasing role the National Federation of Settlements played. Several reasons account for this development. First, as a result of the New Deal, the federal government supplanted local governments as the major provider of welfare programs. That meant that advocacy of better welfare was increasingly conducted at the national level. Second, the general trend toward professionalism highlighted the role of professional organizations. Thus, in the area of welfare advocacy, because the Hatch Act prevented public employees from engaging in political activity, social workers in private agencies, such as settlement houses, had an added need to fill this function. Individual houses were autonomous, but they could often be more effective by unifying their efforts. Therefore, the National Federation of Settlements increasingly took the leadership in setting social reform priorities and then working on an agenda of activities to achieve its goals. This agenda included surveys, publicity, lobbying, and demonstration projects.

In 1946, the National Federation of Settlements (NFS) gave organizational recognition to its long-standing commitment to reform with the formation of the Social Education and Action Committee. At about the same time, the NFS also designated a staff position for Social Education and Action. The inspiration for this arrangement may have come from a similar one in the Presbyterian church, in which the NFS's executive director, John McDowell, was active.

Fern Colborn, who was the National Federation's director of Social Education and Action from 1950 to 1961 and continued working for the NFS in other capacities after that, was particularly effective. Prior to joining the National Federation, Colborn attended the University of Pennsylvania School of Social Work and directed Beth Eden House in Philadelphia as well as worked on the Social Education and Action staff of the Presbyterian church. While working for the National Federation, she wrote a number of pamphlets and articles plus two books, *The Neighborhood and Urban Renewal,* for use by both settlement workers and housing officials, and *Buildings of Tomorrow,* the only book on the architecture of neighborhood centers. On her retirement in 1968, she received praise from Robert C. Weaver, Secretary of the Department of Housing and Urban Development, and Wilbur J. Cohen, then Under Secretary of Health, Education, and Welfare, for her work on behalf of better housing and welfare programs. President Johnson had earlier honored Colborn's work on behalf of Model Cities by inviting her to the bill-signing ceremony.[3] Whenever the National Federation was involved in a project of some substance, Fern Colborn was likely to be the main force behind it.

Among the activities of the Social Education and Action director were informational mailings on issues and bills to member houses plus surveys and publicity. The surveys usually consisted of requests that member houses supply the National Federation with accounts of specific people who were experiencing a particular kind of problem. The purpose was to "put flesh and bones" on statistical data. For example, in 1949, the Joint Congressional Committee set up by the Fulbright Employment Act had collected statistics on urban families earning less than $2,000. It requested settlements to furnish three hundred case studies of actual people living under this limit.[4] Settlement leader Helen Hall coordinated the effort. Her method was journalistic. She rejected some case studies as not heartrending enough and made no pretense about being scientific. Congressmen, who know enough about statistics to know that they can be manipulated, might question the credibility of statisticians. However, settlement workers could add legitimacy and color to the statistics because they lived and worked in low-income areas. When Hall testified before the congressional committee, she talked about people she personally knew. The government published her survey results as "Making Ends Meet on Less Than $2,000 a Year." Senator John Sparkman, chair of the Subcommittee on Low-Income Families, requested this report for use as source material to back a wide range of welfare proposals. While the report did not make definite recommendations, it did point out the need for better wages, wider coverage for unemployment compensation, improved health care, increased welfare and Aid to Dependent Children benefits, higher quality education (including vocational education), more regulation of loan companies and installment buying, and finally, additional recreational programs.[5]

Furnishing survey data was a relatively mild type of advocacy. Basically, two ways existed to influence the political process—the traditional way of working through established channels and the radical way of organized protest. Settlements tended to go the traditional route. An illustration of the two approaches was Illinois' decision to arbitrarily cut Aid to Dependent Children, Old Age Assistance, and General Assistance budgets in 1949 and again in 1950.[6] The University of Chicago Settlement concentrated on providing the National Federation with the case studies mentioned above. However, the initiative for organizing the neighborhood to protest the cuts with the goal of seeing the governor came from another organization in that settlement's area, the Back of the Yards Council,[7] one of the most successful Saul Alinsky groups. The state subsequently granted a slight increase in welfare allowances. In this situation, the Alinsky tactics were more directly effective. However, the traditional settlement tactics were supportive and effective in other contexts.

The National Federation of Settlements further gave direction to settlement house reform efforts through the annual passage of resolutions and later on a "social policy platform." Unfortunately, twice during the conservative 1950s, the NFS's policy of passing resolutions to further social change came under attack. In both cases, the attacks were launched by the NFS's well-to-do board members. Originally, the National Federation board consisted of settlement house workers themselves. However, in 1951, the NFS changed the composition of its board to include lay people active on settlement boards at the local level. At that time, these local board members were drawn almost exclusively from the well-to-do rather than the poor. The NFS hoped these board members would broaden its base of support, financially and otherwise. The trade-off was that these new board members brought more conservative social attitudes with them.

Prior to 1951, a resolutions committee consisting of settlement workers wrote resolutions on national, and even international, issues that were usually passed at the national conference. However, when local, well-to-do board members took on a larger role in the National Federation, one of the first things they did was to question how representative the resolutions were of local (meaning their) attitudes. As a result, the resolutions procedure was revised to require that copies of all resolutions be sent to affiliated settlements forty days or more prior to national conferences. Furthermore, in publicizing the resolutions and sending them to interested Congressmen and government officials, the National Federation of Settlements had to state that they represented the consensus of the national delegate body and not necessarily the opinions of individual houses.[8] However, some board members still objected to the passage of resolutions and the inclusion of opinions in testimony before congressional committees. In 1958, the resolutions procedure was changed again to require that resolutions first pass the National Federation of Settlements board before being submitted to the conference delegates.[9] Since local board

members accounted for around half of the National Federation of
Settlements board at this time, they came close to having a veto over
resolutions. In 1961, the board actually vetoed resolutions favoring
national health insurance for the aged and the Youth Opportunities
Act.[10] Perhaps to keep from having to fight the same battles over
again as the political winds shifted, the federation switched in the
early 1960s from annual resolutions to a "social policy platform" that
didn't require annual passage except for minor revisions. Thus, settlement workers tried to curtail the conservative challenges of board
members.

It may be of some significance that the first resolutions controversy coincided with a peaking of McCarthyism. Although attempts
were made to discredit a couple of settlement leaders, only one apparently lost his job as a result. In April 1949, the board of New
Orleans' Kingsley House forced the resignation of its director, Emeric
Kurtagh. The reason was that Kurtagh's name was on a list issued
by the House Un-American Activities Committee. HUAC accused
Kurtagh of membership in two organizations it called Communist
fronts—the American Committee for Democracy and Intellectual
Freedom and the Southern Conference for Human Welfare. Kurtagh claimed that he had never been a member of the former, although he had sponsored a rally by that group in 1940 and had also
signed the group's petition protesting the release of Bertrand Russell from the City College of New York faculty. Kurtagh said he had
dropped his membership in the second group. In spite of his protests that he was not a Communist and had "been fighting Communism from way back," he lost his job.[11] Luckily, he soon found another as director of Detroit's Tau Beta Community House, a smaller
settlement.[12] Afterward, Kurtagh, who had been a social activist,
avoided social action causes.

In connection with a phenomenon like McCarthyism, professional
associations can play a defensive role in speaking out collectively when
it may be difficult for individuals to do so. In May 1951, the National
Federation of Settlements passed two resolutions. One deplored the
misuse of loyalty oaths and went on to attack the use of the Attorney
General's list of subversive organizations. The National Federation
stated that guilt by association with organizations on the list resulted
in innocent people losing jobs, being ostracized by fellow workers,

and having difficulty in finding employment.[13] The National Federation also criticized the federal government for suppressing Charlotte Towle's pamphlet "Common Human Needs," because the
American Medical Association objected to the statement "Social Security and public assistance programs are a basic essential for attain-
ment of the socialized state envisaged in a democratic ideology, a
way of life which so far has been realized only in slight measure."[14]
Unfortunately, after 1951 and with a changed board, the National
Federation of Settlements was silent on the issue of McCarthyism.

In 1953, when New York settlement workers began getting inquiries from public housing tenants regarding a requirement that they
sign a statement saying that they were not members of organizations
on the Attorney General's subversives list, the settlement workers
turned to United Neighborhood Houses of New York, their local
settlement federation. While United Neighborhood Houses opposed
the loyalty statement,[15] it refused to join other reputable organizations in court actions and publicity efforts.[16] Even so, HUAC criticized United Neighborhood Houses director Helen Harris for her
past connection with the Social Workers' Committee to Aid Spanish
Democracy, for being a sponsor of the American Youth Congress,
and for speaking in favor of such issues as a milk cooperative and
rent control, "the Communist line" according to HUAC.[17] The risk
these professional organizations faced was in being labeled sympathetic to communism and losing financial support. However, in not
speaking out, they made liberal activities more difficult for their
members and supporters.

McCarthyism could bring liberal political activity in the past back
to haunt an individual. In the 1930s, some settlement workers and
volunteers had worked for and given support to the Socialist party's
Workers Committee on Unemployment, which merged with the
Communist party's Unemployed Councils to form the Workers' Alliance. Several years later, the Communists took over the Workers'
Alliance. Frank McCulloch was a Chicago Commons volunteer active
in organizing the unemployed and later in fighting the Communist
takeover of the Workers' Alliance.[18] During the 1950s, he served as
Senator Paul Douglas' campaign manager and then went on to chair
the National Labor Relations Board. When I initially approached
McCulloch about interviewing him regarding his activities organiz-

ing the unemployed, McCulloch was interested; but then he had second thoughts and broke off the correspondence.

Many who lived through the McCarthy era never fully recovered. In McCulloch's case, he moved from being a radical to a mainstream liberal. Others, however, were permanently scared away from liberal social action. The effect of McCarthyism on intimidating the settlement movement in the area of social action is difficult to gauge. That settlement house professional organizations apparently adopted policies of silence on McCarthyism in the early 1950s does indicate some giving in to intimidation and resulting political conservatism.

The controversy over the establishment of the Aid to Dependent Children program in Illinois illustrated the need for a national organization to give focus and impetus to settlement house reform efforts. Individual houses often differed. For example, though it was a federal program, each state had to pass enabling legislation for Aid to Dependent Children to become effective in that state. In 1941, Chicago Commons' head Lea Taylor congratulated Representative Joseph L. Rategan for sponsoring the establishment of the program in Illinois,[19] but the board of the University of Chicago Settlement deliberately refused to endorse Illinois' adoption of Aid to Dependent Children.[20] The National Federation, however, clearly supported the program. Twenty years later, settlement houses nationally complained that for a family to become eligible for Aid to Dependent Children, it was necessary for the father to desert.[21] Fern Colborn, an employee of the National Federation of Settlements, testified before the House Ways and Means Committee in favor of changing the Aid to Dependent Children program to include families where the father remained in the home.[22] The law passed.

McCarthyism and the controversy over passage of resolutions did not stop the National Federation from furthering certain legislation through congressional testimony. Sometimes a National Federation employee, such as Fern Colborn, gave the testimony. The National Federation also acted as the coordinator of testimony from a number of settlement house workers on a variety of issues. Thus, the National Federation contributed to the passage of the 1949 Housing Act, which launched a major program of public housing construction.[23] About that time, the National Federation board decided to divide the responsibility among various houses for going to Washington to testify on behalf of minimum wage laws, inflation, health care, civil liberties, and federal aid to public education.[24] This practice was more or less followed in subsequent years.

To prepare settlement house workers for public hearings, veteran settlement house activist Helen Hall formulated a set of guidelines. First, she advised settlement workers who have the opportunity to influence the choice of people testifying to see that a variety of community elements were represented. Social workers, she thought, made effective witnesses. However, the poor themselves had more impact, bringing "a vividness and reality" to their testimony. Experts in the area of legislation were also important to show that the proposed program was feasible. As for the settlement workers' testimony, Hall advised them to avoid getting caught in technical intricacies by stating that they were speaking from personal observation and experience. The role of the settlement worker was to add honest, human interest material. Surveys and case studies were useful here. Finally, settlement workers should try to get as many people and organizations affected to attend as possible. They could mean the difference in outcome. To illustrate, she described a meat-grading ordinance hearing in New York City. The lawyer opposing the ordinance failed to see the housewives sitting in the back and concluded his arguments by saying that if consumers wanted the ordinance, they would be there. The housewives "rose and cried out, 'We are here. *We are here. We do care!*' " That demolished the opposition.[25] Because settlement workers built up a reputation for reliability and credibility, liberal politicians frequently called on them to participate in hearings.

From the 1930s to the 1960s, Helen Hall was the most frequent settlement house worker to testify at congressional hearings. When Senator Robert Wagner was pushing his Full Employment Act at the close of World War II, he called on Hall to testify, just as he had called on her to testify in the early months of the Great Depression.[26] Some twenty years later, Hall's settlement, Henry Street, did a random sampling of its golden age "Good Companions" group. She discovered the average Social Security check was $66.05 per month, of which $33.50 went for rent. That left around $1.00 per day for food, clothing, transportation, and other expenses.[27] Hall sent the results to Representative Leonard Farbstein. Her survey was printed as an editorial in the *New York Times*, and she used it in testimony before the House Ways and Means Committee.[28] Thus, she contributed to increasing the levels of Social Security benefits. She also testified at other times on consumer protection, housing, and the need for national health insurance.

During these years, the National Federation of Settlements,[29] and especially Helen Hall, put more effort into obtaining some kind of national health insurance than any other measure.[30] Since 1917, the National Federation had sponsored several studies to illustrate their arguments for national health insurance. In 1951, Hall issued a report, "When Sickness Strikes a Family," based on interviews with 553 families in the Henry Street neighborhood.[31] President Truman's Commission on the Health Needs of the Nation reprinted this study in *Building America's Health*.[32] Hall also served on the commission's Panel of Financing a Health Program. Fifteen settlement houses scattered around the country did a similar study in 1953.[33] At that time, the National Federation sent George W. Goetschius to England to write a book-length description of the British National Health Service.[34] Then in 1961, the National Federation asked member settlements to send in material, which became "Case Studies on How the Aged Meet Hospital Bills."[35] Some of Hall's more imaginative ways of agitating for national health insurance were the production in 1939 of a play, "Medicine Show," about the inadequate health facilities available to the poor[36] and the sending of a caravan of senior citizens to buttonhole Congressmen in Washington in 1963.[37] National health insurance remained an elusive goal, but Medicare became a reality in 1965.

In the 1960s, National Federation of Settlements legislative activities became more sophisticated with the employment in Washington of Mrs. Field Haviland. Her job was to keep track of proposed bills and notify the National Federation so that its lobbying efforts would be more effective.[38] In recognition of the National Federation's efforts, President Johnson invited settlement representatives to witness the signing of the laws creating Medicare, the Department of Housing and Urban Development, and new housing programs.[39]

City federations, particularly United Neighborhood Houses of New York and the Chicago Federation of Settlements, lobbied at the state level. Their methods mirrored the NFS's. To challenge public assistance cuts in Illinois in 1950, the Chicago Federation of Settlements collected samples of what the aid cuts meant to actual people in their neighborhoods. A typical family with three children had its aid cut from $103 to $85. That left $40 for food, not enough for all family members to eat regularly. The Chicago Federation sarcastically asked the Illinois Public Aid Commission, "What is the mother to do if she has a headache and no money for aspirin? The answer is, 'Let it ache!' "[40]

Individual settlements also lobbied. In 1962, Hull House head Paul Jans personally conveyed to a meeting of the Illinois Public Aid Commission that his board thought the welfare department should make birth control information available to its clients,[41] a change in policy which was soon made. On another occasion when the Illinois General Assembly delayed relief checks while it argued over aid-grant ceilings, Hull House threatened to take on conservative legislators in their home territory by sending speakers to the churches where downstate legislators were members. Jans believed that even the most conservative legislators were "not in favor of people starving. They just don't believe it's happening."[42]

In addition to formal testimony at hearings, settlement workers cultivated politically influential people who could be of assistance in their efforts on behalf of the poor. An excellent example of this activity is Helen Hall's relationship to Mr. and Mrs. Herbert Lehman. As a young man, Herbert Lehman led a boys' club at Henry Street Settlement. He prospered and became governor of New York, and Hall campaigned for Lehman's election to the Senate. In the early 1950s, he chaired the Senate Subcommittee on Health. Meanwhile, Mrs. Lehman was an active Henry Street Settlement board member. The Lehmans regularly made substantial gifts to the settlement and also donated the money to build "Pete's House," a postwar addition to the Henry Street buildings which was named in honor of the Lehmans' son killed in World War II.[43]

At the city level, settlements also cultivated local politicians. For years, Stanley Isaacs was both a New York councilman and president of United Neighborhood Houses of New York's federation of forty-six settlements. Isaacs was also an advocate of better welfare programs.[44] In Philadelphia, William J. Green served on the board of the Greater Philadelphia Federation of Settlements until he took office as mayor in 1980. Occasionally, aldermen and councilmen along with other government officials served on the boards of individual settlements as well. With influential board members, middle-class staff, and poor clientele, the settlement was in a position to bridge class lines. The access it offered different groups to each other was useful in furthering social action.

Most National Federation of Settlements efforts in social action involved the poor only passively. Usually, testimony was given in Washington about the poor by settlement workers, not by the poor themselves. About the closest the National Federation came to involving the poor directly prior to the 1960s was through the Washington legislative conferences organized approximately every two years beginning in 1946. The conferences had two purposes. First, they gave settlement neighbors a chance to express their opinions directly to their Congressmen in Washington. Second, they provided settlement workers with an opportunity to educate their neighbors in the legislative process.[45] Usually several hundred people took part; but because of the expense, few neighbors in attendance were from very far west of Washington, D.C.[46] Also, delegate participation was essentially as passive listeners until 1970, when some Welfare Rights Organization members tried confrontation, and several meetings with Congressmen were disruptive.[47] The conferences were generally more education-oriented than action-oriented.

THE ROLE OF INDIVIDUAL SETTLEMENTS

Because individual settlements were autonomous within the national movement, that autonomy lent an added dimension to settlement house social action efforts. It was largely at the local level that settlements involved their neighbors in direct participation in reform efforts. This participation was of a relatively mild nature until the War on Poverty popularized direct action. The autonomous nature of individual settlements also meant that some houses, if they so chose, were freer to carry on certain controversial activities. Settlement activity in the area of birth control illustrated the value of autonomous settlements being able to individually tailor their policies to suit widely different neighborhoods. The demonstration project method of social reform was also best adapted to individual houses. Given the National Federation's aversion to government grants and government-sponsored projects, the freedom of member houses to engage in government-sponsored activity was important. Thus, in spite of growing activity at the National Federation level, individual settlement houses retained their significance.

On the local level, settlements sought to involve their neighbors in social action through the traditional program. In the early days of the settlement movement, a number of houses staged forums or lecture/discussions on social issues. Some of these continued into the 1940s. The Hull House Forum featured sessions on "Relief," "Race, Nationality, and Democracy," and other topics.[48] The typical forum flitted from topic to topic and never went beyond passive education to direct action. Sometimes the groups got sidetracked into self-help projects, as was the case with the Hill District People's Forum at Irene Kaufman Settlement in Pittsburgh. An interest in housing led to a cleanup, paint, and plaster campaign. This group also organized block parties and other social activities.[49] Another device for involving neighbors in social action was having them write and stage a play about a social issue. The inspiration for this technique was the WPA's "Living Newspaper." A more widely used strategy was interviewing neighbors as part of a social survey to gather data in support of a particular issue like national health insurance. Among forums, dramas, and surveys, the social survey was probably most effective in involving large numbers of the poor and also most likely to have an impact beyond the settlement house neighborhood.

Until the mid-1960s, settlements avoided the radical style of protest; and even then, settlements were reluctant to utilize or encourage confrontation or direct action tactics. An exception in the mid-1960s was South Side Settlement in Columbus, Ohio. There settlement workers became concerned about the level of relief when they realized some of their neighbors were going hungry. The settlement workers began to organize their neighbors, some of whom were on relief, by first calling a meeting. Next the workers accompanied their neighbors to the City Council Committee Relief Hearings, since this body set the level of welfare grants. At first the neighbors just listened, but at the second hearing, one settlement worker described:

> One young man about 32 years old [who] got up and, after
> hearing some of the County Commissioners talk about people
> who were on welfare who don't belong there, about chiseling
> and this kind of thing—well he got up and I guess it took him
> about a half hour to gather up the strength to get up before all
> those people there—and he said that he was unemployed. He
> pulled out of his pockets about 21 different slips from 21 differ-
> ent personell [*sic*] offices where he had looked for work but
> couldn't get work. He didn't want to be on relief but he couldn't
> find a job.

One of the commissioners was sufficiently bothered by that individual to give the man a county job. However, relief in Columbus
was still around 40 to 50 percent of state standards. Another woman
complained at this same hearing about medical assistance:

> I've gone up to the University Hospital for an examination. Three
> years ago I was operated on for cancer and the doctor said to
> me that I need another operation. And you know what he said
> to me, Mr. Commissioner? The doctor said that the Welfare De-
> partment would pay for half of the operation and I would have
> to pay for the other half, in terms of funds available for medical
> care to indigent at that time. You know what I said to him Mr.
> Commissioner? You operate on the half of me that the Welfare
> Department is going to pay for. Because I don't have the money.

South Side Settlement continued to involve its neighbors in meetings with the mayor, state welfare director, and governor. Neighbors
brought state legislators down to the settlement house to talk. When
that didn't produce results, the neighbors (about fifty of them) decided themselves to picket the State House. The settlement also used
volunteers in a voter registration drive. As a result of the "radical"
activity, some right-wing elements threatened to cut the settlement
off from United Fund support, but nothing happened. The settlement's board stood by the staff, partly because conservative board
members had already resigned.[50] While such action did produce some
results in the 1960s, in terms of welfare policies, its most significant
effect may have been the sense of power or control over one's des-
tiny that the protest participants gained.

In another kind of controversy, that over birth control, the individual autonomy of settlement houses was an advantage over other centrally controlled private agencies, like the YWCA. Birth control was so controversial that prior to the mid-1960s, public caseworkers were instructed not to discuss birth control with their clients, nor would public welfare pay for birth control services. Thus, the burden for providing this controversial program lay with private agencies.

Some settlements in ethnic neighborhoods found the birth control issue too controversial to touch. In the late 1930s, local Catholic churches accused Minneapolis' Northeast Neighborhood House of giving out birth control information. The resultant breach between the settlement and the neighborhood churches took five or six years to heal.[51] In 1949, National Federation of Settlements director John McDowell advised Philadelphia's Reed Street Settlement to discontinue its maternal health clinic, which offered birth control services. McDowell asked, "What does offering a service counter to religious teaching of the largest group in the neighborhood do to the settlement's relations to that neighborhood?" Reed Street reluctantly relinquished the clinic.[52]

However, other settlements successfully provided birth control services. Some loaned space within their buildings for birth control clinics. Neighborhood residents would be more likely to use clinics housed within an accepted neighborhood agency. Planned Parenthood established a number of these clinics in Chicago settlements. Abraham Lincoln Centre on Chicago's South Side had a clinic dating back to the 1930s.[53] Methodist-sponsored Newberry Center had a clinic since the early 1940s.[54] Newberry's sister center, Marcy, began a Planned Parenthood Clinic in 1947.[55] In 1961, Henry Booth House, which became one of the components of Hull House, began its clinic.[56] Kingdom House, a Methodist-sponsored agency in St. Louis during the early 1960s, was the most unusual case I came across. There the settlement caseworker actually distributed birth control supplies, which she received free from a board member.[57] When Planned Parenthood had trouble winning acceptance in a certain St. Paul neighborhood, it asked to station a Planned Parenthood representative in a settlement's Well Baby Clinic. After some hesitation, the settlement granted permission.[58] Protestant sponsorship and/or a receptive neighborhood were essential to these activities.

Besides housing some clinics, settlement houses occasionally lent their voices as advocates to make birth control more widely available. In 1953, United Neighborhood Houses of New York protested the exclusion of Planned Parenthood from the Welfare and Health Council. The council excluded Planned Parenthood because the Catholic agencies threatened to withdraw. United Neighborhood Houses' response was to then let the Catholics leave.[59] In the early 1960s, both Hull House Association and Abraham Lincoln Centre supported the movement to get Cook County Hospital and public health clinics to offer birth control services to indigent women.[60] Cook County subsequently pioneered in changing welfare practices in the area of birth control. On the other hand, the National Federation of Settlements did not go on record favoring the dissemination of birth control until 1965.[61] With a few brave exceptions, most of the houses that got involved with birth control advocacy and services prior to 1965 were in the non–Community Chest cities of New York and Chicago. There, without Community Chest funding, each settlement had maximum autonomy to respond as it saw fit.

The Planned Parenthood clinics illustrate the demonstration project method of reform. Settlements saw a need, they instituted a small-scale demonstration project to prove its worth, and then they hoped society would make the service available to everyone. In their early days, a number of settlements established medical and dental clinics. However, the growth in publicly funded health care services has meant that most of these settlement clinics have become a thing of the past. Likewise, settlements often ran small job placement services until the United States Job Service was established in the 1930s. Since then, settlement efforts have focused on encouraging neighbors to use the government agency. Helen Hall had a special interest in consumer issues. She supported a milk cooperative and a credit union at Henry Street. While cooperatives were difficult to sustain, a well-managed credit union could go on for years. In the early 1960s, emphasis switched to consumer clinics, with their educational programs and individual counseling for people in difficulty. In all cases, while providing these small projects, settlements worked to gain major public support to solve the problem, whether it was better public health services or "truth in lending" and other consumer protection laws.

An excellent example of the demonstration project method was

Meals-on-Wheels. The program began in 1954 at a Philadelphia settlement, the Lighthouse, then under the direction of Paul Jans. Its purpose was to deliver on a daily basis hot meals to people in their own homes who for one reason or another, such as poor health or disability, were unable to shop and cook for themselves.[62] The service was partially staffed by volunteers, partially grant-funded, meant to be a demonstration project, and well publicized. By 1957, it had spread to Columbus and New York City. The Lighthouse received inquiries from social agencies in almost every state.[63] The program continued to spread in the 1960s and has survived the demise of the War on Poverty.

Prior to the 1970s, the National Federation of Settlements was not particularly demonstration-project-oriented itself. During the Korean War, it did receive grant funds from the United Community Defense Services, a private agency, to do community organization in a couple of defense towns, Warner Robins, Georgia, and Moses Lake, Washington. Also, in the late 1960s, the National Federation got private funding for the Mississippi Project, which involved the establishment of community centers and community organization in rural Mississippi. Generally, the NFS seemed to feel that the demonstration project method was most appropriately carried on at the local level by individual settlement houses. Furthermore, until the 1970s, the National Federation avoided government grants. It may have been concerned about its political independence or about the danger of becoming too dependent on an unstable source of funding or unsuccessful in a couple of attempts to gain federal funds. However, individual settlements were quite eager for government funds and quite willing to cooperate with various government programs. The fact that the NFS largely stayed out of this activity meant that it avoided competition for funds with individual settlements.

While they engaged in a variety of cooperative efforts with government, settlement houses tried to stay out of the relief-giving business themselves. Nevertheless, a number of houses had small emergency funds to help families out until they could get on public relief programs. Some settlements also collected donations of food and used clothing, which they distributed to the poor. These activities were incidental to the regular settlement program.

In addition, settlements also provided various kinds of supportive services to women on welfare. Chicago's McKinley House had a sewing program to help ADC mothers stretch their budgets by making their own and their children's clothing.[64] Two other Chicago settlements housed a Cook County program to train welfare mothers in homemaking, budgeting, and child care.[65] Since one of the reasons women on ADC had difficulty getting off welfare was that they couldn't find jobs paying enough to meet both their living and their day care expenses, Cleveland's Merrick House sought federal funds in 1964 to subsidize the children of ADC (now called Aid to Families of Dependent Children or AFDC) mothers in its nursery.[66] In addition to trying to improve the welfare system, settlements also tried to help their neighbors cope with the system as it existed.

Because welfare has never been popular with the taxpayers, welfare departments do not advertize their services and are quite closemouthed about discretionary grants, such as extra clothing allowances. This reticence created another role that private agencies, such as settlements, could fulfill. Welfare-conscious Marillac House sponsored a panel for its neighbors describing available welfare services.[67] People who were denied welfare or had other welfare-related problems turned to Marillac for assistance. They asked the settlement's help in learning why they were denied assistance, what they could do about delayed welfare checks or lost money, and where they could get household items not covered by welfare. Because Marillac was seeing about four or five of these people per day, the Cook County Department of Public Aid temporarily assigned one of its workers part-time to the settlement.[68] In most houses, the job of acting as an advocate for welfare clients with the welfare department fell to the personal service worker or whoever was providing casework on the settlement staff.[69] While this activity was highlighted during the War on Poverty, settlements had always engaged in it.

The settlement house movement went about seeking to improve welfare programs primarily through a consensus method. In 1939, Chicago Commons head Lea Taylor described how Chicago settlements mobilized their board members and generated publicity to pressure Illinois into granting an adequate relief budget, not 65 percent of minimum subsistence. She made a point of saying, "There has been no protest or disturbance on the part of the relief clients."[70] To settlement workers, the way to achieve reform continued to be through established channels. The settlement's chief professional organization, the National Federation of Settlements, was increasingly prominent in leading the way with resolutions, surveys, and coordination of congressional testimony. Local houses provided grassroots support, and at times carried out demonstration projects and organized their neighbors. The autonomy of the individual settlement house was occasionally an asset—for example, in tailoring controversial programs like birth control to specific neighborhoods and in departing from the National Federation's practice on government grants and cooperative efforts. In fact, along with the growing prominence of the National Federation, the increasing role of grantsmanship at the local settlement level and its pressures for professionalism represented the major changes in the movement's traditional consensus approach to welfare reform. As such, settlements helped to broaden the base of support necessary to achieve higher levels of welfare benefits, greater acceptance of birth control, and the eventual adoption of Medicare, Medicaid, and other gains in the health and welfare field. However, their slow, consensus, establishment-oriented methods of achieving social change were being seriously questioned.

CHAPTER 7

SETTLEMENT HOUSES
LOSE INFLUENCE:
THE SOCIOLOGICAL ATTACK

———•———

T HE SETTLEMENT HOUSE METHOD OF WORKING FOR reform was relatively mild and oriented toward seeking consensus across class lines. In the decades following the Great Depression, sociologists and others launched a serious attack on that method. Basically, their attack centered on the charge that settlement houses were not so much democratic agencies as they were institutions of social control. By far the most influential attacker was the leading promoter of conflict-style community organization, Saul Alinsky. His ideas were reinforced by other leading sociologists, and by civil rights and labor activists. Weakened by poor public relations and constrained by financial dependence on a conservative United Way, settlements were in a difficult position to defend themselves.

SAUL ALINSKY VERSUS THE SETTLEMENT HOUSE:
1939–1965

To understand Alinsky's attack, one must remember that historically settlement house workers had a tendency to speak for their

A portion of this chapter appeared as "Social Change: Settlement Houses and Saul Alinsky, 1939–1965," *Social Service Review* (September 1982), 56: 346–365.

neighbors in the slums. That carried more credibility with the larger community when settlement workers actually lived in the settlement neighborhoods. However, as residence of settlement workers in the settlement houses declined and virtually disappeared after World War II, settlement workers did not change their methods of social action. They continued to hold conferences, pass resolutions, write their Congressmen, testify at hearings, "interpret" the poor to the rest of the community, carry out demonstration projects, organize community councils, and run their usual programs. And generally, they refused to listen to what radical community organizer Saul Alinsky was telling them—the settlements were no longer in touch with their neighborhoods; they didn't know the influential neighborhood leaders; they didn't know what the neighborhood really wanted.[1] Alinsky also stressed a conflict as opposed to a cooperative approach in bringing about social change. Thus, Alinsky and the settlement houses were in opposition to each other.

Even though Alinsky's reputation grew at the same time that community organization was emerging as a separate discipline in social work, professional community organization prior to the 1960s betrayed little of Alinsky's influence. When Alinsky was organizing the Back of the Yards Council in 1939, the National Conference on Social Welfare was trying to define community organization.[2] In the 1940s, the University of Pittsburgh School of Social Work developed its specialization in social intergroup work. This program emphasized relationships among groups and did not stress mobilizing for community action in terms of effective pressure tactics. Pittsburgh's approach fit in with the trend toward the establishment of community councils. These were typically sponsored by welfare federations, the policymaking and money distribution arm of the Community Chests, although settlement houses occasionally took on the task of assigning some of their professional workers to these councils.

Before the 1960s, most community organization graduates went to work for United Funds. Also, it was hardly a booming specialty. Only seventy-eight social work graduates in 1960 had specialized in the field. When they organized and staffed community councils, their main goal was the coordination of social services through meetings attended largely by social agency professionals,[3] precisely what Alinsky had criticized fourteen years earlier as "monthly social get-togethers for a small group of professional people who wallow in their egos as self-anointed saviors of the people and commiserate with one another on the poor benighted people of the neighborhood who don't have sufficient intelligence to know what is good for them."[4]

Alinsky also criticized community councils for acting as the tools of conservative business interests that donated to private agencies. Alinsky claimed that in the 1930s, employers in the Mohawk Valley got settlement houses and other agencies to set up a community council, which then accused CIO organizers of being outside Communist agitators. He claimed the tactic was repeated in 1965 when he was denounced as an outside agitator on arriving in Rochester to organize FIGHT (Freedom, Integration, God, Honor, Today). As Alinsky saw it, he was more of an "insider" than those denouncing him because the black community invited him to come to Rochester, and "that's more than any other agency can say."[5] In other words, community councils formed by settlements and United Funds or Chests did not represent the poor.

From the settlement viewpoint, a certain amount of dominance was often necessary. Many times the instigation for the formation of a social action group came from the community worker. For example, when a group of merchants mentioned a poorly drained street, a settlement worker suggested they organize a committee and complain to the city departments involved. The merchants were quite surprised when the committee complaint brought results.[6] Another settlement-based community organizer had no success until he hit on the idea of promoting flower boxes. From there the worker interested his group in creating tot lots, and then in housing code enforcement.[7] To be effective, community workers often had to overcome the fact that they were of a different religion and nationality or race and were regarded as "outsiders" by those they were organizing.

One of the problems in community organization was that not all neighborhoods were homogeneous. In cases where a neighborhood was split by rival nationality or racial groups, some settlements thought they they had to exert control to try to get the groups to work together. At Hull House, the Mexicans distrusted the Greeks so much that they were unable to form a coalition strong enough to preserve their neighborhood from demolition.[8] In Philadelphia, Friends

Neighborhood Guild felt it had to take the lead in a certain neighborhood because of rivalry and lack of leadership among thirty small groups.[9] While settlement workers didn't like to think of themselves as domineering, they did think their domination was sometimes necessary.

Occasionally, settlement neighbors formed their own groups, then turned to the settlement for professional leadership. In 1958, the stated goal of Manhattanville Community Centers was to develop "indigenous leaders . . . to act on behalf of their own community needs and problems."[10] The settlement worker could help with formal organization and the development of leadership, and help the group members become more articulate. However, if the worker became too dominant, he or she could defeat the goal of stimulating indigenous leadership in the neighborhood.

The War on Poverty stressed "maximum feasible participation" of the poor in policymaking roles. Depending on how appointments were handled, a settlement board could put neighbors in policymaking positions as well as given them access to influential people in the larger community. Traditionally, boards contained wealthy businessmen, professionals, and other socially prominent people. Prior to the advent of the Community Chest, settlements depended on boards for fund-raising. That situation has persisted in the non-Chest cities of New York and Chicago, but elsewhere since the Chest appeared settlements have been free to pick board members for qualities other than their reputations as donors and fund-raisers. In spite of a growing tendency to appoint more neighborhood people, almost all settlement boards remained dominated by well-to-do people into the 1960s. While many were undoubtedly conservative, others were "innovators and even critics of the conservatism of their economic and social peers."[11] These well-to-do people provided the settlement with the means and contacts whereby the settlement house could interpret itself and its neighbors to the larger community.

However, pressure to appoint neighbors to the boards came from a variety of sources. In 1943, Cleveland's welfare federation requested settlements to appoint representatives from organized labor as well as from neighborhood racial and nationality groups,[12] but the response was token.[13] Sometimes when they were appointed, the local members were not especially influential, even in their own communities. Also, Paul Jans, who in 1959 headed a Philadelphia settlement, complained that as more neighbors appeared on boards, the settlements lost influence in the larger community.[14] Nevertheless, the trend gained added impetus in the 1960s from the War on Poverty's requirements for citizen participation. A number of settlements wanted federal grants, and neighbors on their boards were a help in getting them.[15] Generally speaking, a mixed board with some truly representative people from the neighborhood appears to have been the best arrangement, provided a settlement didn't depend on its board for money.

In summarizing the settlement approach to social action, the major change was the replacement of residents with professional workers. Settlement workers continued to stress reform through traditional channels. These included passing resolutions at the National Federation level, doing surveys, testifying before congressional committees, educating their neighbors through conferences and forums, forming them into social action groups and community councils, and occasionally admitting them to board membership. However, it is also important to note that several traditional approaches are largely absent. Occasionally, settlement workers got involved in politics by endorsing and working for candidates, but this kind of political involvement was relatively minor. Also, although some of the original settlement leaders, most notably Jane Addams, author of the classic *Twenty Years at Hull House,* had been superb publicists for the movement, publishing books and articles and being widely quoted in the press, this sort of talent had largely disappeared from the settlement movement. Increasingly, the public was more interested in what the poor themselves had to say than in what settlement workers had to say about the poor.

Meanwhile, toward the end of the Great Depression, an alternative approach to the cooperative one used by settlement houses emerged. This approach to community organization stressed conflict and giving the poor the power to speak for themselves. The man chiefly responsible for this conflict approach was Saul Alinsky. He specialized in organizing people who were thought too apathetic, too down-and-out, to do anything about their situation. His tactics involved going into a neighborhood on a temporary basis, finding indigenous leaders among the poor themselves, shaking people out of their apathy by personalizing social problems, building anger against a "villain" or finding a scapegoat, pitting the poor against other groups in conflict situations, setting concrete and attainable goals, utilizing direct action tactics, and eventually withdrawing his leadership to let the people's organization carry on under its newly found power. Alinsky was a superb publicist of his methods, a speaker much in demand, and, like Jane Addams, author of a classic, *Reveille for Radicals*. Through his Industrial Areas Foundation, he was in the business of creating conflict-style community organizations. Between 1939 and 1965, four of the organizations he created came into contact with settlements. Thus, settlements had several opportunities to become involved in an alternative approach to social action. Each of the four settlements responded differently.

The first of the settlements to have an experience with an Alinsky group was the University of Chicago Settlement, located in the neighborhood of Alinsky's first people's organization, the Back of the Yards Council. The Welfare Council of Chicago regarded the formation of the Back of the Yards Neighborhood Council in 1939 as "a natural reaction to the up-to-then traditional community council," in which middle-class professionals sought to minimize conflict. The Back of the Yards thrived on conflict.[16] However, several years passed before conflict openly erupted between the council and the University of Chicago Settlement, located in the council's territory. In the fall of 1939, the settlement had invited Saul Alinsky, the organizer behind the council, to speak on juvenile delinquency and his organizing efforts,[17] but it made no effort to join the Back of the Yards Council. Sociology professor Ernest W. Burgess gave a warning of what was to come in an interview in April 1943. Burgess said settlement houses were still in "the 'Lady Bountiful' stage of work and were controlled by board members from outside their communities." Lucy Carner of the Welfare Council replied to Burgess' criticisms by saying that older agencies might more readily learn from Alinsky's area projects if these agencies were not attacked by the projects. Prophetically, she warned, "If the Area Project finds that opportunity for success depends . . . on discrediting other agencies, it can probably do sufficient damage to their reputations to put them out of business."[18]

The fight erupted in the spring of 1944 when the Back of the Yards Council opposed the suggestion that the Infant Welfare Society move into the University of Chicago Settlement. The council charged that the settlement was anti-Catholic because settlement staff had helped Catholic women get divorces, had given out birth control information, and had made derogatory remarks about the Catholic church. The Back of the Yards Council also accused the settlement of being antilabor because it had denied use of its facilities to the CIO and had opposed a strike the neighborhood strongly favored. In addition, it accused the settlement of being anti-Semitic for allowing the local Kiwanis Club, which excluded Jews, to use its facilities. Finally, the council claimed that the house had "done nothing for the neighborhood" and was not developing indigenous leadership. Alinsky suggested that the settlement sell its building to the Back of the Yards Council, which badly needed facilities. The settlement categorically denied the charges and refused to sell.[19]

The settlement then tried to find a way out of the conflict. Board members held a series of interviews with the settlement's supporters, including President Hutchins of the University of Chicago, who suggested the settlement leave the neighborhood if it felt the council was so strong that the settlement couldn't function. He went so far as to suggest that the settlement consider relocating in "the Negro district where the need is so great."[20] The suggestion was significant because ten years later Hutchins' successor forced the settlement to stop using the name "University of Chicago" and urged the university community to keep its charitable efforts closer to home. The university was by that time in a major struggle to hold the line against deterioration in Hyde Park. Since the bulk of the board had always been drawn from the university community, the loss of university support in 1955 was devastating.

In 1944 and 1945, the settlement's board was equally stubborn in ignoring what Saul Alinsky and the local Catholic bishop had to say. When the board decided to get neighborhood opinion, it deliberately selected people who had already expressed their dissatisfaction with the Back of the Yards Council. They rather inanely justified their biased selection by saying, "The favorable side of the picture had been painted by members of the Council itself."[21] In the end, the settlement requested to join the council and was rejected. The settlement also announced good intentions to appoint neighborhood people to its board, but never did so to any significant extent. Furthermore, its reputation never fully recovered from the attack.

The University of Chicago Settlement did become a member of the Back of the Yards Council in 1947, but it was never able to successfully define its area of responsibility in relation to the council or other neighborhood groups. What good feeling existed between the council and the settlement seems to have been based on personal relationships. For example, settlement head worker Bert Boerner was elected chairman of the Back of the Yards Youth Committee,[22] and his successor, Daniel DeFalco, served as chairman of the Council Recreation Committee.[23] Settlement membership had declined during the council attack; it revived with council membership, and churches resumed sending their groups to the settlement gym.[24] The council also offered occasional token financial support, such as four hundred dollars in 1947 to help repair the house roof.[25] However, when the settlement requested major help from the council to continue operating in 1962, it was not forthcoming. In the opinion of the council, the neighborhood churches had developed sufficient recreational programs for the area,[26] implying the settlement was not needed. The settlement, which had been lax in keeping up its contacts with the Back of the Yards Council,[27] faded out of independent existence a few years later to be absorbed by Chicago Commons.

The only case of a settlement inviting Saul Alinsky into its neighborhood to put together a "people's organization" was that of Hudson Guild in New York City's Chelsea district. The New York Foundation had hired Alinsky to do a preliminary survey in the mid-1950s. However, because of Alinsky's controversial reputation and the attitude of United Neighborhood Houses of New York, the foundation requested that Hudson Guild act as the sponsor for the area project and work out a proposal with Alinsky's assistance. According to Alinsky biographer P. David Finks, social workers were concerned that Alinsky's "rough and tumble organizing approach would alienate supporters of neighborhood-based social agencies, and perhaps even stir up ethnic warfare among whites, blacks and Puerto

Ricans."[28] Initially ignoring these concerns, the guild's director, Dan Carpenter, agreed to devote half his time as project director, and Alinsky was hired as project consultant. That meant that Alinsky would spend forty-eight days per year for three years in New York City advising the director (Carpenter), training staff, and guiding the organization. Alinsky not only fulfilled his contract, but donated his services free of charge for a fourth year, and his Industrial Areas Foundation also donated that year a Spanish-speaking organizer. The outcome of their efforts was the Chelsea Community Council, which at its height contained representatives from ninety organizations. However, nineteen months after it was formally organized, nearly half the participating organizations (the non-Catholic ones) withdrew in protest over the conflict the council generated. Eight months later the Chelsea Community Council disbanded.

Several explanations were offered to explain the failure. Dan Carpenter complained about Alinsky's methods of generating internal conflict and pitting one group against another. In fact, Carpenter himself became one of Alinsky's targets. Sanford Kahn, a community organizer for the project, cited a number of other reasons. Father Dunn, whom Alinsky supported as president of the organization, may have been the wrong man for the job. Also, Kahn conceded the failure to find or develop indigenous leadership. Finks cited the low opinion Alinsky and Monsignor John O'Grady had of the settlement house's general ability to involve its neighbors. The response of settlements that Alinsky always took the side of settlement neighbors in disputes rather than act on the merits of the issues merely underscored the clash in methods between Alinsky groups and settlement houses. Alinsky probably felt that he failed in Chelsea because he had to work through an established social agency.[29] Hudson Guild, on the other hand, depended on a variety of other agencies, including city government, for funding. It had to protect its goodwill with those agencies.[30]

However, what comes through in all accounts was the diversity of the neighborhood. Protestants, Catholics, and Jews were all strongly represented. The neighborhood contained Puerto Ricans, blacks, and whites and people of all income levels. In other words, it was almost a complete contrast to the homogeneous, working-class, Catholic Back of the Yards neighborhood. When Dan Carpenter and his Protestant, middle-class followers favored a subsidized housing project that was too expensive for Chelsea's poorer residents, council president Father Dunn and his Catholic followers opposed him. Carpenter and the white-collar minority were ousted from the council. It is debatable if the Chelsea Community Council accomplished anything constructive in its short existence.[31] In other words, Chelsea raises the question as to how applicable Alinsky's methods are to neighborhoods without much homogeneity. It also raises questions as to the role of the settlement in neighborhood conflict. Should the settlement be neutral or take a position and become a potential target?

When Saul Alinsky was doing a preliminary survey of Chicago's Northwest Side in 1961, Chicago Commons director Bill Brueckner invited him to dinner, a meal that with conversation stretched on for eight hours. In his thank-you note Alinsky wrote, "I had two regrets—one of major proportion to wit that twenty years had gone by before this meeting (but let us try to make up for lost time) and the other a minor regret as to the kind of music you and I could have made in Chelsea if you had been there."[32]

Alinsky went on to put together the Northwest Community Organization, which included Brueckner's Chicago Commons and some other settlements as members along with businessmen, neighborhood organizations, and Protestant and Catholic churches. This particular "people's organization" made a scapegoat out of the local ward committeeman, Matt Bieszcat, who told the Alinsky organizer bluntly, "Look, sonny, I own this area. Just keep your two cents out of it." The Northwest Community Organization didn't, of course. When the local alderman refused to get after the city sanitation department to increase street cleaning and garbage collections, a hundred residents swept up beer cans, dog drippings, and other debris into a trailer, then dropped the filth next to a tavern "owned by the alderman's wife." As a result, street cleaning in the neighborhood increased. One of the group's major victories came in 1963, when Mayor Daley appointed eleven of its members to the local fifteen-member Conservation Commission. The commission's goal was urban renewal through rehabilitation, not demolition, of buildings.[33] Bill Brueckner was one of the appointees.[34]

Brueckner gave the Northwest Community Organization steady

support from the beginning. He urged an older, smaller neighborhood organization, the Near Northwest Side Planning Commission, to work within and to support the Alinsky group.[35] Within the Northwest Community Organization, Brueckner and his director of Emerson House, Clarence Lipshutz, functioned as conciliators, helping to minimize internal conflicts. In 1965, Clarence Lipshutz, who lived at Emerson House, was elected president of the Northwest Community Organization.[36] This project represented the most successful cooperation between the settlements and an Alinsky organization.

However, Brueckner considered the Northwest Community Organization a failure.[37] By 1965, the group hadn't developed indigenous leadership at the top level. It wasn't that Chicago Commons "hogged" the top positions or tried to dominate the organization. Rather, with "establishment" leaders included at the start and with conflict minimized by them, no alternative leadership developed.

Nevertheless, by the mid-1970s, the Northwest Community Organization had weathered a transition to roughly 50 percent Puerto Rican membership. To its city planning and sanitation concerns, it had added a number of welfare and Hispanic issues, such as bilingual education. Its methods continued to reflect the Alinsky protest philosophy. However, it was also unique among Alinsky groups in that it continued to have a number of people not of the community in staff-organizing positions. Unlike the other long-lasting Alinsky groups, it also avoided ongoing administrative projects, instead bouncing from local issue to local issue.[38] Still around in the mid-1980s, Commons' head Frank Seever regarded it a minor factor in the neighborhood.[39]

A final example of a settlement in relation to an Alinsky organization is the case of Baden Street Settlement in Rochester and FIGHT. When FIGHT began organizing in 1965, Baden Street Settlement hesitated in giving its support. Meanwhile, the director of Rochester's Community Chest announced that no Chest funds would be used to support FIGHT, directly or indirectly. That meant that any agency staff working with FIGHT would have to do so on their own time. FIGHT retaliated by accusing the Chest of putting undue pressure on the settlement not to support Alinsky's efforts, and FIGHT publicly demanded the ouster of both the settlement and

the Chest directors. When the settlement board finally decided not
to apply to join FIGHT, two of Baden Street's board members, one
of whom was elected executive vice president of FIGHT, resigned.[40]
Subsequently, Baden Street discontinued all community organization activities.[41] FIGHT went on to put pressure on the local poverty
board[42] and also Eastman Kodak to hire more poor people.[43]

Thus, several settlements had some rather bad experiences with
Alinsky organizations. Except for Chicago Commons, the tendency
was for a settlement to end up as a scapegoat at the hands of an
Alinsky group. Perhaps the underlying reason why this happened
was that the structure of the Alinsky groups was almost entirely opposite that of the settlements. Settlement houses were staffed by
professionally trained social workers, who regarded their jobs as permanent and so were more likely to dominate their organizations and
withdraw their support if an organization got beyond their control
and adopted goals which met with settlement house disapproval, such
as keeping the neighborhood white. Alinsky, on the other hand, relied on talented, but not graduate school educated, organizers who
were sent into an area on a temporary basis to form a group and
then pull out, leaving the group to set its own goals. Settlement houses
had outsiders, representatives of the "establishment," on their boards.
Alinsky groups regarded outsiders with suspicion. Settlements sought
to build a bridge between the rich and the poor. Alinsky groups
were clearly on the side of the poor and accentuated class conflict.
The settlement building symbolized its permanent nature. Alinsky
groups didn't get bogged down with a large, expensive physical plant.
Settlement houses preferred a consensus approach to problem solving. Alinsky emphasized conflict. Since both were interested in improving the lot of the poor, it is unfortunate that they didn't work
more in concert with each other. However, at the time, Alinsky may
have been too much in the vanguard for most settlements.

In the 1960s, social work schools developed a new community organization curriculum oriented toward achieving social change. Along
with civil rights and labor union tactics, this curriculum embraced
Saul Alinsky's theory and techniques. However, having had several
experiences as Alinsky targets, settlement houses took the opposite
stand from that of the schools. In 1965, the National Federation of
Settlements put together a kit that contained a number of articles

and documents critical of Alinsky's methods. Among the items was Dan Carpenter's criticism of Alinsky's undemocratic, divisive tactics in Chelsea. The kit was designed for use with local social service agencies concerned about an Alinsky group in their community and for use in social work schools. It was only distributed on request and is as forward as the settlements became in their counterattack.[44] In the ensuing years, the social work schools' new community organization curriculum burgeoned in popularity. A generation of social workers trained in Alinsky methods spread his philosophy, and settlements were further isolated. Thus, Alinsky also drove a wedge between the social work schools and the settlements.

In their 1973 manual on how to do community organizing, George Brager and Harry Specht offered an explanation of why Alinsky groups used settlements as targets. In selecting a target, a conflict style group must take into consideration the nature of the retaliation it will provoke and the "counter-resources" of the target. "The settlement house—which, for a time, was the bête noire of Alinsky's contest tactics—was an easy mark," the two wrote. "It did not have the power to retaliate, and if it did, it could not have been repressive because of its value system."[45] Being the ideal Alinsky target did nothing to strengthen the settlement's reputation, and a battered reputation meant the loss of crucial grants.

Although the idea for Mobilization for Youth originated with a settlement house, by the time the federal government funded the action phase of the project, control had shifted away from the settlements to a board dominated by the New York School of Social Work. The shift was deliberate. Many social work professionals, including the Mobilization staff, criticized settlement houses for "having middle class standards,"[46] for appearing intimidating to the hard-core poor unaffiliated with organizations, and for being unwilling to share power.[47] In other words, the pre–Great Society program most influential in pointing the way for the War on Poverty regarded settlement houses as too old-fashioned.

In some respects, Alinsky succeeded where settlements failed. Alinsky gave the apathetic poor a sense of power through direct action and confrontation tactics, tactics generally avoided by the settlement houses. Alinsky's approach was more spectacular and dramatic than that of the settlements. Alinsky did reach people with whom the settlements had had no success. Given the right circumstances, the conflict method could also produce specific results, particularly in the 1960s. The same people could hardly implement conflict and cooperation simultaneously; yet the settlements with their cooperative approach and Alinsky with his conflict approach could have indirectly reinforced each other and made a significant contribution toward reform. After all, Alinsky's conflict tactics were meant to be a prelude to negotiation, and the goal was resolution of the problem. To a certain extent, the settlements' defensiveness about Alinsky may have been motivated by the settlement houses' desire to protect their own turf from a rival community organization.

Finally, the settlement house offers a kind of permanence or stability absent in the Alinsky groups. During periods of conservatism, reform efforts—whether of the conflict or cooperative model—may be ineffective and gains nonexistent; but the settlement house, through its recreational program, maintains a neighborhood relationship and continues its social change values and commitment. While settlement houses may have lost the Alinsky battle in the short run, they may well have won out over Alinsky in the long term. Certainly, some houses are healthier in 1986 than many Alinsky groups, and Alinsky's philosophy is in some discredit. However, it is important to keep in mind that Alinsky was in vogue in the crucial decade of the 1960s; settlements were not.

In his highly regarded *Street Corner Society: The Social Structure of an Italian Slum,* William F. Whyte reinforced Alinsky's criticism that settlement houses were alien to the poor. Whyte observed that none of the settlement workers in the Italian neighborhood he studied (with one exception) knew Italian. Street corner groups were hostile to the settlement. Even among upwardly mobile neighborhood residents, Whyte quoted one as saying of the settlement workers: "They consider us scum. . . . They'll talk to us with every consideration, but behind our backs they consider us scum."[48] Furthermore, the upwardly mobile neighbors who were most likely to use the settlement house were also the ones most likely to move out of the neighborhood, leaving the settlement behind.

Herbert Gans elaborated on Whyte's criticism. In a somewhat skewed account of the origins of the settlement movement, Gans claimed settlements did not come into being until Jewish immigration began to be heavy. Settlements, he said, experienced their greatest success with Jews because Jews were oriented toward achieving middle-class status through education; and settlement houses could help them achieve this goal. Settlements were geared toward helping the poor become middle class.[49]

But what happens when the poor reject middle-class values and goals? Gans claimed that the settlement house just didn't reach those people. Increasingly, the poor (blacks, Puerto Ricans, etc.) were in that category. However, settlement house workers "wanted to change the slum-dwellers, not understand them."[50] They might give lip service to the need for sensitivity to the cultural differences of the poor, but, according to Gans, settlement workers "express little sympathy for the behavior of their clients or for the reasons for that behavior and do not side with them in their grievances and needs."[51] Furthermore, in designing programs, settlements neglected to first consult their neighbors to learn their needs and wants or to give them a role in program formulation. Likewise, in supporting new legislation, settlements did not consult the poor to be "sure that the legislation [was] what the poor [needed] and [wanted], and not just middle-class estimates of what [was] best for them."[52] Gans concluded, "The settlement house never realized how little it understood its neighborhood."[53] The most effective approach, Gans thought in 1963, was through experimental "super-agencies," such as Mobilization for Youth. Gans completely ignored the settlement contribution to these agencies while advising settlements to support the super-agencies and "to fight for the social and economic policies necessary to reduce poverty and racial discrimination"[54]—as if settlements hadn't been doing that for some time. It must have been galling to settlement house leaders to listen to Gans gloss over their efforts.

In his popular *Urban Villagers*,[55] Gans portrayed settlement workers using recreational services with missionary zeal to attract their neighbors into the house. Once there, settlement workers hoped they would absorb the middle-class social norms of the staff. However, what struck Gans about a settlement in Boston's West End was the hostility teenagers directed against the house. They deliberately and frequently broke house-owned phonograph records and used bad language with the staff. The settlement also differed with its neighbors in that it supported urban renewal. Gans saw the problem as a clash between different social and cultural values, with the settlement workers as the outsiders trying with missionary zeal to win converts in the slums over to middle-class norms and values.

Settlements did attempt to defend themselves against these attacks. After his 1963 attack, National Federation of Settlements director Margaret Berry wrote Gans a four-page letter in which she defended the settlement house promotion of middle-class norms as preparing disadvantaged youngsters to obtain jobs from middle-class employers.[56] After Gans' article appeared in *Social Work* in 1964, Berry wrote another rebuttal. Her published editorial mentioned that 42 percent of settlement workers had M.S.W.s, and the essence of their professional training was to discipline themselves so that they did not impose their will or values on their clients. To Berry, for a settlement to become a "protest agency of the poor" was to segregate the poor and cut off opportunities.[57] However, possession of M.S.W.s did little good when the settlement movement found itself in conflict with key professional leaders. The major problem was that Alinsky and other critics had focused attention on the fundamental dilemma of the settlement house—was it to bridge class lines or just represent the poor?

PUBLIC RELATIONS AND FINANCIAL PROBLEMS

The economist and future head of the Department of Health, Education, and Welfare, Wilbur Cohen, chaired a settlement house conference in 1958 in which he wrote, "Some say the settlement's finished."[58] Cohen didn't agree, but he pointed to a major public relations problem. Much of the public either had no idea what a settlement house was or had little regard for the settlement as an effective reform-oriented, social agency.

Symbolic of the problem was the decline of the movement's best-known settlement, Hull House. Following Jane Addams' death in 1935, the house developed financial and leadership problems. Head Charlotte Carr and board president Louise Bowen were both strong personalities who frequently held different political views. Repeated clashes resulted in Carr's sudden resignation at the end of 1942. Carr publicly claimed she was forced out because Mrs. Bowen opposed her liberal political activities.[59] Most settlement workers rushed to Carr's defense, since they were concerned about settlement workers' freedom to act in controversial situations. The Hull House staff and resident body was divided and additional resignations followed, one of which was Bill Brueckner's.[60] Meanwhile, the Hull House board maintained that the reason for Carr's departure was her inability to live within a reduced budget. In the end, the publicity tarnished Hull House's image, and the settlement movement was left with a diminished flagship.

Poor public relations contributed to settlement house financial problems. Outside of settlements in New York and Chicago, since the 1920s most houses had depended on their local United Way (formerly called the Community Chest) for support. In order to stay in the good graces of the Chest, a settlement house had to avoid controversy. These problems persisted into the post–World War II decades and became especially severe when Alinsky and others raised settlement neighbors' expectations for controversial social action. Margaret Berry recalled her shock when a private caucus of delegates to a Chest meeting got a phone call from a Chest official telling the group to rescind a resolution it had passed or face progressive, annual reductions in the Chest's campaign goal. If the group refused to bow to the will of Chest officials, it would be responsible for curtailing its own funding as well as the funding of other private agencies.[61]

Other examples of Chest or United Way officials squelching social action included when a Minneapolis settlement worker was organizing a campaign against local banks for redlining. The local banks got United Way to force the settlement to fire the worker. However, the worker had the support of other neighborhood groups, including some sponsored by the housing authority. These groups vented their wrath at the settlement, charging that it was out of touch with the neighborhood.[62] Yet, another example of United Way influence was the statement of a settlement executive that while settlements usually hire their own staff they sometimes have "to contend with the restrictive approval of United Way boards (if the Way board does not like someone, that person does not get hired)."[63] Finally, Margaret Berry recalled a couple of cases where United Way pressured settlements not to let certain groups meet on their premises. However, usually the pressure was more indirect with timid agencies trying to stay out of trouble by going overboard on avoiding controversy.[64] To maintain Chest or United Way funding, even in the 1960s, most settlements avoided controversy. In avoiding controversy, however, they missed opportunities to act as neighborhood advocates. That kind of forceful, courageous image usually went to the Urban League, tenants' unions, and welfare rights organizations. The latter two, especially, were independent of United Way funding.

Another problem was that the Community Chest often gave a low-priority rating to settlements. Initially, settlements blamed that on their poor public relations. A common response was to strengthen their city-level federations of settlements to get the settlement story before the public and present a united front when dealing with Chest officials.[65] However, because settlements tended to be multipurpose in nature, they usually turned up in several places on Chest service priority rankings, and ended up in the middle or lower range of funding. Chest or United Way officials traditionally gave low priority to neighborhood organizing. In the 1950s, Chest officials feared that settlements might "rile the troops up too much," and so were afraid to give settlements much, if any, money for this activity. When community organizing became popular in the 1960s, Chests and foundations often chose to fund the new, indigenous groups as opposed to settlement house activity.[66] Perhaps these newer groups posed an immediate political threat. Also, perhaps the newer groups, because they lacked the stability of the settlement house, were less of a long-term threat. Whatever the reason, settlement workers found it increasingly difficult to convince Chests, and later United Ways, that settlements were really needed.

Finally, the Community Chest itself may have obscured the settlement image by eliminating the need for member houses to raise their own funds. Raising its own funds forces an agency to be visible. It has to explain itself to the public to get donations. However, the Chest or United Way did the campaigning instead. It might feature settlements in a percentage of its advertising, but even then, settlements would share the limelight with the soliciting Chest.

People living in New York and Chicago probably have the strongest image of what a settlement house is. Because joint fund-raising is extremely weak in these two cities, settlements have had to rely on their own campaigns to raise money. In 1957, the city federation of New York settlements began soliciting foundations on behalf of member houses. Also, the Chicago Federation of Settlements solicited professional and business people in a "United Settlement Appeal."[67] These, as well as individual house fund-raising efforts, got the settlement image before the public.

In sum, professionalism turned out to have a negative side for settlements. Three influential thinkers, Alinsky, Whyte, and Gans, all claimed that settlements were not well accepted in their neighborhoods and failed to meet the needs of, or even to serve, the really poor. The National Federation's defense that the settlement workers, by virtue of their professional training, would not impose middle-class standards on their clients only partially met this criticism. Settlements did not always meet the needs or respond to the wants of the poor. However, they did function under serious constraints. For example, to remain in the good graces of their major funder, United Way, they did have to be careful about engaging in controversial activities. Also in professionalizing, the settlement had abandoned its most unique feature—residence. Just what a settlement was, or should be, was a subject for debate. On the one hand, this flexibility was healthy; but on the other hand, if settlement workers themselves weren't too clear about what a settlement house was, or what they should be doing, they could hardly present a strong defense of themselves to the public. Yet if settlements hadn't professionalized, they probably would have lacked the legitimacy to survive the sociological attack as well as they did. However, the damage of this attack on settlements would be apparent in their treatment by the prototype War on Poverty program, Mobilization for Youth, and by the War on Poverty itself.

CHAPTER 8

FIGHTING THE EFFECTS
OF POVERTY:
FROM JUVENILE DELINQUENCY
TO THE GREAT SOCIETY

"DO AREA KIDS CLIMB THE ECONOMIC LADDER? ARE they on it at all? If not, why not?"[1] Around 1950, these were questions Rochester's Council of Social Agencies posed to settlements but did not pursue at that time. Settlement workers were, and always have been, concerned with the effects of poverty. However, in the 1950s, public attention and the resources needed to attack poverty were directed toward other problems. Settlements could try to influence public opinion, but the most effective way to utilize the increasingly available grant monies from the government and private foundations was to go along with the social concerns of the times.

Since World War II, each decade seems to have had its dominant social concern. In the 1970s, it was environmental issues. In the 1960s, the War on Poverty received massive funding. And in the 1950s, the emphasis was on juvenile delinquency. This concern was related to rising delinquency statistics, a situation reflecting the growing proportion of adolescents in the population. Delinquency prevention, with its conservative emphasis on law and order and traditional family values, also fit the temper of the 1950s. Thus, delinquency prevention was one of the few social concerns for which grant money, both public and private, existed. Some of this tendency toward faddishness is reinforced by the growth of governmental grant monies. Public support for attacking these problems induces politicians to appropriate money for the grants, and the grant projects then give a certain dynamic quality to their problem areas, in turn generating additional support. The growth of grant funding also expanded the influence of professionals who served as grant reviewers.

For settlements, involvement with delinquency prevention was a natural thing to do. They had always worked with youngsters and had a long history of advocating various child welfare measures. Progressive Era settlement workers were instrumental in launching the juvenile court and put much effort into combating child labor. Thus, when delinquency emerged as a popular issue after World War II, settlements renewed their efforts in this area. For settlements in the 1950s, a grant proposal dealing with juvenile delinquency was likely to be funded. Given grant program guidelines, an attack on poverty, unless tied in with juvenile delinquency, was unlikely to even get written. Delinquency, however, could be tied to poverty by blaming it on lack of economic opportunity. Settlements played a crucial role in making this connection. As a result, by the mid-1960s, the goal of increasing opportunity through the War on Poverty had enough public support so that the juvenile delinquency rationale was no longer needed.

WORK WITH JUVENILE DELINQUENTS

In the 1940s, what settlement concern existed for juvenile delinquency tended to spring directly from people with whom settlements came in contact. During World War II, some members of a notoriously tough juvenile gang patronized Chicago's Bethlehem House. One of the seventeen-year-old gang members died, his neck severed, either while attempting to rob a store through a broken window or having been murdered by being pushed through the window. Some time before, that youngster had tried to beat up Bethlehem's director for disciplining another gang member. The year following the death of the seventeen-year-old, four other members of that gang appeared before juvenile court, one of whom, on being released from the state detention school, killed another fourteen-year-old member of the same gang. The settlement director blamed the house's failure to work successfully with these youngsters on the World War II shortage of male volunteer club leaders. Such club leaders, he felt, would have provided positive role models and perhaps have averted the tragedies.[2]

Another factor drawing the attention of settlements to delinquent youngsters was the appointment of Russell Ballard as head of Hull House in 1943. Ballard previously headed the Illinois State Training School for Boys at St. Charles. As director of Hull House, he emphasized youth programs. Ballard believed that if a youngster learned to play a musical instrument or create something artistic, his self-esteem would increase; and he would develop positive social attitudes and not become delinquent.[3]

However, in the 1940s, Ballard's concern with delinquency was not widespread among settlement houses. When a Cleveland probation officer asked University Settlement to accept an unruly youngster, the board hesitated. Its reasons were twofold. First, the board feared that the delinquent would be a negative influence on other settlement youngsters. Second, the board was afraid that the delinquent might give the settlement a bad reputation. Their attitude seemed to be that the offending youngster should get psychiatric treatment somewhere else before coming to University Settlement.[4] Most settlements in the 1940s were either not very involved with delinquents or managed to sidestep the problem.

In the 1950s, settlement house interest in work with delinquents picked up sharply. For example, when a University Settlement club member and mother of a fourteen-year-old told the settlement director that her son was scheduled to appear in juvenile court for burglary, head Eleanor Bonham offered to help. She played a supportive role, accompanying the mother to juvenile court, interpreting the court's decision to refer the family to the Youth Bureau for casework, helping the woman overcome her fears of the Youth Bureau, and supporting the youngster's desire to join the Catholic church.[5] As public interest in juvenile delinquency rose, settlements discovered that working with delinquents added to their image as a useful social agency; and furthermore, grant money for this purpose was increasingly available.

Throughout the 1950s, settlement leaders worked to get more federal funding for juvenile delinquency projects. They testified repeatedly before congressional committees. In 1950, Russell Ballard spoke to the Senate Finance Committee on behalf of a $12 million appropriation to the Children's Bureau for probation, detention, and institutional services. He talked about seeing "many children and youth lose their way because circumstances denied them their equal chance."[6] Irving Kriegsfeld told the Senate Subcommittee on Juvenile Delinquency in 1954 about the involvement of Boston settlements in special projects.[7] John McDowell's testimony before that committee the following year foreshadowed President Kennedy's Committee on Juvenile Delinquency, which did so much to lay the groundwork for the War on Poverty. McDowell favored the establishment of "a Federal Advisory Council on Juvenile Delinquency" and also argued for a "total community approach,"[8] the latter being indicative of the "saturation of a neighborhood with social services" concept of the future Mobilization for Youth and the War on Poverty. Again in 1959, Fern Colborn of the National Federation staff testified before the Juvenile Delinquency Subcommittee, describing settlement projects and seeking major federal funding.[9] Finally, in 1961, Chicago Commons head Bill Brueckner testified in favor of the Juvenile Delinquency and Youth Offenses Control Act, which provided major grants for experimental projects.[10] This testimony helped to pave the way for massive federal spending for social services, some of it channeled through private agencies, which characterized the antipoverty program.

Settlements were among the first to make explicit the connection between juvenile delinquency and poverty. In May 1957, the National Federation of Settlements passed a resolution calling attention to the "inevitable correlation" between delinquency and indigence, economic insecurity, inadequate schools, bad housing, and chronic disease.[11] After World War II, juvenile delinquency theory had stressed the delinquent subculture. In the 1930s, sociologists Clifford Shaw and Henry McKay had organized the Chicago Area Projects, which sought indigenous neighborhood leaders to fight social disorganization and thus curb the growth of juvenile delinquency. Saul Alinsky, in the 1930s a Chicago criminologist, came out of this tradition. In fact, Alinsky, who was a student of Shaw's, was supposed to be organizing adolescents to prevent delinquency when he organized adults into the Back of the Yards Council instead. Alinsky would have some influence on Mobilization for Youth and a great deal on the War on Poverty. Meanwhile, the National Federation in 1957 built on the Shaw and delinquent subculture theories by pointing to the settlements' neighborhood approach and calling for funds for research and demonstration programs.

Settlements were also involved in a couple of early experiments coordinating and concentrating social services in given areas to reduce delinquency. In 1957, Friends Neighborhood Guild received Community Chest money to launch Operation Poplar. The project had counseling, youth, and community organization components. Among neighborhood agencies receiving funds and cooperating in the work were the Girl Scouts, Boy Scouts, YMCA, Big Brothers, Family Counseling of the Episcopal Community Services, and Crime Prevention.[12] This project preceded the larger and more influential Mobilization for Youth.

In addition to seeking funding, in the 1950s settlements utilized two relatively new approaches in dealing with delinquency. One was the so-called "detached" or "floating" worker, who worked with groups or gangs outside of an agency setting on the gang's own territory— be it street corners, pool rooms, or whatever. The second approach, which was less prevalent but more influential in relation to what was to come in the Great Society, was the use of indigenous leadership. Settlements carried out detached worker projects in New York, Chicago (Hard-to-Reach Youth), Philadelphia, Cleveland (Unreached Youth), Minneapolis, St. Paul, and other places. These projects were usually privately funded, although in New York, Youth Board staff worked closely with settlement houses.

The Unreached Youth Project in Cleveland's Friendly Inn was fairly typical. A gang of thirteen-to-fifteen-year-old boys, numbering about twenty, plagued the settlement neighborhood. They engaged in a lot of vandalism and stealing, which local businessmen were reluctant to complain about for fear of retaliation. Friendly Inn hired a twenty-nine-year-old black science teacher, Richard W. Cooper, who also had a strong background in college athletics. Cooper, who was employed on the project fifteen to twenty-five hours per week, used athletics to get and hold the boys' interest. He made his first contact by meeting three boys while in a neighborhood market and asking them if they would like to form a baseball team. They responded to Cooper in part because he had access to athletic equipment. He was also able to bribe the youngsters into good behavior by having the resources to take them to an occasional Cleveland Indians baseball game.[13] Cooper worked with this group for two and a half years. He talked to them about school, drinking, and community standards, and visited their parents. He got the youngsters into municipal baseball and basketball leagues and into Friendly Inn. None went to jail, and all either graduated from high school or were about to at the end of the project. Cooper succeeded because of his strong interest in young people, his persistence in helping them,[14] and probably because he himself was an excellent role model.

The Unreached Youth Program continued at Friendly Inn through the 1960s and on into the 1970s.[15] In other settlements, however, detached worker projects were cut back as popular interest in delinquency waned in the 1960s. Chicago Commons devoted four staff positions to a Hard-to-Reach Youth Project in 1956, but only one position in 1960.[16] Association House, another Chicago settlement, combined the detached worker approach with specialized family services in the mid-1960s.[17] However, most telling in 1966 was the comment of a Philadelphia settlement worker: "The past summer was exceptionally quiet due to most of the youngsters in the [Special Youth] project obtaining employment."[18] The jobs came through the Great Society's Neighborhood Youth Corps, with youths working at two Philadelphia settlements. To a large extent, the 1960s replaced detached workers with jobs and "opportunity."

The employment of indigenous workers (members of the target population or the poor helping the poor) and storefront centers were other hallmarks of the Great Society. One of the men who served frequently on key federal grant review panels in the early 1960s, Bill Brueckner, experimented with both the indigenous worker and storefront approaches at Chicago Commons. In 1955, the Commons hired as its indigenous worker a former city bus driver, Dan Nagel. Previously Nagel had, on his own, organized a series of twenty-five groups and gangs with about 400 youngsters ranging in age from thirteen to twenty-five into the Northwest Youth Council. The council had a board composed of gang leaders, some elected, some self-appointed, and a small bank account. According to Brueckner, the council's "original purpose was to fight, to get some place against the odds provided by the 'adult world,' to retaliate where they found obstacles when they were looking for agency services such as the use of ball fields, gyms, meeting space."[19] The council first came to the attention of the Commons when it asked the settlement to endorse their efforts to obtain a playing field. The Commons gave the young men money for playfield equipment,[20] and eight months later hired their leader, Dan Nagel.[21] Nagel provided an invaluable bridge between the Commons and youth who had previously ignored the settlement. He remained on the settlement staff for roughly half a dozen years, going back to the Chicago Transit Authority in the early 1960s.[22]

Nagel sought a certain degree of independence from agency identification. It was easier to reach some youngsters operating out of a cheap storefront than in an established, well-equipped agency. The Commons ran a drop-in center on the second floor of a storefront from 1956 to 1960.[23] How it worked is described as follows:

> The worker was crowding in some paperwork before dashing out for supper. A young man came in. The worker rose and greeted him. They both hitched themselves up on a desk, and the young man blurted out: "My girl is going to have a baby. How can she get rid of it?" There were some questions that had to be asked, and some help that had to be arranged. This one worked out that the family kept the healthy baby, and the boy voluntarily contributed to the support of his child. [This was 1959.][24]

Although the Commons discontinued its drop-in center, the concept held appeal for the 1960s. The prototype antipoverty program, Mobilization for Youth, included some settlement-house-based detached workers; but in 1966, Mobilization for Youth switched to the storefront drop-in center concept as the more effective way to help out troubled teenagers.[25] In 1969, Cleveland's Alta House experimented with a drop-in center supervised by neighborhood adults.[26] The purpose of the drop-in center was to provide a setting where youngsters could bring their problems, whether they were personal ones, job or school related, legal, or medical. If necessary, the drop-in center could put the youngster in touch with other appropriate agencies or resources.

By the 1960s, increasingly teen problems were related to drug abuse. In her autobiography, Helen Hall described her exasperation with police who neglected to arrest drug pushers and courts that repeat-edly let off drug pushers either without a sentence or with a light one.[27] A settlement colleague, Janet P. Murray, complained, "You are never sure when the policeman on the beat is tied in somewhere and misuses the information, so that there is a leak to the distribu-tors or a shakedown of the youngster who has been 'hooked.' "[28] Hall's settlement, Henry Street, did run a drug abuse clinic,[29] as did Chicago's Erie Neighborhood House.[30] Usually, though, settlements referred drug addicts seeking help elsewhere. The problem was where. Hall lamented the lack of effective drug treatment facilities for teen-agers. To call attention to the problem, Henry Street worker Ralph Tefferteller tape-recorded conversations with neighborhood addicts and published excerpts in *Addict in the Street*. Hall called this book Henry Street's "most far-reaching contribution" toward resolving the drug abuse problem.[31] However, most settlements found it wise to isolate drug users from their regular members to protect the latter.

Still another approach to juvenile delinquency was to try to revi-talize parent-child relations. Henry Street began a project in 1956 that stressed work with parents and home visits.[32] In 1961, the Vin-cent Astor Foundation gave United Neighborhood Houses, the co-ordinating agency for New York settlements, a million dollars to spend over a three-year period in nine settlement neighborhoods. The set-tlements were to follow the Henry Street approach; Henry Street was one of the nine funded settlements, and Helen Hall, Henry Street head, was one of three consultants on the prevention of juvenile delinquency chosen by the Astor Foundation.[33] Thus, Astor en-dorsed the parent—child approach.

In the case of some delinquents, their family situation was so bad that alternative living arrangements had to be found. To fill such a need, Friends Neighborhood Guild established Franklin House in the mid-1960s as a temporary home for delinquents released from state institutions who could not be returned directly to their families.

As Franklin House evolved, delinquents sent there as an alternative to a state correctional institution occupied some of its dozen spaces. Teenage boys whom the court removed from their homes who had no other place to go occupied other places. Department of Welfare payments met half of Franklin House's budget, and an anonymous foundation paid the rest. All admissions were channeled through the Welfare Department.[34] About the same time in Chicago, Association House rented an apartment, which it used to house half a dozen homeless teenage boys.[35] However, this type of residential treatment facility was more characteristic of institutions treating emotionally disturbed children than it was of settlements.

MOBILIZATION FOR YOUTH TIES POVERTY TO DELINQUENCY

A philosophical connection existed between settlement houses and Mobilization for Youth (MFY). Both shared a community organization emphasis and a commitment to solve social problems through social science. In terms of its activities, MFY duplicated the settlement house approach. For example, settlement houses combined specific services with efforts to achieve broader social changes. MFY offered specific services, such as legal aid clinics, while at the same time stressing community organization and advocacy to bring about more basic reform. In his account of Mobilization for Youth, *Professional Reforming*, Joseph Helfgot commented, "Among the assorted traditions in social welfare, MFY was most identified with the settlement house movement."[36]

Besides philosophically, that identification also extended to MFY's origins. The idea for Mobilization for Youth can be traced back to a Henry Street Settlement board meeting in June 1957. Present were several guests, including Jim McCarthy of the New York City Youth Board and Jack Kaplan, husband of a Henry Street board member. Kaplan suggested that Henry Street head Helen Hall "pool together all they felt should be tried to cope with juvenile delinquency, and he would underwrite the cost of the research." McCarthy and Henry Street board president, Winslow Carlton, put much effort into the initial proposal. They thought this program to saturate the neigh-

borhood with social services was "best undertaken under the auspices of the settlement . . . in as much as this is the generic community agency, having program interests ranging from individual
help through broad social action."[37] At that time, they hoped that
New York University would be able to supply the research compo-
nent of the project.[38]

A second grant from the Kaplan Foundation in June 1958 allowed
Henry Street to hire Jim McCarthy to work full-time on the project
proposal. That summer, he and Helen Hall met with National Institute of Mental Health officials in Washington. The NIMH expressed
interest in funding "the Pre-Delinquent Project, which was embed-
ded in the plan." Hall and McCarthy declined, saying what was important about MFY was "its attack on the multiple causes of delinquency over a wide geographic area." They "wanted to get away from
the piece-meal approach" in "an effort to saturate a whole poverty
area with services enough to change its social climate."[39]

James McCarthy not only was primarily responsible for writing the
early proposal drafts, but he effectively promoted MFY in Washington. McCarthy's background included an M.A. in social work from
Fordham University,[40] work at Henry Street prior to joining the New
York City Youth Board,[41] deputy director of the Youth Board, and
director of Big Brothers. Helen Hall attributed congressional support and appropriations to McCarthy's ability to informally reach
Congressman John Fogarty of Rhode Island,[42] then chairman of the
House Appropriations Committee. McCarthy had an uncle who had
been Congressman Fogarty's teacher at Notre Dame,[43] and Mc-
Carthy himself had graduated from Notre Dame in 1938. Henry
Street and other interested MFY sponsors shrewdly engineered Fogarty's "education" with a well-publicized political shindig announc-
ing MFY's existence, arranging contacts from other "big-name" politicians, and other lobbying efforts.

Settlements played the key role in lobbying city and federal politicians. Besides Jim McCarthy's contacts, Henry Street had strong
ties with the Lehmans and New York settlements had a durable relationship with the mayor's office and with other Tammany Hall politicians.[44] One tactic used in 1959 was to put on a media event to
announce the establishment of MFY; be sure Congressman Fogarty
would be there; then have the mayor, senators, and other influential

people attend to impress on Fogarty he wasn't alone. The importance of MFY was emphasized to Fogarty when he saw front page coverage of the event in the *New York Times*. The Ford Foundation gave Henry Street a small grant for these lobbying efforts, and Fogarty's committee came through with major support for juvenile delinquency projects in general and MFY in particular.[45]

However, the relationship of MFY to the settlements began to be undercut. National Institute of Mental Health review panel criticisms of the initial proposal were that it lacked a research design and theoretical underpinnings. Henry Street remedied these defects with the addition to the project staff of Richard Cloward and Lloyd Ohlin, both of the New York School of Social Work at Columbia. Cloward and Ohlin had received favorable reviews of their book *Delinquency and Opportunity*, in which they claimed that slum youngsters became delinquent because they saw their legitimate aspirations being blocked by a lack of social, economic, political, and educational opportunities.[46] "Opportunity" became the key word for MFY, and later for the War on Poverty. Thus, MFY priorities were shifted in the planning stage from rehabilitative programs to education and jobs for youth. At first, a grant from Henry Street board member Stephen Currier financed Cloward's and Ohlin's participation. Cloward and Ohlin became the principal investigators of the project's research arm.[47] Another professor from Columbia, George Brager,[48] replaced Ohlin in 1960.

A theoretical contradiction had also undercut the original Henry Street proposal. Henry Street called for a saturation of the Lower East Side with social services, but these services tended to be of the traditional type already there. If these services were effective, then why was the delinquency rate increasing at such an alarming rate? How could one expect more of the same services to solve the problem? What was needed was a new approach if large-scale funding was to be justified. The original Henry Street proposal did not mention an opportunity structure, nor was the sociological perspective clear-cut.

Some of the problems facing settlements that have been discussed earlier also soon undercut Henry Street's leadership of MFY. The social work profession had a low opinion of settlement houses. Alinsky, Whyte, and Gans were leading sociologists who had been quite public in their charges that settlements didn't represent their neighborhoods. Richard Cloward added to this criticism. Cloward and the others were all authors of widely read books. The settlements hadn't produced an author of a major book in decades. They had been relatively late to hire M.S.W.s, and they lacked prestige within the social work profession. On top of their professional difficulties, the settlement movement was in a state of flux. When residence in the house for settlement workers disappeared, they lost their most clearly identifiable characteristic. Furthermore, as many neighborhoods changed, settlements had to adjust to a new clientele. Thus, settlements found it difficult not only to define themselves, but also to defend themselves. Finally, in speculating on Henry Street's loss of leadership of MFY, one should remember that Helen Hall at this time was in her late sixties, female, and lacked an M.S.W. Her influence and that of settlements in general was probably less as a result of all these factors.

As the MFY proposal made its way through various drafts toward funding of the action phase, which didn't begin until 1962,[49] Henry Street and other settlement houses found their role increasingly downplayed. Mobilization for Youth incorporated independently,[50] and Columbia University and the independent MFY board, which had twenty members of which thirteen represented settlements in 1958,[51] was enlarged in 1961 to include eleven representatives chosen by Columbia's New York School of Social Work.[52] The National Institute for Mental Health's review panel engineered this Columbia takeover.[53]

The Mobilization staff, hired by the Columbia group, criticized settlement houses for "having 'middle class' standards,"[54] for appearing intimidating to the unaffiliated people they were seeking to reach,[55] and for only attracting those low-income people who were already on their way up and out of the ghetto.[56] As established agencies, they said settlements were also unwilling to share power with newcomers.[57] The Lower East Side Neighborhood Association (LENA), an organization consisting largely of professional workers from around ninety community groups,[58] was bypassed for approximately the same reasons. LENA was essentially a meeting ground for agency staff. The kind of community organization that most interested MFY was working directly with the disadvantaged, rather than through "establishment" intermediaries. MFY did give LENA a small contract for work with existing community councils, and settlement houses got a contract for a predelinquent program.[59] Thus, Columbia's New York School of Social Work captured control of the project.

The Columbia takeover of MFY illustrates the key role of professionalism in grantsmanship. MFY portended the increasing role federal grants were going to play in private agencies. In evaluating grant proposals, however, the federal government needs knowledgeable but disinterested reviewers. It finds these in abundance in academe. However, one thing these academic reviewers are likely to promote in their evaluations is professionalism. Columbia University had professional prestige; the settlements did not.

The Columbia takeover happened in spite of Chicago Commons head Bill Brueckner's involvement with the chief funding agency, the National Institute of Mental Health. Besides testifying before the House Subcommittee on Education in favor of the Juvenile Delinquency and Youth Offenses Control Act of 1961,[60] Brueckner also reviewed grants, including the MFY proposals, for the National Institute of Mental Health and the President's Committee on Juvenile Delinquency between 1959 and 1965.[61] Margaret Berry of the NFS staff had introduced Brueckner to Cloward in 1959, and Brueckner reported being "much impressed."[62] However, Cloward was not impressed with the settlements. It is significant that in his 1967 account of the planning period, Cloward began with 1959, totally neglecting the settlement contribution,[63] which included coining the name "Mobilization for Youth." One wishes Cloward had at least acknowledged the grace with which the settlements relinquished control while continuing their lobbying efforts to make the now-Columbia-dominated MFY a reality.

The interaction between the settlements and MFY is worth exploring. Not only were the functions of the two similar, but MFY had used the settlements in key ways. The original project idea was theirs. Also, the political connections to get the grant funds appropriated were largely the settlements'. MFY was the demonstration project for the War on Poverty, and the MFY staff was aware of the need to publicize the plight of the poor and campaign for more general reforms—just like settlement house workers. However, to get major funding for MFY and later the War on Poverty, proponents had to offer something new to justify massive expenditures. What MFY and the War on Poverty offered was an emphasis on involving the poor in policymaking and in community organization through a confrontation approach. The settlement approach was consensus. Thus, underneath the rhetoric and professional concerns, a fundamental difference in how one approached community organization separated the settlements from MFY. Given the success of MFY and the subsequent War on Poverty, settlements would subsequently question the degree to which they supported the consensus idea and partly change their community organization practices. In that sense, the settlements did learn from MFY.

The degree to which MFY divorced itself from the settlements can be seen in the action phase of the program. MFY began action projects in 1962, with a staff of around three hundred. Action programs were grouped into four categories: Community Development, Educational Services, Employment Services, and counseling. MFY added a fifth category, Legal Services, in 1964,[64] although Henry Street had urged the inclusion of legal services in its original proposal.[65]

The target group for Community Development was those people who didn't belong to any formal organizations or participate in community affairs. MFY initially tried new organizations, such as an association of Pentecostal ministers, and also tried to involve purely social organizations, such as storefront athletic clubs, in community action projects.[66] By 1963, Community Development was switching to issue-oriented mass protests as a way of involving the unaffiliated. The key issues were housing, the schools, and government money for a work-training program.[67] With a couple of exceptions, settlement involvement was peripheral or nonexistent. About the only active settlement cooperation was in the predelinquent program. No wonder Helen Hall complained that the MFY staff was unwilling to be influenced by her or others.[68]

MFY's housing protests began with the formation of ten housing clinics to help tenants file complaints with the Department of Buildings. Two settlements, Educational Alliance and University Settlement, each housed a clinic.[69] Because of the difficulty in getting some tenants to fill out forms and the slowness of the Buildings Department to act on the complaints, the University Settlement Housing

Clinic, along with MFY and the Negro Action Group, sponsored a meeting to organize an illegal rent strike. No other settlements were directly involved in the rent strike which followed. The strike did not produce immediate results, although a legal crackdown on land-lords reluctant to make repairs occurred the following year. How-ever, the strike left tenant associations in its wake, giving MFY the satisfaction of having organized some of the unaffiliated.[70]

In another area, delinquency prevention, Hamilton-Madison House got a grant from MFY to run its Preadolescent Program. The settle-ment enrolled youngsters from eight to twelve, who were judged delinquency-prone and unserved by other agencies, in a program of athletics, trips, tutoring, and job finding. Older youths from MFY's Urban Youth Work Corps served as part of the program's staff.[71] This program took place at Hamilton-Madison in 1962–63,[72] and it foreshadowed later Great Society tutoring and Neighborhood Youth Corps programs.

Not only were settlements largely pushed aside during this signif-icant phase of MFY, but at least one MFY staffer complained that settlements were not concerned with poverty. Wyatt Jones, MFY's assistant director of research, told an Albany group that Henry Street was reluctant to work with the poor, and that "one even sees Cadil-lacs at this agency." Presumably, he meant Cadillacs in front of Henry Street's playhouse, which attracted a wide audience for its produc-tions.[73] Jones also told the Junior League the "Henry Street Settle-ment served 10% of the population . . . and left the impression that 'Mobilization' was the only organization dedicated to the attack on poverty. He gave no recognition to the fact that . . . Henry Street Settlement . . . had conceived the idea of MFY."[74] MFY criticism of traditional agencies was common as MFY clamored for funding for new approaches to solve the problems of poverty.

One result was that MFY alienated a lot of people. City politicians were upset because they did not control MFY's purse strings. MFY was getting $1.5 million from the Department of Labor for a work-training program when the city-sponsored jobs program, JOIN, was turned down for additional funding.[75] MFY was undercutting the established institutions with its own direct federal government–pri-vate agency relationship.

MFY's issue-oriented mass protests also made it controversial and were probably the major reason why some city politicians and the press launched an attack against the organization in the late summer of 1964. In utilizing mass protest techniques, such as the march, boycott, and pickets, MFY was seizing on tactics the civil rights movement had already used successfully. Furthermore, it was discovering that these tactics could attract otherwise unaffiliated people, whereas more acceptable means of social change, like a meeting run according to *Robert's Rules of Order,* did not.

The opposition struck at MFY with charges that it was harboring Communists.[76] Out of around 350 employees, it did turn out that one had belonged to a Communist-dominated union while working as a machinist (but not while at MFY),[77] and another had been the Socialist Workers party candidate for attorney general two years before.[78] It took several months for MFY to clear itself of the Communist charges. Given the flimsiness of the charges and the resultant furor, one observer wondered if publicly funded agencies could conduct militant, social action programs for any length of time.[79]

The other aspect of the attack on MFY charged the agency with fiscal mismanagement. These charges boiled down to $2,100 in unaccounted-for funds. Jim McCarthy had dined out extensively at MFY's expense, and he did repay the $1,500 for which he was responsible. Rather than announce his interracial romance with another MFY staffer, McCarthy cited health reasons, resigned, and married.[80] Bert Beck, who served on a review panel examining the charges and who subsequently headed MFY and then in 1967 replaced Helen Hall as head of Henry Street, felt that while some grounds did exist for fiscal complaints, "the heart of the crisis . . . was obviously related to the social-protest activities."[81]

MFY's defense of itself was hampered by the fact that its board was too large to play an active role in the agency. MFY's top administrative staff made almost all the decisions with little or no board input. Furthermore, as a matter of policy, MFY had tried as much as possible to avoid working through existing agencies, such as the settlements. However, when the attack came, MFY needed the endorsement of these agencies. In spite of having been badly treated by MFY, the settlements gave their public support at the crucial time. Helen Hall summarized the situation:

> The deliberate hostility, lack of skill, and, often, arrogance directed toward what they [MFY] termed the "Establishments," left them with few friends able and willing to defend them when the attacks came. The Settlements, having started them out, stood by MFY because we felt that the idea was more important than their mistakes. Also, important innovations had already been started which would have been destroyed if the attacks had been successful.[82]

Although MFY continued in existence after the 1964 attacks, it lost its innovative significance. Its primary contribution was that it pointed the way for the Great Society programs that were to follow. Settlement participation in MFY programs remained relatively minor. Three settlements housed MFY legal clinics. These were essentially referral stations to Legal Aid or MFY Legal Services for the indigent.[83] Settlements also housed three preschool centers. At these centers (which helped to break down male-female stereotypes by successfully using some male aides), mothers met to discuss their problems while their children played.[84] By 1967, MFY programs were essentially down to Legal Services and Job Training and Placement.[85] When MFY's director since 1965, Bert Beck, accepted the position of head of Henry Street in 1967, both organizations decided to have Beck head them simultaneously.[86] Thus, the settlement that gave birth to MFY also sheltered it in its waning days.

In evaluating MFY and the settlements' role in relation to it, what stands out is that during MFY's most significant phase settlement houses played a relatively minor role. MFY was the prototype program for the War on Poverty because it offered a new approach to poverty—participation of the poor through confrontation-type community organization. Its message was to solve poverty by giving the poor power through participation. If the settlements had remained in charge, with their emphasis on consensus and working through established channels, the sense of something new, exciting, and unique would have been lost. That sense was needed for War on Poverty funding. However, because of their underlying commitment to the same goals as MFY, the settlements stood by MFY in spite of being used by the Columbia group.

SETTLEMENT PROGRAMS LEADING TO
THE WAR ON POVERTY

While MFY was the major settlement contribution toward shaping
the direction of the War on Poverty, well before 1964 settlements
did engage in a variety of other programs that also had significance
for antipoverty and citizen participation. At a 1958 settlement house
conference, future HEW Secretary Wilbur Cohen posed the question: "Will poverty be a thing of the past? If America has the capacity to eliminate poverty in the next few years, what must settlements
do to make sure that it is eliminated for our neighbors?"[87] One answer was more participation of the poor in shaping welfare programs. In the 1940s, settlement workers began to give attention to
the development of indigenous leadership. To further the trend, in
1957 the National Federation of Settlements proposed a workshop
on citizen participation.[88] By then, activist citizen groups were starting to show new vitality in some settlements.

Another hallmark of the 1960s was the Peace Corps and its domestic counterpart, VISTA (Volunteers in Service to America). The
government used settlements in Philadelphia and New York City as
settings for Peace Corps training. At Philadelphia's University Settlement, trainees headed for Ceylon got experience organizing young
adult activities.[89] At Henry Street, trainees worked with Spanish-
speaking people. The Henry Street trainees were first introduced to
the Gouverneur Clinic health services. They were then given the assignment of "connecting Puerto Rican families with these services."[90]
Settlement efforts with the Peace Corps were soon transferred to
VISTA.

The National Federation of Settlements took the lead in developing a liaison with federal officials that led to VISTA. In 1961, the
director of the National Federation, Margaret Berry, was appointed
to the President's Advisory Committee on Juvenile Delinquency. Following a conversation with the director of the committee, David
Hackett, the National Federation submitted a proposal that showed
how domestic volunteers might be used effectively in ghetto neighborhoods.[91] Based on a survey of settlements around the United States,
the National Federation proposed that VISTA (called the National
Service Corps in its planning stage) volunteers be used in community

organization, programs for delinquents and predelinquents, expansion of services to the elderly (e.g., Meals-on-Wheels), and work with multiproblem families. Settlements also offered to provide supervision and an organizational base that volunteers could use to gain entrée into slum neighborhoods.[92] The VISTA objective of trying to stimulate disadvantaged people to improve themselves and their environment by having volunteers actually live among the poor was very much in the settlement tradition. The VISTA input also showed the National Federation's liaison role with Washington at its best.

The War on Poverty placed a lot of emphasis on using the poor to help the poor. That was also the idea behind the Good Companions Health Service, a federally funded project at Henry Street Settlement. Starting in 1963,[93] the project used elderly volunteers to help out home-bound oldsters with shopping, visiting (loneliness), cleaning, and cooking. The goal was not only the well-being of the helped but to broaden the horizons and improve the mental health of the volunteers. It achieved a fair degree of success.[94]

Because the War on Poverty was concerned with opportunity, it tried to increase what the poor got out of education through both tutoring and motivational programs. Again, forerunners of these programs can be seen in settlements. In 1957, Hudson Guild began a program of individual and group tutoring.[95] Three years later, Philadelphia's Houston Community Center started its Opportunity Club for eight-to-twelve-year-old youngsters who were capable of doing better work in school. By 1966, the Opportunity Clubs had spread to four settlements and were funded by the Board of Education.[96] Chicago's Firman House ran a motivational program starting in 1962 for high school youngsters called Education for Life. The program featured trips to restaurants and museums plus sessions with politicians, a professional ball player, a disc jockey, a registered nurse, and the Chicago School Board. All ten of the original members went on to college.[97] Also in 1962 in Pittsburgh, Kingsley House offered an after-school study hall with Carnegie Institute of Technology volunteers.[98] These programs were similar to the Upward Bound and tutoring programs of the subsequent War on Poverty.

Education was to lead to jobs, and again settlement programs preceded the War on Poverty. The Jobs for School Youth program at

Friends Neighborhood Guild illustrates the progression from a job-finding emphasis to job training. Jobs for School Youth started in 1962 to keep potential dropouts in school by finding them summer work. The boys were organized into work crews to do unskilled interior and exterior maintenance jobs. The guild, however, had trouble finding sufficient employment for the work crews.[99] Therefore, in 1963, it instituted a training program to teach the boys how to spackle, wallpaper, and paint walls, and refinish floors. Among the future Great Society bureaucrats familiar with the activities of the guild were Seymour Wolfbine, director of Manpower Training at the Department of Labor, and Robert Weaver, Secretary of Housing and Urban Development.[100] The guild also urged influential Congressmen to support federal funding for similar job programs.[101]

Other settlements ran other job-training projects. In Cleveland in 1961, Phyllis Wheatley staged a "Charm Conference" designed to make black girls more employable by focusing on attitude, manners, and appearance. However, the same settlement also offered a training course in power machine sewing, which would increase the employability of women in the apparel industry.[102] In 1961, Chicago's Olivet Community Center ran a program similar to the future Neighborhood Youth Corps.[103] Anticipating the Job Corps, Neighborhood House in North Richmond, California, got a grant from the Rosenberg Foundation to run Supreme Services, a janitorial training and placement project for hard-core unemployed youths.[104] The New York City association of settlements, United Neighborhood Houses, was in tune with the War on Poverty's more direct approach when it voted in 1963 to do all possible to change the emphasis from job-counseling programs to paid on-the-job training.[105]

As in so many other cases, settlement workers formally testified and provided behind-the-scenes input to make federal job-training programs for youth a reality. In her testimony before a Senate subcommittee on the Youth Employment Opportunities Act of 1961, United Neighborhood Houses head Helen Harris recalled her experience as head of the 1930s Youth Administration in New York City. She talked about teaching skills and good work habits to youngsters who were "downhearted, unsure of themselves, without skills and most often without the faintest notion of the rudimentary requirements of getting and holding a job."[106] That bill failed, but the following year, Washington officials requested National Federation input on a new Youth Employment Opportunities Bill.[107] With settlement help, the War on Poverty was approaching.

SETTLEMENT ACTIVISM IN
THE CIVIL RIGHTS MOVEMENT

Professional social work values were said to respect the attitudes of clients and traditionally tended to emphasize individual, problem-oriented services at the expense of social reform. However, the social work profession also adopted a pro–civil rights stand. While it is correct to say that professionalism in general had an inhibiting effect on social reform, civil rights is the major exception to that generalization. The reason may be that professionalism stresses learned skills, not personal characteristics; and racial prejudice should not be allowed to overshadow or devalue those learned skills. Also, changing neighborhoods and a growing professional commitment drew settlements more deeply into the larger civil rights scene.

Their involvement began very mildly in the early 1950s with the traditional letters of protest and ended the decade with direct action participation in marches and picketing. For example, in the spring of 1950, three staff members and two black teenagers from Chicago Commons traveled to New York by car, staying overnight in Toledo, Ohio. They discovered that the YMCA in Toledo would not accommodate an interracial group. About the only avenue of protest they saw open to them was to write to the national headquarters of the Y as well as the Toledo Y.[108] That style of protest would change.

The Supreme Court decision to desegregate schools came in 1954, but it was slow in being implemented. To put pressure on the federal government to enforce this decision, the Youth March for Integrated Schools took place in April 1959. The twenty-six thousand who assembled in Washington, D.C., for the demonstration included a contingent from New York settlement houses. At Hamilton-Madison House, a couple of board members opposed the settlements' participation, considering the march a rather undignified way to promote integration. These board members were overruled when another Hamilton-Madison board member, former Manhattan bor-

ough president Stanley Isaacs, pointed out that "such a demonstration receives local and national attention that sitting around a table
in New York could not produce."[109] For the settlement house youths,
the excitement of the trip must have been enhanced when their buses
were stopped by police outside the city, then escorted in convoys of
ten to the Washington Monument for the demonstration. While they
didn't necessarily listen closely to all the speeches, those who were
there felt a strong sense of unity in a great cause.[110] The march
drew youngsters from both black and white settlement clubs.[111]

Another phase of the integration campaign was sit-ins to integrate
lunch counters in Southern stores. Chains such as Woolworth's and
Kresge's were special targets. Civil rights sympathizers in the North
could contribute to the effort by picketing those stores in their own
communities. This happened in New York City, and again settlement youths joined the effort. At Hamilton-Madison House, young
people formed a group to work for civil rights that passed around
petitions, picketed Woolworth stores, and raised money to help activists who were fighting for integration in the South. This group of
about thirty young adults had as its president a twenty-one-year-old
Puerto Rican exterminator, as its treasurer a young black man, and
as its secretary a white female journalist.[112] Hudson Guild also had
a similar group.[113]

By 1963, the focus of the demonstrations in Washington was on
equal opportunity for jobs. At least a dozen New York settlements
sent delegations to the August 28, 1963, March on Washington for
Jobs and Freedom. In New York, a rally at City Hall in which around
a thousand settlement youths heard Mayor Robert Wagner endorse
the goal of equal job opportunities preceded the march.[114] During
this march, which was a high point in the civil rights movement, two
Hamilton-Madison House staff members were arrested for blocking
traffic. That incident prompted the board to question the motive of
the demonstrators "in terms of 'showing off' or satisfying their own
personal needs." As a result, the board warned the staff that they
were not to carry on civil rights activity in the name of the house
nor could they continue to carry on this activity on settlement time.[115]

Perhaps because of the curtailment of civil rights activity, a young
Hamilton-Madison staff member, Michael Schwerner, left the settlement to work for CORE in Mississippi. He was one of three white

civil rights workers shot and killed in the summer of 1964,[116] apparently with the approval or collaboration of local authorities in Mississippi.[117] Schwerner had gone to Meridian, Mississippi, to try "to establish a center along settlement lines," but was working on a CORE voter registration drive at the time of his murder.[118] It was as a worker fore CORE, and not as a settlement worker, that Schwerner became a martyr for the civil rights cause.

Latent settlement conservatism surfaced in another way. During the 1950s, blacks put almost no pressure on the settlement movement to do more for them. That began to change in the early 1960s. In 1961, United Neighborhood Houses of New York received a million dollars from the Vincent Astor Foundation to run a juvenile delinquency prevention program in nine settlements. None of the nine were located in the major black ghetto of Harlem. The omission was doubtless due to the fact that in spite of efforts to increase services to blacks, most settlements were originally established at locations where the workers could serve white ethnic groups. There was still no settlement in central Harlem. Therefore, several members of the Harlem Neighborhoods Association made a special appeal to United Neighborhood Houses to use part of the Astor funds to establish a new settlement.[119] United Neighborhood Houses resented the appeal to do more, pointing out that most of the houses involved in the project did serve some blacks.[120]

The Harlem group had much better success getting money from the federal government. Within six months, the President's Committee made planning funds available to Harlem Youth Opportunities Unlimited (HARYOU) under the direction of a Harlem Neighborhoods Association member, Kenneth Clark.[121] By 1964, HARYOU had become a multimillion-dollar poverty program, but settlements were in no position to take advantage of increased funding for Harlem's social services. By the time of the War on Poverty, settlements had tasted direct action tactics and they had digested some of the civil rights movement, but their support for direct action and black power was only halfhearted at best.

Settlement houses played a crucial role in translating the 1950s concern for juvenile delinquency into the 1960s concern for poverty.

As ghetto-based agencies with a tradition of social activism, they were in a position to experiment and agitate for better programs. Furthermore, the growing availability of both public and private grant sources made much of this experimentation possible. Some of the settlement approaches to delinquency, such as the use of indigenous leaders and storefront drop-in centers, foreshadowed the War on Poverty. Their small-scale experiments with tutoring and youth employment programs were also significant. Finally, the settlement role in creating the prototype antipoverty program, Mobilization for Youth, and in defending MFY after MFY repudiated its initial settlement leadership deserves more recognition than it has received. However, the fact that Mobilization for Youth, during its initial action phase, was hostile to settlements as traditional, establishment-oriented, consensus-seeking (and, therefore, ineffective) agencies was also indicative of the problems settlements would face in the War on Poverty. Likewise, the settlement commitment to integration as opposed to black power and the settlement's affinity for consensus methods as opposed to direct action would undermine the settlement movement. Settlements had begun to pay a price for their reputation as agencies of social control.

CHAPTER 9

THE WAR ON POVERTY
"SAVES" THE SETTLEMENTS

———•••———

THE WAR ON POVERTY SHOULD HAVE BEEN THE opportunity for which the settlements had been working. It was the culmination of post–World War II reform efforts. The cornerstone of the antipoverty program was the Economic Opportunity Act passed in 1964. In addition to establishing the Office of Economic Opportunity, which housed many new programs, the law also provided for "maximum feasible participation of the poor" in policymaking roles at the local level. The most innovative programs were those that stressed community organization of the poor into what often amounted to effective pressure groups. The War on Poverty favored neighborhood-based service centers, supported the use of paraprofessionals, and sought to break the cycle of hereditary poverty by focusing on youths and blacks. It provided educational and job-training programs and a variety of other services to the disadvantaged. In addition to trying to find new approaches to fighting poverty, it made major funding available to local service agencies. In fact, one of its chief effects was to develop the direct federal government/private agency relationship through major expansion of federal grant monies. Since settlements had always had a broad conception of their function and were neighborhood-based agencies with some experience in community organization among the poor, they expected to benefit from the War on Poverty as well as contribute to it.

THE WAR ON POVERTY ATTACKS
THE SETTLEMENTS

Richard Cloward, formerly of Mobilization for Youth and on the Columbia social work faculty, did much to crystallize the widespread hostility toward settlements. In a 1965 statement before the Senate Select Committee on Poverty that was reprinted as an article in *The Nation,* Cloward recognized the settlement method as one of consensus, bringing different ethnic and class groups together within its structure in order to solve community problems through communication and cooperation. However, Cloward saw the interests of Puerto Rican slum dwellers as being in opposition to those of Jewish landlords, and it was hardly in the self-interest of Italian political machine leaders to promote voter registration among blacks. To Cloward, strategies of coalition and conciliation would fail to "bring the poor into the mainstream of American life." According to Cloward, what the poor needed was "a heightened awareness of conflicting interests and the means to organize separately."[1] Cloward very much reflected War on Poverty theory and tactics as well as the social work profession when he attacked the heart of the settlement method of consensus.

The War on Poverty also fed charges that settlements failed to serve the really poor. Besides the MFY attacks, staffers from another prototype program for the War on Poverty, ABCD in Boston, took the position that settlements could not be trusted to run neighborhood service centers or other poverty programs because they were not sufficiently close to the poor. Also, in 1965, Helen Harris, head of the New York federation of settlements, complained, "Cloward has been running down the settlements ever since he started working for Mobilization for Youth five years ago. He claims we do not work with the poor."[2] What Cloward was actually saying in 1965 was that social service agencies tended to reflect the values of their controlling well-to-do board constituencies more than they reflected the values of the poor they were supposed to help.[3] By the fall of 1965, criticism of the settlements' orientation was so strong that settlements could no longer ignore it.

Thrown on the defensive, settlement workers acknowledged their problems while trying to contain the charges. Juliet Brudney of the

New York federation conceded, "Not every settlement house has concerned itself with the needs and aspirations of the disadvantaged, and not every program of those settlements who tried to work in this field was effective." However, she claimed it was grossly inaccurate "to call settlements 'representatives of the establishment' or 'social welfare colonialists.' "[4]

Settlements had the uneasy feeling that some truth existed in the charges. Helen Harris was bothered by the difficulty that many settlements had in finding just ten youths each that were poor enough to be referred to the Neighborhood Youth Corps.[5] She was also concerned that Brooklyn settlement houses resisted giving the poor a larger role in managing their programs.[6] The result was a negative neighborhood reaction toward the Brooklyn settlements.[7] Negative neighborhood reaction meant that many settlement proposals would fail to receive funding.

The major theme of the War on Poverty was empowering the poor. Social workers and others who were developing a grass-roots approach to community organizing saw established agencies, like the settlements, competing with new antipoverty groups for federal funds. Richard Cloward claimed the old-style agencies were making inroads on their local antipoverty councils. To illustrate, he cited thirty-one New York settlements with Neighborhood Youth Corps programs, twenty requesting Head Start operations, and thirteen planning community action programs, plus a number of others with various other projects. Cloward clearly thought the settlements were more interested in expanding their programs than in seeing that competing antipoverty agencies flourished.[8] This attitude was widely shared by academics, antipoverty officials, and the poor. As a Columbia social work student in the 1960s who wrote his Ph.D. dissertation as part of the Brandeis research group evaluating community action programs in the War on Poverty recalled, "It was kind of a joke among us, both at Columbia and in the Brandeis research group, that the War on Poverty revived the settlements."[9]

By far the most visible effect of the War on Poverty was the sudden influx of federal money into settlements for all sorts of programs. In November 1965, the National Federation of Settlements estimated that settlement houses had over $10 million worth of OEO (Office of Economic Opportunity) grant money.[10] The influx of money was the result of the large amount available and not of a favorable attitude toward settlements as such. In some cases, the use of settlements for antipoverty programs was clearly reluctant.

Hull House, which by 1965 had made the transition to an association of several houses in different neighborhoods, was one of the most successful recipients of poverty program grants. This money enabled Hull House to almost double its services in 1965 and 1966.[11] By September 1965, Hull House had received nine grants totaling over a million dollars and had added around 150 staff members. Among these grants was one to train VISTA volunteers. Another was for a Head Start program. A third, STREETS, was designed to prepare predelinquent girls "for marriage and motherhood" through cultural programs, charm classes, special counseling, vocational guidance, job training, and preparation for baby-sitting. Under its Neighborhood Youth Corps contract, Hull House provided eligible youngsters with a variety of work experiences, ranging from typist to assistant club leader. (This program was almost identical to the National Youth Administration, in which settlements participated in the 1930s.) Other grants were for Meals-on-Wheels, the training of indigenous neighborhood leadership, and additional nursery school projects.[12] Smaller settlements got fewer grants, but the proportional impact was comparable. Thus, some privately funded settlements were now dependent on federal grants for up to 50 percent or more of their budgets.

While settlements benefited from the antipoverty funds, so did a lot of new competing agencies. The War on Poverty officials distrusted established agencies and blamed the social work profession for perpetuating poverty. So, where feasible, antipoverty funds went to start new agencies that in some cases duplicated settlement functions. For example, community organization had been a settlement specialty; but as a result of the War on Poverty, settlements now found a number of other competing agencies doing that. A longtime settlement head, Camillo DeSantis, recalled that prior to the War on Poverty, the settlement was the place to go for the help. Then the antipoverty program in Minneapolis funded "citizens' community centers." Local poverty officials successfully blocked attempts to link these centers with settlements. The centers were independent, citizen-controlled, and lacked well-skilled staff. Like so many new antipoverty agencies, they were transitory. Within three years, these citizen-controlled centers were out of business. Some of their backers were so activist that they didn't think things through. They just practiced confrontation. Had they used settlements, some of the floundering of the new agencies could have been averted. Settlements were not successful in "rabble-rousing," but they knew the power structure and they had administrative and planning expertise. However, for those new agencies that did survive the War on Poverty, rather than identify with the settlement movement, they competed with it.[13]

One difference between the settlements and the new antipoverty agencies was that the antipoverty agencies were quicker than the settlements to reflect the emergence of minorities. The War on Poverty promoted the concept that the poor should have policymaking roles because, as poor people, they would have special insights into poverty. That concept was extended to the idea that only Indians can work effectively with Indians, alcoholics with alcoholics, and so on. In some ways, this concept is true, but the War on Poverty carried it to an extreme. A professional degree was not as important as having the right background to identify and empathize with the group to be helped. Furthermore, these poor and minority groups were so distrustful of settlement domination that they rejected a professional/nonprofessional partnership. They wanted to run their own agencies, and sometimes they lacked the leadership to make these agencies successful. Furthermore, they left behind the attitude that minority identity was more important than neighborhood identity. Since the settlements wanted to unify rather than fragment neighborhoods, the War on Poverty did have a basic philosophical difference with settlements. Thus, while settlements did benefit from War on Poverty funding, when one considers the overall effects of numerous other new competing agencies receiving funds, the net effect of the War on Poverty may well have been to contribute to the demise of the traditional settlement house movement.

SETTLEMENT HOUSE ATTEMPTS TO COORDINATE THE WAR ON POVERTY

Along with the money available to settlements, the amount of influence, coordination, or control the settlements would have over the poverty program was important. On the national level, settlement leaders continued to maintain and cultivate political contacts. For example, Helen Hall served as a program proposal evaluator for the federal government. In a letter to federal bureaucrat Esther Peterson, she criticized the tendency to rank programs for women last.[14] Occasionally, on the local level, settlement leaders appeared on an advisory or policymaking committee. In 1964, both the director of Baden Street Settlement and his assistant served on a ten-member committee advising Rochester's city manager on possible poverty program participation.[15] Also, Winslow Carlton of Henry Street's board joined a mixed group of agency representatives and indigenous leaders from poor neighborhoods on the New York City Council Against Poverty.[16] However, these activities were not extensive enough to indicate major settlement influence.

Shortly after the passage of the Economic Opportunity Act, the National Federation of Settlements attempted to assume a coordinator role. It first tried the idea of submitting a master contract containing the proposals of member houses, but the Department of Labor quickly nixed that approach. The National Federation then proposed a grant whereby either the Department of Labor or the Community Action Program would underwrite two additional National Federation staff people to help member settlements write antipoverty proposals.[17] That also went nowhere. However, beginning in April 1964, the National Federation on its own sent information bulletins about the Economic Opportunity Act to member settlements, provided consultation to members on their grant proposals, and did follow-up checking on these proposals in Washington. Furthermore, the National Federation directly stimulated a number of settlement house Neighborhood Youth Corps proposals. Attempts to formalize this liaison role with a federal grant, however, continued to fail. What settlements were slow to grasp was that the federal government was interested in local community input and approval by the poor and not the involvement of a national, professional organization.[18] While Cloward and others were too quick to dismiss settlements, the settlements were not easily moved beyond their "top down" organizing, consensus methods, and social control tendencies to adopt a more grass-roots approach.

In a few cases, the antipoverty program co-opted settlement personnel. For example, North Richmond, California, wanted the associate director of Neighborhood House on the staff of the Council of Neighborhood Services before having that agency contract with Neighborhood House to run a nursery and a tutorial program. Thus, the council insured control over these settlement-based programs.[19] In Philadelphia, a University Settlement staff worker organized poverty council elections and town meetings, but as an employee loaned to the city and not as a settlement house worker.[20] Perhaps the most influential settlement worker to take another position was the director of New York City's federation of settlements, Helen Harris. In 1964, she became the city's coordinator of the Job Corps[21] and also chaired "the city's screening board for anti-poverty proposals" until resigning in frustration in 1966.[22] However, the co-opting of settlement personnel was not extensive, nor were the co-opted workers all that influential on behalf of settlements.

Conflict often occurred between settlement houses and their local poverty boards because the poor tended to classify settlements with the social service "establishment," and because they associated settlements with a kind of top-heavy community organization in which direction seemed to come from the settlement workers rather than the poor. Even when settlements forwarded proposals framed by the poor themselves, poverty councils often refused to fund them because they assumed the settlement was just using the poor as a front. Settlements and poverty boards also clashed over the poor's frequent preference for protest over service, lack of regard for professional qualifications, tendency to hire themselves while ignoring conflict of interest charges, and, occasionally, anti-Semitism. These antipoverty workers persisted in regarding settlements "as 'the establishment' and the enemy."[23]

Philadelphia is an example of a city whose settlements had their bid to play a local coordinating role rejected. The Delaware Valley Settlement Alliance submitted a proposal in 1964 that encompassed a number of subsequent Great Society programs, which would have been *run out of settlement houses*. The programs included legal aid, preschool education, housing rehabilitation, employment education and counseling, family counseling, and community organization. Residents of the settlement neighborhoods were to be employed as preschool aides, homemaking aides, and instructors.[24] The proposal was not funded. Instead, settlements found themselves trying to work out a relationship with their local Community Action Councils.[25] Thus, the settlement houses traded control by welfare councils and United Funds for control by poverty boards. The poverty boards were perhaps the more difficult with which to work, in part because of the distrust bordering on paranoia that they often exhibited toward established agencies. The settlements, for their part, probably could have been more adventurous in following the lead of the poverty boards sooner. After all, one reason the poverty boards were created was to bypass the "establishment."

The Pittsburgh experience was happier. Early in the antipoverty program, Kingsley House established its neighborhood Economic Opportunity Office, hired a coordinator, and formed a representative neighborhood poverty council. Kingsley encouraged participation of the poor, gradually withdrawing from the leadership role. Thus, Kingsley was able to maintain a contractual relationship with Community Action Pittsburgh and serve as the local poverty program's delegate agency in its neighborhood.[26] A genuine willingness to relinquish control seems to have been the key to cooperation. As a result, the relationship of settlements to their local antipoverty board varied by city, with settlements being the major agency group under the local board in some cities.

DIRECT ACTION

It was very important for settlement-created or -sponsored agencies to be nonsettlement directed. A model of such an organization was Milwaukee's Triple O (Organization of Organizations), started by Northcott Neighborhood House. Northcott was founded in a predominantly black neighborhood in 1961 and headed by a black minister, Lucius Walker, who had an M.S.W. In developing its Poverty Advisory Council, Northcott tried to avoid the self-appointed, middle-class leadership found in most civil rights organizations. Instead, the staff worked to identify and become acquainted with existing neighborhood interest groups. The next step was house-to-house calls, talking to people about their concerns and organizing block groups. These block groups and indigenous leaders then formed the basis of Northcott's Poverty Advisory Council. The council was to advise and assist Northcott on grant proposals and programs, study poverty, and inform the neighborhood.

Because the Northcott Council was concerned that the poor lacked representation on the governing board of Milwaukee's Community Action Program (CAP) agency, the council called a rally. At the rally, Triple O was formed. Triple O was successful in getting one-third of the seats on the CAP board assigned to poor people. Initially, Triple O was dependent on Northcott for staff, space, clerical help, and other expenses. As it matured, Triple O attained independence through outside grant support. Among the reasons for Northcott and Triple O's success were the steadfast support of Northcott's funding agency, the Methodist church; the support of the local National Association of Social Workers chapter, which gave Walker its "Social Worker of the Year" award; and the county welfare department, which contracted with Northcott to locate families to adopt black children.[27] Northcott enjoyed widespread support.

Often, settlement participation in the broadly based community organizations was resented. The old-style neighborhood councils did not enjoy much support. They were really meetings of the executives of neighborhood-based social service organizations. The Lower East Side Neighborhood Association (LENA) in New York City is an example of a council dominated by the staffs of neighborhood settlements. It continued to function in the 1960s. However, it and other traditional councils were increasingly regarded as irrelevant and unrepresentative. Settlements were also occasionally asked to send a staff or board member to serve as an appointee to antipoverty committees. In 1964, the mayor of Philadelphia gave such an appointment to the president of the Delaware Valley Settlement Alliance.[28] However, boards and committees consisting entirely of agency staff appointments were perceived by the poor and also regarded by the federal government as not meeting the requirements for the participation of the poor themselves. No matter how conscientious or informed the staff or board representative might be, if the person was not himself poor, he just was not as legitimate a representative of the poor as one who was.

It was not just the type of membership of a group but also its methods that were very much an issue. By the 1960s, settlement houses were slowly learning the lessons of Saul Alinsky; but since they preferred to work within the established political system, settlement workers were drawn rather reluctantly to the support and utilization of direct action tactics. A 1967 NFS Training Center study claimed that if the poor were unable to communicate effectively through the usual means with the political establishment, "resort to militant strategies is necessary and deserves the support of settlement houses."[29]

One of the settlement workers who took advantage of the greater acceptance of direct action was Kevin Riordan from Philadelphia's Lighthouse Settlement. In 1969, Riordan led two dozen women and ten children in a sit-in at the Philadelphia Housing Authority. The Authority was buying houses for use as public housing. The demonstrators demanded that neighbors be involved in the decisions over which houses were to be bought. Initially, the housing authority threatened to lock the demonstrators in the offices over the weekend; but after hearing from a lawyer, it relented and signed an agreement granting the demonstrators their demands.[30]

When the National Welfare Rights Organization was founded in 1967, it could draw on the experience of some local groups in settlements that had lobbied the state legislature for increased welfare benefits or had boycotted ghetto merchants to protest higher prices. In Philadelphia, settlement staff were active in organizing and assisting Welfare Rights groups. The Welfare Rights Organization was careful to maintain control, and wouldn't let settlement workers working with them meet unless the Welfare Rights Organization itself had representatives present.[31] Among the Welfare Rights projects that enjoyed settlement worker participation was a 1969 sit-in at Philadelphia's United Fund to pressure the United Fund into "dealing honestly and effectively with the basic causes of poverty, exploitation, ignorance and discrimination."[32] What settlements had to offer Welfare Rights groups was settlement credibility and stability. Besides initiating groups, settlements could also offer staff and material support; but if a group was to succeed, the welfare recipients had to run it.

Launched by Martin Luther King and carried out in the aftermath of his assassination, the Poor People's Campaign had settlement house support. In this massive and lengthy demonstration to revive the waning support for antipoverty programs, poor people from around the United States converged on Washington and camped out there for a couple of months. The National Federation urged its member settlements to assist this effort through fund-raising and in other ways.[33] Cooperating settlements donated money to the demonstrators, opened their facilities to Poor People's Campaign organizers, and offered staff assistance.[34] Philadelphia settlement worker Allen Bacon also urged settlement workers to apply more traditional pressure and write their Congressmen on behalf of the antipoverty program.[35] However, in the end, the hoped-for legislation was not forthcoming.

In spite of the vogue for direct action, settlements were most comfortable with traditional pressure tactics. When a Cleveland settlement worker discovered that the city was dragging its feet on a rat control program because a local councilman thought his constituents didn't want it, the settlement worker got neighborhood residents to call and write the councilman's office and pass around a petition. As a result, the rat control program was instituted.[36]

Settlements probably would have been more in the vanguard of social action if they had not been United Fund (now called United Way) agencies. United Funds and other local sources of financial support pressured settlements to emphasize the provision of immediate services as opposed to social change activity. A speaker at a neighborhood organization conference observed, "The more a settlement is involved in social action, the greater the problem in raising money. . . . The agencies which can best afford action programs are those with politically liberal and geographically distant sources of money."[37]

During the 1960s, a lot of money was available to settlements, not only through the federal government but through private foundations. However, these grants were not a complete way around United Fund conservatism. Houston's Neighborhood Centers Association worried that federal- or foundation-funded settlement projects might on occasion prove embarrassing to its local United Fund. They did not, as members of the United Fund, wish to be the cause of adverse public opinion which could negatively affect the United Fund, and so Neighborhood Centers Association proposed a system of joint consultation with the United Fund on controversial programs and actions.[38] It wasn't long before United Funds across the country demanded the right to review grant proposals of member agencies prior to submission to granting agencies.

BLACK PRIDE, BLACK POWER, AND CIVIL RIGHTS ADVOCACY

Meanwhile, the civil rights movement was moving beyond integration into black power and militant confrontation. Traditional settlement house methods of consensus and advocacy through establishment channels increasingly failed to satisfy the black community. Thus, settlements were faced with a series of dilemmas. Should they abandon their traditional philosophy of consensus in favor of black power and direct action tactics? And when direct action degenerated into riots and violence, what role should settlements play? Above all, how could settlements most effectively serve their clientele and further the civil rights movement?

Settlements serving a black clientele with a predominantly black staff and board were in a unique position to foster black pride. In so doing, programs featuring the arts were common. Typical was Wharton Centre's exhibit of "Negro Life" by local artists and its black theater group.[39] Rochester's Baden Street Settlement planned to show the creations of a black fashion designer, and also recruited African students from the University of Rochester as volunteers.[40] Some feeling existed that black males were better able to generate racial pride than black females, for in 1968, the head of Hull House Association, Paul Jans, listed as one of his goals "to have competent black *male* executives in administrative charge of centers serving the black community" (italics added).[41]

One of the by-products of the 1960s race riots was the establishment in several northern cities of radical black settlements. In Minneapolis in 1966, The Way was founded. After eight years of working at the center in various capacities (black history instructor, football and boxing coach, and counselor), Harry (Spike) Moss became executive director in 1974. His lack of a professional degree didn't bother him. He said: "Being black, that's all I need." Moss went on to echo the militant line, remarking, "The only thing I've been shown is that the system only responds when a person gets out in the streets and gets down and rebels to get what he needs." As for The Way's clientele, Moss said, "Pride—they have that now. They didn't when we started."[42] However, because The Way served only one particular group and did not embrace the settlement philosophy, the Minneapolis social work establishment did not recognize it as a settlement nor did The Way identify with the settlement movement. It was also quite controversial.

The settlement philosophy was to bring different groups together to try to get them to get along. However, racial pride and the resulting trend toward different centers for different racial groups was a different approach. Not only did black pride cause a dilemma for the organization of settlements, but the confrontation that characterized black power clashed at times with the settlements' methods of advocacy.

However, traditional advocacy did not always work. Furthermore, the settlement role as advocate did not go unchallenged. The United Crusade of San Francisco warned member agencies "to refrain from the use of United Crusade funds for purely political purposes."[43] In St. Paul, when a board member of Hallie Q. Brown House criticized director Alice Onque for involving the house in the debate over *de facto* segregation in the schools, she said, "The minute we stop being involved . . . we might as well put a lock on the door."[44] If the opposition got too strong, a common retreat was to take the position utilized by the Chicago Federation of Settlements that agency employees retained the right to speak out and take actions as private citizens, whether or not their position was agency-endorsed.[45] Of course, they did so on their own time as individuals and not in the name of the agency. That was essentially the line of defense the Columbus Federation of Settlements used when some realtors criticized a settlement head for certain activities on behalf of open housing.[46] The opposition that was perhaps hardest to meet was that which came from the settlement's own neighborhood. When Gads Hill director Meta Schwiebert refused to take part in a meeting opposing integration of a local school, the community council vice president asked her, "What would you think if no one came to Gads Hill tomorrow?"[47] These were some of the conservative forces pressuring settlement personnel to limit their involvement in civil rights.

Advocacy styles changed in other ways as well. The 1960s was a decade in which direct action tactics—rallies, demonstrations, sit-ins— got a lot of sympathetic media coverage, and many people regarded them as more effective than traditional means of advocacy. However, direct action tactics were also controversial and could cost an agency financial support. Settlement use of direct action was limited, which reinforced the image many people had of settlements as being old-fashioned and ineffective. Therefore, the settlements that did utilize direct action tactics and their experiences are particularly noteworthy.

The outstanding example in the mid-1960s was Chicago's Marillac House. The settlement was established in 1947 when the Daughters of Charity, a Catholic order, bought an old Episcopal orphanage. The neighborhood was then about 90 percent Catholic and 95 percent white. However, it changed rapidly, and by 1965, was about 2 percent white and 98 percent black. The sisters reached out to their new neighbors, only 10 percent of whom were Catholic, and placed more emphasis on community organization.[48]

Community organization at Marillac included direct action. In June 1965, civil rights activists demonstrated against Chicago school superintendent Ben Willis because he refused to allow blacks in overcrowded schools to transfer to better ones. The demonstrations were met with police arrests. One of those arrested was a priest, who requested that the sisters at Marillac join the demonstration the following day. Six did and were arrested. A rumor then spread that the police were subjecting the sisters to "disrespectful treatment." The sisters, whose arrest had been featured on the evening news, denied the rumor at a press conference following their hearing.[49] The nuns were subsequently convicted of blocking traffic. When they refused to pay the twenty-five-dollar fines levied against them, the judge sentenced them to jail. Two black attorneys not associated with Marillac House intervened to pay the fines. One of the attorneys explained to the press: "I do know what they do to prisoners at the House of Correction. They strip them and they search them and I didn't want the sisters subjected to that."[50] The episode cost Marillac financial contributions from supporters who objected to the nuns' militant behavior. However, the settlement found other friends. To further a fund-raiser, Mayor Daley proclaimed Marillac Day.[51]

The following summer, Marillac staff decided to participate in a Martin Luther King rally. To encourage their neighbors to do so as well, the settlement not only advertised the rally, but provided rally-goers with a free lunch and free transportation.[52] In the wake of Martin Luther King's assassination, when widespread vandalism occurred in the neighborhood, "Marillac House, protected by Negro teens and adults, suffered not even a broken window."[53] Marillac was one of the outstanding settlement houses in the civil rights struggle.

Another form of direct action in which several settlements participated was the school boycott. As part of the effort to end segregation in the Chicago schools, a boycott was organized in the fall of 1963. Hull House Association supported the boycott by offering classes in black history and minority problems for the boycotting youngsters during school hours. Of Hull House's two settlements in black neighborhoods, classes at one were completely full and the other reported its attendance at between sixty and one hundred.[54] A second boycott occurred the following year, and Hull House Association again operated "Freedom Schools." This time the head of the Chicago Community Fund personally reprimanded the director of Hull House.[55] However, the agency does not appear to have lost financial support; and it did gain favor with CORE, the NAACP, and other civil rights groups.

As militant groups took the lead in seeking social change, it became necessary for some settlements to establish working relationships with these groups. In 1966, less than half the agencies received requests to use facilities from civil rights organizations.[56] When the requests did come, the houses were often unfriendly. Wharton Centre's board considered CORE "way out" and so denied its request for space in the building. Wharton, however, was willing to work with the Urban League on public assistance standards.[57] When a Black Muslim appeared at Henry Booth House, the settlement allowed him to "give his 'line' " to a group and was undoubtedly relieved when the Muslim "left without making a conversion."[58]

Toward the end of the decade, civil rights challenges to settlements became more serious. By 1968, Philadelphia's Germantown Settlement was aware that many blacks regarded settlement services "as too limiting, structured, professionalized and, in a way patroniz-

ing." Therefore, when a group of twenty young men, calling themselves the Young Afro-Americans, demanded that the settlement turn
over its Waring House branch to them and provide money for staff,
the settlement board and staff gave the key to one of the Waring
House rooms to the Young Afro-Americans.[59] Waring House placed
added emphasis on serving youth, and besides the Young Afro-
Americans, began serving a group known as "the Brickyard Gang."[60]
Apparently, relations between the two groups soon got out of hand,
and Germantown Settlement temporarily suspended services at Waring House in December 1968.[61]

In the aftermath of King's assassination, Philadelphia's Houston
Community Center established a branch in the black community run
by "an Advisory Committee of local people." In the fall of 1968,
when rioting occurred in the neighborhood and blacks feared for
their safety, Houston organized "a *patrol* of Whites in the White
community and Blacks in the Black community . . . for three days
and nights to prevent violence."[62] Later on, Houston Center allowed
Black Panthers to use the settlement for a breakfast program. Local
merchants donated food, and adult volunteers along with the Panthers served needy youngsters. The program itself was innocuous
enough, particularly since the Panthers were not even allowed to
distribute their proviolence propaganda at the breakfasts. Houston
Center may have been the only settlement in the United States, and
was the only United Fund agency in Philadelphia, where the Panthers actually ran a program.[63]

Settlements tend to function as builders of bridges, interpreting
one group to another, and drawing groups together to talk out their
differences. Therefore, it is not surprising that when settlements got
caught in the race riots of the 1960s, they played the roles of con-
ciliator and neighborhood communications center. Also, while generally deploring confrontation, settlement workers used the riots to
argue for more social programs.

Baden Street Settlement in Rochester was the first settlement to
be engulfed in a riot. During the riot, the interracial staff continued
the usual settlement program, and they also went out into the neighborhood, attempting to talk to people.[64] Following the riot, the black
assistant settlement director, Art Ferrell, met with those businessmen

most hurt by the rioting to encourage them to reopen. Because of this activity and because he was outspoken in favor of "law and order," neighborhood blacks circulated a petition to "get rid of him."[65] Sidney J. Lindenberg, executive director of Baden Street Settlement, made light of the petition while putting together a radio interview program designed to increase community understanding of racial problems.[66] The general consensus was that more efforts were needed to create opportunity in the ghetto.

When riots hit, other settlements acted as message centers. In 1964, Wharton Centre rounded up local leaders to distribute fliers during a riot, "urging people to stay off the streets."[67] During rioting following Martin Luther King's assassination, Chicago's Association House also set up a communications center.[68] Message centers were important because rumors could feed a riot, and accurate information was the best way to combat rumors.

One effect of the 1960s violence was to make it difficult for white volunteer or temporary workers to live in black ghetto neighborhoods. Chicago's Beacon House began the summer of 1966 with twenty-five college student workers. During the riot, the house suspended program activities and sent the student workers to live outside the neighborhood. Only ten returned to carry out their program responsibilities, and none resumed living in the settlement house.[69] That same year, Sister Mary William sent away from Marillac two white VISTA workers because of the way they responded to hostility expressed against them.[70]

Generally speaking, settlements in riot areas suffered very little or no physical damage; and few attacks on settlement personnel occurred. An exception was Friendly Inn during the 1966 riot in Cleveland. A female worker was beaten and a male worker damaged a tendon while trying to stop some commotion.[71] Also, during rioting that same summer, Newberry Center in Chicago suffered extensive window breakage.[72] Those were apparently the worst incidents directed against settlements.

Needless to say, settlement involvement with such black power groups as the Black Muslims and the Black Panthers was minimal. Militant black settlements, such as The Way, were also reluctant to identify with the settlement movement, probably because of its "social control" aspects. The gulf between the still predominantly white settlement houses in the mid-1960s and an increasingly militant civil rights movement reflected differences in goals as well as methods.

USE OF PARAPROFESSIONALS

The War on Poverty also raised some questions about the trend toward professionalism in social work, including settlements. In addition to emphasizing neighborhood organization and direct action, the War on Poverty questioned the professional qualifications needed to perform certain social service jobs and also recognized the special contributions that neighborhood people could make. Settlements had always used volunteers, but not until the 1930s did they use workers drawn from their surrounding neighborhoods. During the Great Depression, the WPA and NYA (Works Progress Administration and National Youth Administration) assigned people on their work relief programs to settlement houses. The NYA would be revived in the form of the War on Poverty's Neighborhood Youth Corps, and again settlements were among the host agencies providing jobs. This time, however, the use of indigenous workers would be in an environment that was increasingly coming to value the paraprofessional.

In other ways, the use of paraprofessionals in settlements actually predated the War on Poverty. In 1961, Home Toberman Settlement House in San Pedro, California, developed a "friendly visiting" program in cooperation with the local welfare department. The settlement recruited neighborhood volunteers who then worked under a welfare department supervisor. The neighborhood volunteers visited selected welfare mothers. Their purposes were to help the welfare families make better use of community resources and raise their aspirations. The volunteers were generally effective (probably more so than a professional caseworker) in establishing rapport with their clients. Ninety percent of the families so serviced made significant progress in such areas as better health through more use of clinics and in becoming employed.[73]

Some settlement use of paraprofessionals was designed to help its neighbors become more employable. Beginning in 1966, Chicago's Marillac House paid workers from its neighborhood, which it used as group leaders. The program was called Leadership Through Learning. In its first summer of operation, Marillac paid neighborhood people the minimum wage to do "everything from showing movies to adults to taking kids to the beach." As part of their training, the settlement put the workers through the Gabriel Richard Institute's leadership training course.[74] The institute concentrated on developing self-confidence and public-speaking ability. In the second year, one of the settlement's neighbors did so well that he was accepted into a training program to become a Gabriel Richard instructor.[75] Marillac developed the Leadership Through Learning program because it perceived a need for activities that would build self-confidence, a sense of personal worth, and a desire for self-improvement.[76] Philadelphia's Houston Community Center had a similar program, but it was tied more closely to eventual employment in the city's Department of Recreation. The settlement hired neighborhood people as cultural and recreational workers, then encouraged them to use their work experience in applying for jobs with the public recreation department.[77] These programs were targeted toward unemployed adults.

Settlements also wanted to help ghetto youth get jobs, and so became actively involved in employing Neighborhood Youth Corps workers. In 1964, the Labor Department asked the National Federation of Settlements to find jobs for ten thousand people between fifteen and twenty-one years of age.[78] In the 1965 programs in Philadelphia, the settlements employed in-school youth fifteen hours per week as clerk-typists, junior group leaders, playground and gym assistants, program aides, nursery aides, and in maintenance.[79] Two years later, the Philadelphia settlements had shifted to employing school dropouts for thirty-two hour weeks in entry-level clerical and maintenance jobs.[80] This shift was typical of what was happening nationwide as the antipoverty program sought to reach the hardcore poor. In terms of supplying paraprofessional workers to settlement houses, the Neighborhood Youth Corps had the greatest impact of the antipoverty programs. Thousands were employed in settlements.

Another Great Society program that augmented settlement house personnel was VISTA (Volunteers in Service to America). In 1965, some Chicago settlements provided field placements as well as a place for VISTAs to live during their six-week training program. The training also included seminars led by some of the top people in the settlement house movement, such as Bill Brueckner of Chicago Commons; Arthur Hillman, head of the NFS Training Center; and Margaret Berry, the NFS executive director.[81] The VISTA philosophy that well-to-do people would be more effective helpers of the poor if they actually lived among them was the same philosophy held by the early pioneers of the settlement house movement. By the time of the War on Poverty, nearly all settlements had abandoned the residence in the house or neighborhood idea. Thus, it is significant that VISTA would revive it. In 1966, settlements in Cleveland, Cincinnati, San Diego, and San Antonio joined the Chicago settlements in running VISTA training programs and altogether that year trained 253 VISTAs.[82] The following year Hull House alone trained 371 VISTAs.[83]

After their training, VISTAs received eleven-month assignments in disadvantaged areas. Some worked in settlements, particularly in New York and Chicago. At Henry Street Settlement, VISTAs carried out projects related to finding jobs for youths[84] and encouraging school dropouts to complete their education.[85] In Chicago, VISTAs supplemented settlement services by providing additional personnel for children's play groups and adult block organizations, and VISTAs made longer hours for recreational facilities possible.[86] One Hull House VISTA organized a tutoring project for Spanish-speaking youngsters.[87] The largest number of VISTAs Hull House Association had scattered among its half-dozen centers at any one time was sixty-one in the fall of 1966.[88]

However, the VISTAs also presented problems. Both Henry Street and Hull House felt that VISTAs needed more supervision than they were getting.[89] Hull House had to dismiss three VISTAs for allowing a group to smoke marijuana.[90] Also, a number of VISTAs questioned whether what they were doing was worthwhile.[91] Philadelphia's Germantown Settlement had used VISTAs in several programs in 1967, but anticipated none in 1968.[92] Generally speaking, VISTAs disappeared from the settlement scene around the country about that time. Perhaps it was too much to expect the altruistic spirit to continue strong among young people in the face of the war in Vietnam, and perhaps the early VISTA program should have been more selective in those it admitted and provided more supervision for those it kept.

ANTIPOVERTY SERVICES IN SETTLEMENTS

Along with paraprofessionals, the War on Poverty placed additional services in settlement houses. Of all the Great Society programs and emphases, those relating to education seemed most compatible with the settlement house tradition. In their earliest days, settlement houses had offered supplemental education to immigrants as the latter sought to adjust to and move upward in America. Thus, when the Great Society proposed supplemental educational programs to break the cycle of intergenerational poverty, settlement house participation came naturally.

Thanks to federal funds, supplementary preschool education designed to compensate for the effects of poverty began in settlement houses around 1965.[93] Head Start was one of the most popular antipoverty programs. To a certain extent, settlements had always helped neighborhood youngsters with tutoring. In Philadelphia, the school board funded a settlement-based program emphasizing group experience for elementary students with behavioral problems; a private foundation funded a jobs and tutoring program for teens; and two other foundations financed settlement programs to motivate youngsters to go on to college.[94] The War on Poverty made educational enrichment programs more common in settlements.

Although the War on Poverty hoped to break the cycle of intergenerational poverty by concentrating on youth, some educational efforts were made with adults. Forest Neighborhood House in the Bronx reported a program called "Operation Second Chance." It offered help with basic skills such as reading, writing, and mathematics to adults in order to make them more employable.[95] Another New York City settlement, James Weldon Johnson, offered basic literacy classes to mothers on welfare.[96] In addition, the Older Americans Act funded a variety of self-help and social service programs for senior citizens in settlement houses.

Besides educational programs, settlements also occasionally housed legal aid and welfare projects. Chicago's Olivet Community Center provided space and acted as fiscal agent for a Neighborhood Legal Assistance Center.[97] Some settlements developed joint programs with their local welfare departments to provide supplementary social services. Six Philadelphia settlements housed welfare department personnel who took applications for assistance and provided counseling, the purpose being to make these services more accessible to their neighborhoods.[98] In cooperation with the Cook County Welfare Department, Chicago's Marcy Center provided additional services to selected families on relief.[99] Again, in Philadelphia, Western Community House served breakfast to neighborhood children "who would normally go through the whole school day without food."[100] Thus, settlements came to resemble multiservice centers.

In an August 1966 speech, President Johnson called for "the establishment—in every ghetto in America—of a neighborhood center to service the people who live there."[101] A variety of demonstration projects followed which emphasized social service delivery at the neighborhood level, but not the development of a neighborhood relationship. Thus, the evolving multiservice centers were not all necessarily settlement houses. When Tau Beta Settlement in Detroit merged with two others to form the Neighborhood Service Organization, it became a multifunctional agency working closely with the schools, police, and welfare department. It gave up its own permanent building locations in favor of "a mobile and flexible service program." Therefore, its director, Emeric Kurtagh, considered it "a mutation of the settlement." The usual concept of a "multiservice center" was a neighborhood-based, one-stop center offering a variety of accessible and coordinated social services. Many of these services were public, but settlements had occasionally provided housing for public services earlier. In Cleveland, out of ten projected multiservice centers in 1968, the federation of Cleveland settlements planned to establish four or five.[102] Elsewhere, settlements were less successful in identifying themselves with the multiservice center trend.

The most tangible impact the War on Poverty had on settlement houses was the money made available to construct new settlement facilities or renovate existing ones. The Housing and Urban Development Act provided funds to cover up to 75 percent of the cost of neighborhood facilities. Among settlement houses to benefit from this and other federal programs for new community centers were

Neighborhood House in St. Paul,[103] Kingsley House in New Orleans,[104] Dixwell Community House in New Haven, and Clinton Square Center in Albany.[105] In other cases, such as in Topeka, Kansas, the War on Poverty actually provided funds to start a new settlement house.[106]

Unfortunately, the War on Poverty was short-lived. Settlement houses began to feel the impact of budget cutbacks as early as 1967. Several New York settlements in that year submitted proposals to employ and otherwise assist the elderly that were rejected. Also turned down at that time were Grand Street Settlement's proposal for education and training for teenagers and proposals for the establishment of neighborhood centers in South Brooklyn and the South Bronx.[107] At the same time, because of cuts in funds, Hull House eliminated all arts programs; cut its predelinquent girls program, STREETS, by 60 percent; and severely reduced its program to train indigenous neighborhood leaders.[108] Since many settlement houses had reallocated their staff and building resources to accommodate federal and foundation-funded projects to the extent that these programs sometimes amounted to over half their budgets, the sudden withdrawal of the funds wiped out many of their activities. Friends Neighborhood Guild had little of its core program left by 1968.[109] The demise of the War on Poverty meant severe readjustments for many settlements.

Emerging from the short-lived War on Poverty, settlements were different. They were more oriented toward seeking grant money, especially from the federal government, but also from private foundations. Their attitudes toward community organization showed more sensitivity to the participation of their neighbors in a policymaking capacity. They were more likely to appoint neighbors to settlement boards and hire them as paraprofessionals on their staffs. To the traditional settlement methods of advocating social change, settlements could now add experience with direct action tactics and black power. The War on Poverty's emphasis on breaking the cycle of intergenerational poverty had given added meaning to settlement house programs. Perhaps the most valuable legacy of the War on Poverty to settlement houses was to give them a renewed sense of purpose.

However, one can question whether the War on Poverty really "saved" the settlements. In 1983, I had the opportunity to ask Richard Cloward if, given the transitory nature of organizations of the poor, more use shouldn't have been made of settlement houses. Cloward adamantly disagreed. Yet he had just mentioned settlement house cooperation in his 1983 efforts to promote voter registration among the poor. In disparaging settlements, Cloward and others in the War on Poverty and the social work profession did shake them up. Unfortunately, they also did serious, and perhaps irreparable, damage. One result was a widened gulf between settlements and the social work profession that translated into fewer field placements, a peaking of the hiring of M.S.W.s, and less rapport in general between settlement houses and the social work profession. That, combined with extreme dependence on unstable funding sources, left the settlement houses extremely vulnerable.

CHAPTER 10

THE LEGACY OF
THE WAR ON POVERTY
THE BLACK ASCENDANCY WITHIN
THE SETTLEMENT HOUSE MOVEMENT,
FRAGMENTATION, AND
THE CONSERVATIVE SOCIAL CLIMATE

———•-•———

THE WAR ON POVERTY HAD RAISED SOME fundamental challenges to the settlement house's traditional methods and left behind a legacy of criticism and pressure for change. Settlement critics questioned the movement's traditional reliance on consensus methods and certain tendencies toward social control. These critics asked if enhancing minority identity wasn't more important than bringing the neighborhood together. They raised doubts about the relative contributions of professionals as opposed to paraprofessionals. Then came the conservative, political reaction to the War on Poverty. The settlement was ready for change.

THE BLACK ASCENDANCY

In the aftermath of the War on Poverty, the most striking development was that blacks displaced whites as the dominant leaders of the settlement house movement. This changeover from a predominantly white to a predominantly black leadership occurred within a context of political conservatism and cutbacks in funding. Indeed, blacks may have moved into settlements in large numbers at this time because of cutbacks in other types of community organization. Just as men had earlier displaced women in the settlement movement and redirected it, so black leadership again redirected the movement. Both with respect to individual blacks and blacks as a group, one can ask how black styles, perceptions, priorities, interests, and resources differed from the earlier leadership. What have blacks brought to the movement? And how is the settlement house movement and the National Federation of Settlements (renamed United Neighborhood Centers of America) different as a result?

The black ascendancy to a dominant, leadership position reflected a change in the composition of settlement neighborhoods. A 1968 National Federation of Settlements survey of ethnic and racial composition of neighborhoods of member agencies showed that out of 229 settlement neighborhoods that were predominantly or all one racial or ethnic group, 95 were white, 104 were black, 24 were Latin-American, 4 were Puerto Rican, and 1 was Oriental. While in 1968 the number of black social workers in settlements was almost as great as the number of whites, the number of white settlement administrators was almost double that of black administrators. As for boards, the survey didn't do a racial breakdown, but did indicate that roughly 25 percent of agency board members either worked or lived in their settlement neighborhood, and this trend toward neighborhood representation was increasing.[1] It would be only a short time before the administrative leadership of settlements more or less reflected the racial composition of their neighborhoods.

Many of the new black settlement heads had M.S.W.s, but not all. For those that did have the M.S.W., they had added status within the social work community. However, the War on Poverty's emphasis on paraprofessionals and the questioning of just what practical effect the degree had in a neighborhood made it possible for some blacks without the M.S.W. to assume leadership positions. One of these, Jim Cook of Minneapolis' Sabathani Community Center, had a bachelor's degree from Carnegie-Mellon and claimed that he didn't miss the M.S.W.[2] On the other hand, many black settlement heads had the M.S.W. and some had the Ph.D.[3]

Usually, these black administrators were men. Minneapolis' Phyllis Wheatley House was only one example of a settlement originally established for blacks that went from black female to black male leadership. While one can blame the social work profession for a male administrative bias, what may be more important is the different outlook and past experience of black women compared with white women. For black women who had historically found employment easier to obtain than black men and who resented the black matriarchal family image, progress to them was seeing black men move ahead.

These new black settlement heads brought certain qualities to the settlement movement. Among blacks that chose to utilize it, the black rhetorical style could be forceful, emotional, ministerial, and exciting. Blacks could set forth a case well. However, it is my observation that most black male settlement heads favored a low-key, business-like, almost formal image. On the other hand, blacks as a group seemed to have more difficulty with administrative matters, such as dealing with boards, raising money, and writing grant proposals. In part, this situation may have resulted from a reluctance to accept white help, perhaps because of the danger of white control. Yet by themselves, blacks sometimes lacked the necessary administrative skills and influence.

Another difference in values and style revolves around salary and perquisites. Not only black males but others from a disadvantaged background who have achieved professional status have emphasized material reward. Tony Wagner, who grew up in a settlement neighborhood, strongly defended his $65,000 salary, and also defended the approximately $75,000 paid to Jerome Stevenson, a black and former United Way of Chicago official hired in 1985 to replace Walter Smart. However, Wagner did support United Way of Minneapolis' criticism of radical black settlement head Harry "Spike" Moss' Lincoln Continental, purchased with agency funds. As Wagner noted, the United Way staff have agency cars too; but theirs are Novas. The perquisites and the salaries may signify a loss of altruism or may reflect the fact that these workers are men presumably with families to support. The emphasis on high salaries may also reflect the need of professionals from disadvantaged backgrounds to validate their professional status with materialistic rewards. They will take an almost belligerent "I'm worth it" attitude in defending salaries that may be high in proportion to an agency budget. The salary becomes a matter of pride. Likewise, considering that these are agencies strapped for funds, holding settlement conferences in expensive hotels also becomes an issue of status or pride for them. With hefty salaries comes a vested interest in the job, and a corresponding desire to avoid controversy or to "play it safe."

Another problem had to do with the black social action agenda. In the past, black settlement workers were at times more activist than their white counterparts. However, blacks were frequently so caught up in racial issues that they had considerable difficulty moving beyond their own agenda to a broader community agenda. Whites, on the other hand, may be more inclusive in their thinking. Boards reflect this principle. Black agencies tend to have boards that are predominantly black. In white settlements, the boards are usually evenly split between the neighborhood and the outside community. However, one can still ask to what extent whites will accept blacks as representative of the whole community. Part of the black impact on the settlement movement recently has been redirecting it toward black pride and away from the traditional purposes of bridging class and racial lines.

The black ascendance to leadership was accompanied by a corresponding departure of a generation of whites from the settlement house movement. In 1968, Fern Colborn ended a seventeen-year struggle with Social Education and Action on the National Federation staff and retired. Among the former chairs of the Social Education and Action Committee was Irving Kriegsfeld, who had left his position as head of Rochester's Baden Street Settlement to work for a housing organization in Cleveland. Also leaving the field by 1968 was another former Social Education and Action chair, Reinhard Gutman, who joined the staff of the National Council of the Protestant Episcopal Church. Charles Liddell in 1968 abandoned the directorship of United South End Settlements in Boston to a black, Ken Brown. Liddell then replaced Bill Brueckner, who retired as head of Chicago Commons. No sooner had Liddell arrived at the Commons than the black social workers' opposition scared him off, and he left.[4] That year Liddell was secretary of the National Federation of Settlements. He had worked in settlements since 1947 and had been especially active in efforts to improve low-income housing.[5] He returned to Boston, and in 1981 was executive director of Traveler's Aid there. Others who yielded leadership positions to blacks included Dan Carpenter, who retired as head of Hudson Guild in 1973, and Frank Seever, who ran Henry Street for a short time, leaving after a sit-in in 1978.[6] However, the most prominent departure and the one that signified the "changing of the guard" more than the others was the resignation of Margaret Berry as head of the National Federation of Settlements, to be replaced by Walter Smart, a black.

A longtime settlement leader who was one of the few whites to remain on the board of the National Federation of Settlements after blacks took over that organization was Camillo DeSantis. According to DeSantis, some of the whites voluntarily left their settlement directorships and others were forced out. Over a period of time, the general white settlement leaders' reaction was "to hell" with the blacks. If they think they can do a better job, let them. Many of the whites felt betrayed. They had prided themselves on working for better human relations. They had worked with blacks for years. The abrupt black takeover "was a slap in the face" to many whites. In spite of the predominantly black nature of the majority of settlement neighborhoods, whites responded by holding back, by not supporting the National Federation.[7]

From a black social work educator's perspective in 1970, the settlement movement did not stand for the "widening of gaps and must not be trapped into doing so now." She saw the black ascendancy to leadership as "a new revolutionary force acting as a transfusion into the tired, sluggish bloodstream of the [settlement] movement."[8] In other words, the black ascendancy was a test of the white settlement workers' sincerity in bridging class and racial lines. Nevertheless, a significant amount of white bitterness ensued, which may raise some questions about the degree to which the previously white-dominated settlement movement had really supported civil rights.

Margaret Berry never admitted feeling this bitterness, but her resignation was the culmination of the so-called Techni-Culture movement. Throughout her career, Margaret Berry had taken the white liberal position on civil rights. As director of the National Federation, she gave civil rights projects high priority. One of the major grant-funded programs of the National Federation under her directorship was the Mississippi Project. In 1966, the federation secured a grant from the Stern Family Fund and used some of its own funds to support two black social workers in Jackson, Mississippi, and nearby towns. They sought out local leadership, helped establish community centers, developed other community projects, and gave out information about government grants and resources.[9] However, in 1971, while still under Margaret Berry's leadership, the National Federation, in a belt-tightening move, voted to discontinue its financial support of this project.[10]

Meanwhile, blacks first made their presence felt in a major way at the National Federation of Settlements' 1968 conference in Houston.[11] The Techni-Culture movement began at the Midwest Regional Conference of the National Federation the following year. Over 250 settlement-connected people gathered at this meeting in St. Paul. Blacks caucused and put together a list of five demands, of which the major one was for a black settlement workers conference. The Midwest Regional Conference endorsed this idea. Later, the black caucus steering committee voted to enlarge the conference concept to include other minorities besides blacks.[12] With the addition of brown, red, and yellow minorities, the steering committee began referring to the projected conference as "Technicolor."[13] "Techni-Culture," the official name of the conference, evolved from the word "Technicolor."

Margaret Berry was outspokenly sympathetic toward the development of a black caucus within the settlement movement. She saw the caucus as a means whereby blacks could make themselves heard, take responsibility, and demonstrate black pride. While some thought the caucus divisive, Berry thought it would facilitate communication. To her, strong differences of opinion were not to be feared. With patience, common sense, humor, and mutual trust in each other's integrity, she believed the federation would be better for the presence of a black caucus.[14] While the black caucus benefited initially from Margaret Berry's support, it was not about to be beholden to a white woman.

The National Federation of Settlements board voted 25 to 7 in favor of holding the Techni-Culture Conference. Of the seven votes against the conference, five were cast by female board members.[15] It is possible women were more apprehensive about the potential for divisiveness and conflict than men. Some of the "old settlement types" also had reservations, but several endorsed the conference anyway. The National Federation proceeded to raise $75,000 from private foundations to finance the conference,[16] with much of the money going to pay delegates' expenses.

The Techni-Culture Conference took place in Chicago on February 11–13, 1970. Planned for five-hundred delegates, over six-hundred appeared. Margaret Berry admitted, "Arrangements were rather a mess." Because registration lines were so long, delegates had to be admitted to the opening session without registering. Another problem was that keynoter Angie Brooks insisted on speaking about emerging nations in Africa, rather than addressing issues of more immediate concern to her audience. The settlement movement was about to go from white to black domination. To be part of that transition was a lot more exciting than hearing about African problems, regardless of the philosophical connections. The conference's failure to keep to a schedule meant almost no time for the "content" workshops. At the banquet, blacks booed the Rockefeller Foundation's representative, even though that foundation had given $25,000 to support the conference. The conference hotel served grapes, ignoring the boycott of table grapes organized by migrant farm workers, so some conference delegates went from table to table removing the grapes. Other delegates joined a demonstration against Spiro Agnew and, luckily, managed to escape being among those arrested. However, the heart of the conference was in the caucuses held, both scheduled and unscheduled.[17]

Among the unscheduled caucuses was one of around two hundred women. According to Margaret Berry, the women were concerned about antifemale feeling at the conference.[18] Out of ten conference committee members, only one was female.[19] In their caucus, the women talked primarily about setting up an information network to share such items as program ideas.[20] They were hardly as radical on their own behalf as were the minority men.

The black caucus dealt with the board and staff composition of the National Federation and went into power issues. Prior to the conference, the Techni-Culture steering committee asked that a vacant National Federation staff position not be filled until after the conference and that the position be elevated to associate director.

The position was raised. The black group, still acting prior to the conference, gave Margaret Berry a list of candidates, and Berry proceeded to contact applicants. She particularly favored Walter Smart, a black housing official from Boston. However, at the conference, the steering committee caucused and endorsed a current federation employee, Henry Reid. Reid was not Berry's choice. She advised him to take another job offer rather than risk losing the federation position. Meanwhile, a third black male candidate, on seeing the situation, withdrew. Berry went to campaign strongly for Walter Smart and to insist that as executive director, she had the right to pick her staff. She described Smart as an "absolutely straight" human being, one with courage, who has suffered as a result of racial prejudice, who had his home in Georgia burned, but who had worked out the resultant feelings, and was quite at ease with people of any color. She thought Smart worth the $30,000 salary he was asking.[21] The board backed Berry in her decision to let Henry Reid go, but advised her to consult with the Techni-Culture Committee before filling the associate director's position. Nevertheless, Berry proceeded to offer the job to Walter Smart.[22]

By this point, Margaret Berry was on the defensive. H. Charles Sells, chair of the Techni-Culture Committee, claimed publicly that Margaret Berry never consulted him on this appointment. Furthermore, he claimed Berry ignored two names he suggested to coordinate a projected youth conference and that she unilaterally appointed someone else. Sells also accused Berry of approaching candidates for another position, the federation's Washington liaison job, while leading the Techni-Culture Committee to believe that the job was "on ice."[23] Berry hired a black, James H. Sills, Jr., for the Washington position.[24] In self-defense, Berry questioned how representative the Techni-Culture Committee was of the NFS's black constituency.

In May 1970, during the National Federation's annual convention in Sells' hometown of Cincinnati, Berry's position continued to erode. The Techni-Culture Conference Committee recommended that all vacant board slots go to racial minorities. The nominating committee, the membership of which had been elected within the past two years, presented a slate that would have given racial minorities fifteen out of a total of thirty-five board seats and 50 percent of the officer positions. However, blacks packed this convention, threw out the nominating committee's recommendations, and elected their own slate.[25] The result was that the National Federation board went from 30 percent minority representation in 1969 to 62 percent minority representation in 1970. When a light-skinned black, Arthur Logan, who was president of United Neighborhood Houses of New York, called on whites "*not* to assume the burden of guilt which white America properly bears because of the centuries of injustice" to minorities, the convention repudiated him.[26] Berry commented to a local reporter, "The fact that we are having a confrontation here indicates that we are really in the new mold of doing things."[27]

The National Federation went on to elect its first black president, attorney Elizabeth D. (Betti) Pittman of Omaha. Mrs. Pittman, who described her main outside interests as "participating in civic organizations," was active on the board of Omaha's Woodson Center and in civil rights and social service organizations.[28] Busy with her career and a variety of civic and black interests,[29] she did little to bolster Berry's flagging support.

With racial minorities constituting a majority of the board, the Techni-Culture group decided a year after their watershed conference to disband the Standing Committee on Techni-Culture.[30] It was no longer necessary. Black influence in the National Federation was expanding. In spite of a deficit, the federation had reversed its earlier decision and continued to support the Mississippi Project. The project's office was next to Jackson State College, the scene of the killing of four black students in May 1970 in reaction to 1960s protests. The federation felt a special commitment to work with student volunteers there.[31] Also, Margaret Berry bowed to the growing trend toward black domination of the National Federation. In the summer of 1971, she chose to accept a position as executive director of the National Conference on Social Welfare and resigned as executive director of the National Federation effective at the end of 1971. With Walter Smart's assumption of her position as head of the National Federation staff, the black ascendancy within the NFS was essentially complete.

Walter Smart was a professional social worker with a somewhat limited background in the settlement house movement compared with other National Federation heads. Born the son of a postman in Birmingham, Alabama, in 1927, Smart's father wanted him to be a professional. Intending to become a lawyer, Smart attended More-house College for three years, then got married and drafted at ap-proximately the same time. The marriage failed, but an army friend interested Smart in social work as a means of changing society. After earning a B.A. from Miles College, Smart attended the Atlanta Uni-versity School of Social Work, remarried, and received his M.S.W. Both his field placement and his first six years as a professional social worker were spent with Philadelphia settlements. He then left the settlement field to work for the Boston Housing Authority. His de-cision to become associate director of the National Federation of Set-tlements in 1970 was due in part to the strong interests of the fed-eration in housing issues.[32] Smart then moved his family of five sons to the New York suburb of New Rochelle,[33] where he lived while directing the NFS until his death in January 1985. When he became head of the National Federation in 1972, Smart was the only black to head a national organization devoted to social service for all races.

Walter Smart gave the impression of being the kind of man who could smile his way through anything, no matter how rough the sit-uation. He needed that quality. Not only were whites bitter over the black takeover of the National Federation, but Smart had problems retaining black support as well. After three years, some blacks wanted to replace Smart. He confronted them head-on, asking what they had done for the organization. Black factions also appeared. It was as if without the unifying battle against the whites, the spirit of co-operation failed. The federation tried to get the support of addi-tional blacks, including the big, black businessman type, with limited success. It also tried to attract foundation support. However, by the 1970s, being black was no longer enough to attract funding. It was as if the black ascendancy occurred at just the wrong time.[34]

THE DECLINE OF THE NATIONAL FEDERATION
OF SETTLEMENTS

On taking over the National Federation, Smart's main goal was to save the organization, which was in severe financial trouble.[35] Smart inherited an operation with a projected annual income of $345,000[36] and a deficit of $160,000. It represented 192 agencies operating over 300 centers. A 1980 membership list revealed that the number of member agencies had shrunk to 105.[37] In 1984, the organization had reduced its annual budget to $209,000, with a $65,000 deficit. One person who attended the annual conference that year estimated the number of member agencies at 75.[38] The day has passed when one could define a settlement by membership in the National Federation, now renamed United Neighborhood Centers of America. Several factors contributed to the decline.

Part of the problem facing settlements was their image. The attack on settlements as agencies bent on social control by Mobilization for Youth, by sociologists such as Herbert Gans, and by indigenous groups undercut the settlements' ability to raise funds. When the National Federation tried to broaden the definition of its member agencies to include some of the new antipoverty ones, few were interested in identifying with the settlement movement. The chief effect of trying to attract these new agencies was to further muddle the definition of a settlement. Growing numbers of people had no idea what a settlement house was.[39] To try to rectify this problem, Walter Smart placed additional emphasis on publicity and public relations.

One of Smart's major efforts in the area of public relations was to change the name of the National Federation of Settlements. To Smart, the word "settlement" was a handicap. The reference to a building where well-to-do people "settled" in order to help the poor in the surrounding neighborhood was no longer applicable. Instead, Smart sought to emphasize through a name change that settlements were moving from social/recreational programs to a more problem-oriented focus. He recommended "United Neighborhood Centers of America" as the new name. In addition, Smart sought name identification on the part of local settlements with the national office. He proposed that each member agency incorporate the phrase "neighborhood center" in its name and that local federations be known as "United Neighborhood Centers of (name of city)."[40] However, local houses were too individualistic to consider standardizing a portion of their names. Furthermore, the New York federation, United Neighborhood Houses, objected to the similarity to its own name of the proposed name change of the national organization. It actually sued the National Federation to block the name change, but the National Federation went ahead anyway; and in 1979, the new name, United Neighborhood Centers of America, became official. However, the attempt to move in the direction of a franchise through encouraging similar name changes went nowhere.

Smart also sought to promote the visibility of neighborhood centers through a variety of public relations tactics. To familiarize the public with its new name, United Neighborhood Centers (UNCA is the official acronym) launched a public service advertising campaign in donated magazine space. Full-page ads pictured slum children and used the slogan "We're Trying To Even the Odds for People Who Don't Normally Get an Even Break."[41] From the start of his tenure as executive director, Smart emphasized press releases and accepted numerous speaking engagements. He also developed a newspaper column series called "Getting Smart." These columns consisted largely of Smart's analysis of selected national issues, such as health care for the elderly, and did not emphasize settlement houses as such. The columns were mailed to a chain of ninety black newspapers. Finally, Smart encouraged member houses to step up their publicity efforts. In spite of these activities, image recognition has remained a problem with the public.

Smart also tried to counter the settlement house's attackers. For example, Boston settlement houses were active in urban renewal and relocation of slum dwellers. Sociologist Herbert Gans charged the settlements were going against the wishes of their neighbors in these activities. However, Smart worked in relocation in the same city of which Gans wrote, Boston. Smart thought Gans should visit people living in "holes." When these people were given subsidies so they could afford better housing, Gans should have seen the smiles that lit up their faces. Americans move all the time.[42] Smart could speak from more personal experience than Gans and other academic attackers. Unfortunately, writing brilliance and academic, professional standing gave Gans the larger audience.

Besides trying to do something about the settlement houses' image problems, Smart also had to handle that $160,000 deficit. No one, not board members, foundations, government agencies, or member settlements, would give the National Federation a grant to specifically cover that deficit. Smart's solution was to clear the deficit by using the overhead or indirect costs portion of federal grants which the National Federation began to receive. Getting federal grants was something new for the National Federation. According to Smart, Berry thought an agency committed to seeking social change should not get involved with government contracts. Smart, however, felt that support for the really poor was more likely to come from the federal government. In his opinion, private foundations had a certain identity of interest and were somewhat hampered by conservative, establishment boards, as was United Way.[43] While government grants indirectly pulled the federation out of a deficit, they never really allowed for a significant expansion of the National Federation's core services.

Smart's federal grant strategy also had other implications for the National Federation. Member houses had preceded the NFS in obtaining federal grants. The NFS began that activity as federal grants became scarcer. Thus, it was in some competition for grants with its member agencies, which may have added to the divisiveness following the Techni-Culture battle. As for the effect of the federal grants on the National Federation's lobbying role, that is difficult to gauge. Smart continued lobbying efforts, but with less success than Berry. However, he faced socially conservative administrations. Even Jimmy Carter, who did make some liberal proposals, ended up taking conservative actions on welfare. Because of the need of the National Federation to keep the federal grants coming as much as possible, its freedom to take a clearly opposed, "devil's advocate" position in relation to the presidential administrations of the 1970s and 1980s was curtailed. Where rousing criticism may well have been justified, the NFS had to weigh the costs of that against its relations with grant-dispensing bureaucrats. Smart had to walk a fine line and endure rebuffs as social programs and civil rights slid down the federal government's priority list.

The National Federation of Settlements is also underfunded compared with other national social service organizations because it is not a franchise. Local settlement houses existed before the national organization, and they are free to choose whether to belong to the NFS or not. Unlike the Boys Club, Y's, and Scouts, the National Federation cannot compel support for the national office. Each house is legally independent and, in times of budget constraints, can be expected to weigh carefully the cost of dues to the national office against the value it chooses to place on services received from that office.[44]

When Smart took over, the federation had just dropped its training center for financial reasons, but it still provided a variety of services. Besides publicizing the settlement movement and giving it visibility, the National Federation facilitated communication among member houses through its publications and national and regional conferences. It provided consultation for individual houses, ran a placement service that specialized in head worker positions, and engaged in legislative activities. Those activities included lobbying for federal laws and programs, informing member houses of existing programs, helping them develop grant proposals, and providing liaison with federal officials. However, with budget cutbacks, activities such as field service, the placement service, and regional conferences soon disappeared. The dream of the National Federation to be the national agent for individual settlements ran into the historic tradition and value member settlements placed on their local autonomy. The NFS's services just were not that vital to the functioning of individual settlement houses, and so member houses repudiated the moves the NFS made in trying to become more like a franchise.

While this lack of a franchise weakens the national organization of settlements, it does give more autonomy to the local houses and more flexibility to the movement as a whole. Individual houses are free to respond to the needs of their neighbors as they are perceived in those neighborhoods. A house can also choose to get involved in a controversial activity without directly endangering the national movement. Thus, while the National Federation of Settlements is weaker financially than other national social service organizations, it can correspondingly claim to be closer to the grass-roots service delivery level than its counterparts.

The lack of a franchise also makes the National Federation more susceptible to the effects of divisiveness and disenchantment among member agencies. Smart acknowledged that the Techni-Culture fight was a major, bitter, and divisive one. It left member agencies confused, not knowing what the future direction of the national organization would be. Furthermore, once the minorities became the dominant majority in the national organization, they lost their former cohesiveness. Hispanics didn't want to coalesce with blacks, and Hispanics were also divided as a group along social class lines. Then, too, jealousy and rivalry developed among various black settlement leaders. Instead of being enthusiastically supportive, some black settlements dropped out of the national organization. Minority status provided the common goal and goodwill holding the Techni-Culture group together. Once dominance was achieved, rivalries and divisiveness surfaced. Smart felt that he had not nearly as many problems with white cooperation.[45]

Adding to the difficulties of settlements since the War on Poverty has been the lack of support for social work in general. Political conservatism combined with recession-induced budget slashing at social agencies meant that social workers were being laid off, terminated, and not replaced. Few new jobs opened up. Yet New York City's seven social work schools graduated over eight hundred M.S.W.s in 1976 alone.[46] Many of the houses themselves were financially unstable. With social work in general and settlement houses in particular thrown on the defensive, a lessened commitment to the National Federation of Settlements resulted.[47]

That lessened commitment was further underscored by some sharp changes in emphasis within the social work profession during the 1970s and early 1980s. The War on Poverty had sufficient momentum to carry over into the early 1970s. At this time, the profession was emphasizing community organization, social policy, and planning.[48] These emphases didn't last long. By the mid-1970s, the key phrase was "direct service," not "direct action." Community organization jobs and fieldwork placements became hard to find. Social work students avoided that curriculum. One settlement house director noticed that the 1983 National Association of Social Workers convention had almost no workshops on street or poverty programs.[49] Furthermore, in this settlement director's city of Minneapolis, the local social work school did no settlement field placements at the graduate level that year. The school gave as its reason lack of student interest resulting from the absence of jobs in planning and community organization. The school also felt that its lack of settlement house fieldwork assignments was typical of social work schools around the United States.[50] If the social work profession had almost no commitments left to settlement houses, perhaps it is no wonder individual settlement houses had less of a commitment to their own professional organization.

Local agencies began to balk at paying dues to the National Federation. Dues were 1 percent of an agency's budget for those with budgets under $100,000; 1.5 percent for those between $100,000 and $500,000; and 2 percent for those above $500,000. Because the NFS had a serious deficit in the early 1970s, it instituted a crackdown on dues-delinquent agencies.[51] In 1976, the National Federation board voted to drop twenty-two agencies for nonpayment of dues and three others resigned. The losses were especially heavy on the West Coast, with no member agencies remaining in San Francisco.[52] The NFS dropped another eighteen houses in 1977. The most prominent was Chicago Commons.[53] In Minneapolis and St. Paul, where once eight or nine houses had belonged to the national organization, in 1984 the number was two or three.[54] In New York, competing city and state associations resulted in the withdrawal of all but Henry Street from National Federation membership.[55] That meant that the first settlement house in the United States, University Settlement, was no longer a member as the American settlement movement approached its one hundredth anniversary. The loss of Boston's United South End Settlements was particularly symbolic because that house had provided the first office space for the National Federation of Settlements and because the founder of South End, Robert Woods, was also a founder of the National Federation. In explaining South End's decision to leave the NFS, its board president asked, "Where is the 'right' in paying UNCA dues vs. supporting four children in a drastically-cut Day Care Program for a period of one year?"[56] In other words, in a budget crunch, immediate needs of neighbors often took precedence over dues to a distant organization.

Failure on the part of member agencies to place much value on the national organization may have been one unanticipated by-product of the decision of the National Federation to drop field service. Going back to the 1930s, it had been the practice of National Federation staff to periodically make routine visits to member settlements around the country. Not only was an NFS staff member available for consultation on a regular, on-site basis, but the NFS also got a good sense of what was happening at the local level. Field service was what tied the New York City office to member houses and gave the National Federation legitimacy as the voice of the settlement movement. When the National Federation was dominated by what archivist Brian Mulhern called the "old battle-axes" of the movement—Helen Hall, Fern Colborn, and Margaret Berry—they had something to offer in field service from their tremendous backlog of experience.[57] That experience was lost with the coming of Walter Smart and other changes in the NFS's staff.

Actually, the idea of dropping field visits preceded Walter Smart's hiring at the National Federation. Field visits were expensive, and their purposes were usually vague. Therefore, the 1969 New Directions Committee, a National Federation self-study group, recommended that field visits be dropped. In their place, the committee suggested the organization of local "talent pools" consisting of settlement board and staff members who could provide consultation on a problem basis to requesting agencies.[58] When Smart announced the dropping of traditional field service,[59] he was following the recommendation of a previous committee and doing so in the context of a severe budget deficit. In spite of the national office's willingness to consult on an emergency problem basis, there was resentment over the loss of field service. For example, when Minneapolis' East Side Neighborhood Service director was fired, then rehired two months later as a result of local support, and the board president and treasurer then quit, the director's comment to the national office was essentially, "You weren't there when we needed you." At the same time, another Minneapolis settlement director was telling the national office that the level of its "services do not justify the dues."[60] Also, Walter Smart's communications with member settlements reflected this lack of field service. His "Executive Newsletters" analyzing topics like revenue sharing legislation did not always interface with what settlements were doing or could do, nor did they really facilitate communication among individual settlements. Lack of field service contributed to a pattern of communication that was more from the top down rather than a two-sided exchange.

Smart and others in the National Federation realized the need to at least partially try to fill the void left by the dropping of field service. Accompanying the need for more fieldwork was the need some agencies felt after the freewheeling War on Poverty years for some kind of accreditation by an outside body that would mark them as well-run agencies. The National Federation had talked about accrediting settlements in 1960, but did not begin to pursue the idea in earnest until the early 1970s.[61] Accreditation was separate from membership in the National Federation, and members were free to choose whether or not to apply for it. Accreditation criteria focused heavily on agency structure as opposed to program content. Since instituting the program in 1975, accreditation teams looked at the agency's legal basis (including tax exempt status), board selection procedures, annual evaluation or self-study procedures, program development, relations to other organizations, personnel policies, insurance coverage, and physical facilities. A recommendation for accreditation was good for three years initially and was usually accompanied by various suggestions for improvement.[62] Agencies not immediately accredited were given technical assistance to help them meet the National Federation standards.

In implementing the program, a major problem was the national office's lack of resources to staff accreditation teams. That was solved by having one national office staff person on each team, the rest being local agency board and staff people. By carefully coordinating site visits, travel expenses were kept to a minimum. In the first year of the program, forty site visits were made, sixteen houses were accredited, and another fourteen received technical assistance.[63] Thus, through its accreditation program, the National Federation partially revived field service.

If the National Federation of Settlements is to be strong, local houses also have to have strength. Following the War on Poverty, both board and staff members were more likely to have grown up in slum neighborhoods. Such was Goddard-Riverside's program director, José Ramos. Born in Puerto Rico, a teenage delinquent and gang leader, Ramos found his way to Goddard-Riverside. The settlement raised his sights. He began attending night school and was about to receive his bachelor's degree in social welfare.[64] While staff like Ramos could relate in ways to the settlement's neighbors that the old middle-class outsiders could not, they were in other respects limited. In some ways it was harder for them to build bridges to other parts of the broader community or function on the same influential level as the former board and staff members. By the mid-1970s, neighborhood people accounted for more than 50 percent of New York City settlement staffs. Another New York settlement, Hudson Guild, had a board composed of 40 percent who lived or worked in its neighborhood.[65] Walter Smart noted that the national organization draws its board membership from those at the local level. If really outstanding or influential people are not on local boards and staff, their absence will also be felt at the national level.[66] In emphasizing "maximum feasible participation of the poor," settlements may have forgone much of their opportunity to build social class bridges and lost a certain kind of influence in the process.

The National Federation of Settlements has also suffered from the competition of state and local associations, which in turn have not always done well. Of these, United Neighborhood Houses of New York (UNH) has shown the most vitality. Historically, UNH has had a staff and budget comparable to the National Federation. It has also performed many of the same functions, especially in the area of lobbying for legislation. In 1971, UNH had thirty-six member settlements. Rivalry with the NFS became apparent when Tom McKenna replaced Helen Harris as head of UNH and, at about the same time, Walter Smart replaced Margaret Berry as head of the National Federation. In 1976, the rivalry worsened when a black, Joseph Jenkins, replaced McKenna.

The two associations competed for grants. In this area, UNH was more successful than the national organization. UNH's grant proposals seemed to have more focus, more specific service plans, and less administrative overhead in the form of travel and supervision from afar. The national organization was handicapped in doing social service projects by its lack of a local base. UNH was also more successful in getting grant support to carry on its core activities, such as a million dollars from the Vincent Astor Foundation in 1977.[67] Cooperation between UNH and the NFS on grant proposals was a touchy area. In 1978, UNH invited the national organization to do a joint proposal on helping Vietnam veterans with employment and life management; but when the National Federation learned that UNH intended to administer the program nationally, it withdrew.[68]

Local associations also used their leverage to negotiate special dues packages for settlements in their respective cities. At one point, New York settlements were paying 1 percent dues to the national office, but half the amount paid was kicked back to UNH.[69] In the late 1970s, when negotiations over a dues package from New York settlements broke down, all New York settlements except Henry Street withdrew as member agencies of the national organization.[70] The appearance of state federations exacerbated the situation. The California State Association of Settlements and Neighborhood Centers dated from 1962, although it was minimally funded—its income being less than $1,400 in 1978.[71] In 1973, UNH convinced upstate New York settlements to join them in the New York State Association. Part of the rationale was that UNH did a fair amount of lobbying in Albany and could use an Albany office.[72] In 1981, the New York State Association raised $17,000 and hired Susan Russell to be its full-time executive director, based in Albany.[73] Thus, New York City agencies were now paying dues to both a city and a state association, while giving almost no support to the NFS. Walter Smart expressed his concern about where the fragmentation and isolation of the settlement movement would lead in the future.[74]

The financial health of the National Federation of Settlements was also directly related to the financial health of settlements at the local level. The Chicago Federation of Settlements dated back to 1894 and counted among its founders Jane Addams. In the 1970s, it expanded its functions and took on some fund-raising and grant management responsibilities for member agencies. Then, in 1983, the Chicago Federation went into receivership. Hull House claimed the Chicago Federation owed it $250,000, Ada McKinley claimed it was due $170,000, and the national office also was seeking payment of $15,000 in Chicago dues.[75] The practice in Chicago had been for settlements to make one dues payments to the local federation, a portion of which was forwarded to the national office as dues for the Chicago member agencies. The Chicago Federation was in some administrative chaos, with only eight active board members left. Smart offered the help of the national office in developing a new organizational structure for the Chicago Federation;[76] however, as of 1984, the Chicago Federation was dead. Two years later, it showed no signs of reviving.

Although it never played the fund-raising and administrative roles of the Chicago Federation, the Twin Cities Federation of Settlements has also disappeared. The Twin Cities Federation provided a forum for settlement heads to meet regularly. It organized special events, took joint action before the city council, and met with United Way. Then, as settlement mergers accelerated, agency politics turned inward. Settlement heads lost interest in city federation cooperation, and the organization died.

Those local federations that have remained strong have successfully handled fund-raising responsibilities for their members. For example, besides United Neighborhood Houses of New York, the Cleveland federation is strong. In Cleveland, United Way funds the settlements, but the Cleveland United Way has chosen to disburse its funds to groups of agencies, one of which is the Cleveland settlement federation which in turn gives the money to the individual settlements. Thus, the Cleveland federation functions like a merged agency. On the other hand, the complete disappearance of other federations, such as the Twin Cities and Chicago ones, undescores the disarray of the settlement movement and compounds the problems of the national settlement organization.[77]

In recent years, the vitality of the National Federation, renamed United Neighborhood Centers of America, has continued to erode. About a year after Smart's death, the national organization hired Jerome Stevenson, a black who had spent most of his career with Chicago's United Way. Early in his career, Stevenson had worked in a Philadelphia settlement, and he had both an M.S.W. and a master's degree in business administration. Stevenson's hiring coincided with moving the national office to Washington, D.C., where it shares quarters with other national social service organizations. However, as of spring 1986, the national office consisted of only the director, his secretary, and an administrative assistant, quite a drop from the half-dozen professionals plus support staff of the 1950s and 1960s. To try to attract members, the national organization further cut dues to $1,750 per settlement house per year.[78] It remains to be seen if these changes will revitalize the national settlement organization. By the fall of 1986, the organization had added a dozen new houses to its membership roster,[79] arranged for James Craigen of Howard University's Social Work Department to serve as its public policy consultant, and was providing field experience for an M.S.W. candidate from Atlanta University.[80] If the national organization fails, racial divisiveness and other rivalries among settlements will bear much of the blame.

THE SETTLEMENTS AND SOCIAL ISSUES

Because of the pressing problems involved in just holding the national organization together, Smart gave less attention to his second goal of social action. Nevertheless, blacks have been among the strongest consistent advocates of social change within the settlement movement. Part of their impact on gaining dominance was to reemphasize the social change function of settlement houses. They gave added meaning to the official National Federation definition of settlement houses and neighborhood centers as organizations working with people improving neighborhood conditions and bringing about needed change.[81] Unfortunately, the black ascendancy to leadership of the settlement movement came at a time of dwindling resources and lessened support for social activism.

The National Federation's lobbying activities underwent some changes. Margaret Berry had hired a black settlement worker and Wilmington city councilman, James H. Sills, Jr., to man the NFS's branch office in Washington. Sills presented testimony on legislation, provided liaison with Washington agencies for individual settlements, worked in cooperation with other organizations on behalf of legislation, and prepared legislative bulletins to keep member settlements informed of new programs and proposals.[82] However, when Sills resigned in August 1971,[83] the National Federation lacked the resources to replace him and closed its Washington branch. Since then, the National Federation has done its best to carry on this activity from its New York office.

At the Helen Hall memorial service in April 1983, former New York mayor Robert Wagner recalled how Helen Hall personally called on politicians, and while she didn't always get all she wanted, he acknowledged her effectiveness. Walter Smart commented to me afterward that that sort of approach would not work today. To get in the door, it was necessary for Smart to be part of a coalition or group of people representing a number of organizations. Thus, Smart emphasized National Federation participation in such groups as the National Collaboration for Youth, which he chaired in 1978–79. The National Collaboration represents about a dozen national recreational organizations, such as the Y's and the Scouts. It consults with cabinet and other government officials to further legislation in such fields as juvenile delinquency. Its efforts paid off in the form of some grants for the National Federation, individual settlements, and other social service groups.

Participation in the National Collaboration for Youth, however, may have further confused the settlements' image. The other collaboration agencies were all franchise operations controlled by a national headquarters. All the National Federation could do was appeal for *voluntary* cooperation from locally based settlements. Nevertheless, the national settlement staff chose to identify with this group. For example, when in 1985 UNCA hired Jerry Stevenson at around $75,000 to replace Walter Smart, UNCA board member Tony Wagner justified the salary by saying that that was what the heads of other national agencies made. That ignores the fact that Stevenson was unlikely to have more than one or two people reporting to him, and that his agency's budget was minuscule. Furthermore, in lobbying with other social service agencies, the settlements ignored or downplayed the fact that they were more locally controlled or "grass roots" than their other national counterparts.

Settlements have also continued some traditional social change activities and revived others. The passage of resolutions and a social policy platform along with the Washington legislative conferences and seminars have been ways of trying to influence politicians while involving board and staff members in social issues. In the area of community organization, some disillusionment with direct action tactics has occurred, along with a return to more traditional "town meetings." However, the necessity of involving the poor, not just speaking for them, appears to have been a lesson the settlements have learned.

The availability of government grants for certain kinds of activities and not others has also had an effect on settlement programming. Title XX provided money for direct service activities, like day care, but not community organization. Also, money continued to be available for private sponsors of various kinds of low- and middle-income housing projects. Juvenile delinquency prevention and youth employment were other federal priorities that settlements were able to tap into for grants. Many settlements also compensated for staff cuts by taking on federally funded CETA workers. Others got federal funding for new buildings, and a few, like Cleveland's Friendly Inn, found themselves housed in a multiservice center along with several other social service organizations. Thus, up to the Reagan administration, actual settlement house activities had come to be increasingly shaped by the federal government.

However, the political winds continually shift. For those settlements that were heavily involved in government-funded programs, and some were up to 50 to 70 percent of their budgets, the Reagan cutbacks have been devastating. Fortunately, a number of settlements were largely out of federal government programs when the Reagan administration began. As a result, the Reagan impact on individual settlements has been uneven. If anything, it has forced agencies like the settlement houses to rely even more on local support.

At the local level, what settlements encountered by the early 1980s was some availability of funds for specific services to meet specific problems, but no real interest in funding settlements to do social action or strengthen their relationship with their neighborhoods. As one settlement director said, "Nobody's funding geography."[84] Some of the independent, activist community organizations are still around, but tend to avoid the settlement house and still manage to get foundation support. Settlements in the past supplied these organizations with space, typing, printing, advice, and leadership, but received little credit for their efforts. One settlement leader recalled that his house had started five such groups. "When you build them up strong," he commented, "they come after you."[85] Yet some of those groups that remain still call on settlements occasionally for help in finding influential contacts and in other ways, and settlements do help them. Money for this kind of settlement activity is scarce. In one city, neighborhood development in 1984 was number twenty-three on United Way's list of twenty-five priorities, and the foundations preferred to fund the activist groups themselves rather than the settlements. Perhaps smaller activist agencies are more representative, or perhaps they are less of a long-term threat. No agency is really speaking for the entire neighborhood anymore.

One way the black approach to social change has differed most from the previous white leadership has been more direct political involvement at the local level. The ghetto concentration of blacks concentrates their votes for political purposes as well. Furthermore, blacks emerged from the 1960s with a heightened sense of political power. Several black settlement workers, such as James Sills of Wilmington and Bennie Thompson, who ran Tri-County Community Center in Jackson, Mississippi, for three years, successfully ran for political office. Thompson was elected mayor of Bolton, Mississippi.[86] Black settlements have pushed voter registration and actively campaigned for black candidates. During the 1983 campaign, which saw Chicago elect its first black mayor, one settlement was actually answering its telephone with "Washington campaign headquarters."[87] The politics of white settlement leaders had frequently been at odds with their settlement neighbors, but not that of the new black leadership.

Popular awareness of Women's Liberation coincided with the black male ascendancy within the settlement house movement. However, women generally failed to regain lost ground. It is difficult for women who have been oppressed to confront or argue against another oppressed group. Also, without numbers, female support networks may be lacking. Helen Hall, for example, enjoyed the friendship of New York federation head Helen Harris, and the National Federation's executive secretary, Lillie Peck, actually lived at Hall's Henry Street Settlement. By the 1970s, the opportunity for such high-level female support networks was largely absent in the settlement house movement. Consequently, one sees almost no evidence of Women's Liberation activity within the settlement movement, in sharp contrast to the active feminism of the early settlement house leaders.[88]

The few instances of Women's Liberation influence illustrate its limited impact. For example, in 1976, New York settlement house women organized a Women's Issues Conference. The conference organizers took "a 'let's find out' approach rather than a clearly critical one." The 133 women who attended included board members and professional and clerical staff. Conference workshops dealt with sexism in executive appointments and in programming, such as cuts in day care. Among recommendations coming out of the conference was one that male settlement workers be involved in women's consciousness raising.[89] Following the conference, the New York federation formed a Women's Issues Committee.[90] However, in subsequent years, the committee avoided administrative power issues in favor of taking stands on abortion and on the service needs of women settlement house clientele.[91] Another example of Women's Liberation influence in 1982 was Hull House. That historic settlement had a woman director, Patricia Sharpe, and included among its services a battered women's shelter.[92] A third example is Women's Liberation's concern over sex-role stereotyping being applied in a different context. A Minneapolis settlement in 1986 had a Black Men's Focus Group, described as "developing images of black men" and "challenging stereotypes of black males which are based on narrow perceptions."[93] Unfortunately for feminism, these examples are exceptions to the general state of the settlement house movement.

The War on Poverty undermined the traditional settlement house movement and left a different kind of settlement, more appropriately called a "neighborhood center," in its wake. The change was most dramatically seen at the national level. Abruptly during 1970–71, the National Federation made the transition from a predominantly white-controlled organization to a predominantly black one. Bitterness and dissension followed. Many whites dropped out; factions appeared among the blacks, and some of them left too. With the demise of the War on Poverty, the National Federation was already feeling the financial pinch; and in spite of Walter Smart's energetic efforts, its resources continued to erode.

What happened at the national level was mirrored at the local level. So many individual settlements passed from white control to black that the typical settlement was now headed by a black in a black neighborhood with a black board. In some cities with a sizable black population, the settlement house was now regarded as a black agency. Unfortunately, support for black agencies as well as support for settlements in general declined. Henry Street in 1976 depended on public funds for two-thirds of its budget,[94] a vulnerable situation given the political conservatism on social issues that was to follow. However, few settlements went out of business. Instead, many merged. The newly merged agencies often consisted of a series of branches and specialized programs, scattered throughout noncontiguous, poor, and working-class neighborhoods. Gone was the settlement's special identification with a neighborhood. It was difficult even for settlement workers themselves to describe how their problem- and special-service-oriented agencies differed from a host of others in the slums that had no connection with the settlement house tradition. One house might specialize in work with seniors, another in alternative education, a third might provide a senior center in one neighborhood and a day care center in another neighborhood. The phrase "settlement house" no longer seemed appropriate or was even much used in describing the neighborhood center of the 1980s. Likewise, one might refer to a settlement house movement in the past, but nobody was using the phrase "neighborhood center movement" in 1986. The traditional settlement house had lost its unique characteristics and was now simply one social agency among many down in the slums.

CONCLUSION

In *The Backyard Revolution,* Harry Boyte writes about the rebirth of interest in neighborhoods and neighborhood organizing. Thousands of grass-roots neighborhood organizations sprang up in the late 1960s and 1970s. Not once does Boyte mention settlement houses, which may be the ultimate insult. Why, in the midst of all this neighborhood organizing activity, should settlements be declining? Why have they failed to capitalize on the neighborhood trend?[1]

The neighborhood center of today is very different from the settlement house of the early years. Then, a white female college graduate without an M.S.W. headed the typical house. She, or some of her staff, probably lived in the settlement house. The surrounding neighborhood was likely to consist of poor whites. Advocacy to achieve better social conditions followed the established channels of conference resolutions, congressional testimony, and settlement workers speaking on behalf of the poor. In 1986, a black male with an M.S.W. heads the typical settlement house, now called a neighborhood center. He may live out in the suburbs with other professionals and commute to his job. The center's clientele is mostly black; and the poor insist to a certain extent on having a voice in the setting of the center's policies, seek employment on the center's staff, and demand the right to speak for themselves on social issues. Typical of today's daily settlement activities is the program of the first settlement in the United States. Activities at New York's University Settlement in 1986 include Head Start and other day care services; clubs, tutoring, cultural, sports, and community service groups for youth; adult classes in home economics and English; hot meals and social events for the elderly; plus a professionally staffed mental health clinic and family therapy services. Still located on the Lower East Side, this settlement today serves primarily Hispanics. To its 1898 building, University

Settlement has added two satellite centers in neighboring low-income housing projects.[2] The key changes in the settlement movement as a whole are the growth of professionalism, the shift from a movement dominated by women to one dominated by men, the shift from settlements run by whites to centers run by blacks and other minority groups, a changed relationship to the neighborhood, and the fragmentation of the movement.

The growth of the settlements' own professional organization has gone full circle. The National Federation of Settlements was a one-person operation in 1939. After World War II, it went through a period of major expansion. During the 1960s, it had annual budgets of several hundred thousand dollars, a half-dozen full-time specialists, and a training center that offered one-week workshops for different kinds of settlement personnel throughout the year. During the 1960s, settlements commonly sent most of their professional workers at one time or another to the Training Center. Agencies and foundations financed their participation. While there, settlement workers learned more about the settlement philosophy and tradition and came away with a sense of identification with a national settlement movement. Then the Training Center fell victim to budget cuts at a time when much turnover occurred on settlement staffs. Many new people without a settlement house background joined the movement. The kind of identity as settlement workers that the Training Center had provided in the past was not there, and no substitute appeared. Social work schools failed to fill the gap. Following the 1960s, they have done much less with training settlement house workers than formerly.

As the War on Poverty came to an end, the National Federation went through an abrupt change from white to black leadership. In spite of the efforts of director Walter Smart, the organization was unable to overcome the bitterness and divisiveness that grew out of the Techni-Culture movement. Its membership, budget, and services have all eroded. Furthermore, its switch from disinterested lobbyist to federal grant recipient along with the political and social conservatism of the times has blunted its social reform impact. Unfortunately, the National Federation fell under black leadership at about the time when being black no longer meant priority for grant support. Thus, by 1986, the National Federation of Settlements, renamed United Neighborhood Centers of America, was essentially back to being a one-person operation.

Professionalism has also changed the traditional settlement house method. Today no settlement house worker lives in a settlement house. Instead of using the social and political influence that comes with membership in the upper class in the manner of Jane Addams and her contemporaries, today's settlement worker relies on the M.S.W. for prestige and influence. Likewise, instead of using his residence in the neighborhood to establish a working relationship with those he is trying to help and to give legitimacy to his demands for social change, today's professional worker relies on the expertise signified by his M.S.W. degree. His career pattern is different. No longer committed for a lifetime to a particular settlement house or neighborhood, today's professional is more likely to move in and out of the neighborhood center field. With less stable neighborhoods, less reason exists to try to develop long-term neighborhood ties. Also, being male rather than female, today's settlement worker may find more upwardly mobile career opportunities open to him. Since the settlement movement is far from healthy in 1986, the professional is even less inclined to think of settlement house work as a lifetime career. Settlements continue to hire some professionals, however, because the degree is vital to successful grantsmanship, since grant proposals usually require some statement as to the credentials of project personnel. These proposals are then likely to be evaluated by social work academics who will look for the M.S.W. in project directors and principal investigators. Possession of the M.S.W. has become one of the keys to prestige, influence, and funding.

The shifts from female to male and white to black leadership has also had a significant impact on the settlement movement. Certain "female" qualities, such as the emphasis on consensus and the bridging of class and racial lines are less in evidence today. Whites, both men and women, may have yielded control to blacks so readily in part because many had a liberal attitude toward civil rights that was a by-product of their professional training. Also, professionalism had undermined their single-minded commitment to settlements, making them more inclined to move from one type of agency to another. Because of their minority position in American society, black settlement workers always represented a stronghold of social action within the settlement movement. They brought with their ascendancy to leadership a renewed commitment to social reform and a willingness to work more closely with government agencies to enlarge public funding of settlement programs. On the negative side, some have lacked administrative ability and others have tended to limit their social reform agenda to black issues. In the early 1970s, their black leadership made the National Federation of Settlements unique among national social agencies serving all races. However, a trade-off occurred in that the new settlement emphasis on black power meant a lessening of the traditional settlement function of building bridges among social classes. It also resulted in some fragmentation of the movement. The settlement house is less a crossroads for different groups than it was formerly.

Thus, the neighborhood center of 1986 has a different relationship with its neighborhood than did the settlement house of the past. Today's center is more problem-oriented. Services are designed to meet specific needs. Just developing a relationship with a neighborhood is too vague a goal to win funding. In the past, recreation was the major channel whereby a settlement could establish a neighborhood relationship. Today, the local park board and other agencies have even diminished that staple settlement activity. Likewise, social action and advocacy are carried out by smaller, newer, grass-roots agencies, many of which were born in the War on Poverty and somehow managed to survive. These agencies compete with the settlement house; yet, because of the "social control" aspects of the settlement house, they are reluctant to identify with the settlement movement. If the neighborhood center is the result of settlement mergers, it is probably operating in several different neighborhoods. To be the special advocate of one neighborhood is impossible. Gone is the time when one could say that a special relationship with a neighborhood was a distinguishing characteristic of the settlement house or neighborhood center. The result is that today's neighborhood center is a professional, problem-oriented social agency difficult to distinguish from many other, similar agencies that lack an identification with the settlement movement.

Why these changes? Certainly the professionalization of the settlement house is a recurring factor. Not only has professionalization changed the type of settlement house worker as well as the settlement house method, undercutting the settlement house's relationship to its neighborhood; but professionalization has also undercut the settlement's general reputation. Paradoxically, as the movement professionalized, tension grew between settlements and the social work profession. Social work professionals stigmatized settlement house reform efforts as "social control." Furthermore, since the 1960s, the social work profession has done little to train social activists, perhaps because such activity is controversial; but also because professional organizers are usually low paid and increasingly scarce. As for the settlement houses, they have placed less emphasis on offering professional salaries and filling positions with M.S.W.s. Some settlement workers have turned their backs on professional criticism rather than try to answer it or make adjustments. M.S.W.s still hold the leading settlement jobs, but neither settlement workers nor the social work profession seems to see much need for each other today. Yet social work educators might benefit more from the general, non-pathological contact with poor neighborhoods that the settlement offers researchers and students. For their part, settlements could use the stimulation of more professional dialogue and the enhanced credibility and influence that comes with additional professional credentials. Nevertheless, professionalism in 1986 remains an area of tension for the settlement house, something to which it has not fully accommodated itself.

Changing urban neighborhoods are another factor in the settlements' decline along with the War on Poverty. By emphasizing government grants, the antipoverty program changed the pattern of funding settlement houses and left them vulnerable when social welfare slid in public favor. Individually, some settlements remain quite strong, but they are going off in different directions. An all-encompassing national organization is not there. White/black tensions with resentment and distrust on both sides were major factors. Cutbacks in social programs have also exacerbated the situation. Finally, one can conclude that the settlement house has never really recovered from the attacks of Alinsky, Gans, and Cloward. In spite of being locally rather than nationally controlled, in spite of responding to growing minorities among its neighbors with minority leadership, in spite of greater sensitivity to the need for grass-roots democracy, settlement houses still find themselves stigmatized to a certain extent as social control agencies and rightly so.

However, if settlements in the past had not shown certain social control tendencies, would they have been effective catalysts for change? Once they made their commitment to civil rights, they did face much white neighborhood hostility. Also, they did represent their neighbors repeatedly in arguing for a variety of better welfare programs as opposed to letting their neighbors speak for themselves. Even if Mobilization for Youth veered away from the settlement philosophy of consensus toward one of grass-roots democracy and confrontation, Henry Street did initiate the project and did graciously stand by it and defend it in spite of having been badly treated by MFY staff. In fact, the settlements' chief significance may lie not so much in the lives of the individual poor they touched as in their ability to give the rest of society a window through which it can view and better understand poverty. In so many reforms in the areas of civil rights, housing, and welfare, while the settlements weren't always in the vanguard, they were present and they did help to expand support for "progress" in these areas. However, whether one supports the settlements or not may depend on whether one supports the settlements' definition of progress.

What the neighborhood center of the future will be like is open to speculation. Without a strong national agency to coordinate the efforts of local agencies and give them a common identity, the local agencies that survive are likely to develop in different directions with different functions and programs. Eventually, they may feel the need to band together with other agencies on the local and national level. For example, no agency or group is really taking responsibility today for looking at a neighborhood as a total unit and trying to coordinate efforts on that basis. However, should agencies come together, settlement houses may be identifying with agencies that have had no tie to the settlement house movement. Certain settlement houses will no doubt survive; but in changing their functions and methods, the settlement house as a distinctive type of social agency with a movement of its own could conceivably disappear.

At a recent meeting of several settlement heads in Minneapolis, one of them commented that the glue that brought them together was historical.[3] One headed an agency serving blacks, another was specializing in alternative education, a third headed a newly merged agency of six centers scattered throughout the city, and the fourth was emphasizing work with senior citizens. Only one agency belonged to United Neighborhood Centers of America. They had no local federation. They didn't meet together regularly as a group. The local social work school hadn't provided any of them with graduate fieldwork students that year and didn't seem particularly committed to working with or promoting settlements. These men headed healthy, functioning agencies; but except for their agencies' past connections with the settlement house movement, they no longer felt they had much in common. The neighborhood centers that have emerged are individualized agencies that are difficult to distinguish from a host of other varied agencies that have no common settlement heritage. In other words, the traditional settlement house movement as such is only a shadow of its past.

One final question worth raising is whether the social work profession hasn't somehow failed the settlement house. Certainly, more than professionalism was responsible for the decline of the traditional settlement house movement. Yet it was the social work profession that first undercut the settlement method of staff residing in the neighborhood. Then leading social work professionals turned on the settlements and accused them of not being truly representative of their neighborhoods. Today, the social work profession largely ignores a movement that has made major contributions to American reform. If social workers will only remember their own history, they will realize settlement houses were the major element giving early social work a reform mission.

As United States settlement houses reach their one hundredth anniversary, one can ask if perhaps the social work profession doesn't owe the settlement movement some help. The hundredth anniversary of the settlement movement is an appropriate time for the social work profession to call attention to the settlement house tradition, to enhance a sense of identity among these agencies, and to provide some positive leadership in evaluating the future potential of settlement houses. The settlement houses have a certain residual strength, a remarkable past history on which to draw, and demonstrated flexibility. At the same time today, there are neighborhoods and social

reform needs to be met. In seeking to meet these needs, a reconsti-
tuted settlement house movement could provide a partial solution.

Longtime settlement leader Camillo DeSantis thinks one should
look at the basic settlement philosophy and then realize the realities
of today's world. Is the settlement idea still viable? He sees a need
for an agency focusing on a total neighborhood and functioning in
a generalist sense, a place where people can come when they need
help, where professional staff will seek to identify neighborhood needs,
develop neighborhood leaders, and promote social action.[4] I also see
a need for an institution that can serve as a crossroads, a place where
different groups of people can come together, exchange ideas, and
reach a consensus for a better world. Perhaps support for this basic
settlement philosophy will come again.

BIBLIOGRAPHIC NOTE

Many settlement organizations and people have been unusually open and confident of their role in history and so have donated numerous records to various archives, granted interviews, and generated publications. Unfortunately, printed primary sources for the period following the Progressive Era tend to taper off, and are quite meager for the years since World War II. On the other hand, the manuscript collections in public archives for the later period are numerous, and many are voluminous. The leading archives for settlement house collections are the Social Welfare History Archives Center at the University of Minnesota, the Chicago Historical Society, the Urban Archives at Temple University, Special Collections at the University of Illinois at Chicago, and the Western Reserve Historical Society. This study rests largely on manuscripts in these places plus some other depositories. Like the printed primary sources, secondary sources for the recent decades are almost nonexistent. However, I am indebted to numerous writers of books and articles who furnished some material incorporated into this study or whose works generated ideas or insights related to settlement houses and their times. The reader should consult with the endnotes for specific sources.

ABBREVIATIONS USED IN ENDNOTES

AJK	Albert J. Kennedy
CC	Chicago Commons
CHS	Chicago Historical Society
GPFS	Greater Philadelphia Federation of Settlements
HH	Hull House Association
HSS	Henry Street Settlement
LT	Lea Taylor
MFY	Mobilization for Youth
MHS	Minnesota Historical Society
NFS	National Federation of Settlements and Neighborhood Centers
SWHAC	Social Welfare History Archives Center, University of Minnesota
UNCA	United Neighborhood Centers of America
UNH	United Neighborhood Houses of New York
U of Ill., C	University of Illinois at Chicago
Urb A	Urban Archives, Temple University
WRHS	Western Reserve Historical Society, Cleveland, Ohio

ENDNOTES

PREFACE

1. The settlement executives referred to are Marilyn Vigil, head of Neighborhood House in St. Paul; Tony Wagner, head of Pillsbury United Neighborhood Services in Minneapolis; and Fred Williams, head of Hallie Q. Brown. The conference they were planning was the Midwest American Settlement House Centennial, held on May 1–2, 1986, in Minneapolis. Tony Wagner chaired the conference steering committee.

2. Allen F. Davis, *Spearheads for Reform: The Social Settlements and the Progressive Movement, 1890–1914* (New York: Oxford University Press, 1967).

3. Clarke Chambers, *Seedtime of Reform: American Social Service and Social Action, 1918–1933* (Minneapolis: University of Minnesota Press, 1963).

4. Judith Ann Trolander, *Settlement Houses and the Great Depression* (Detroit: Wayne State University Press, 1975).

INTRODUCTION

1. 1946 Directory, NFS, NFS Records, Supp. II, box 49, fol. 1, SWHAC

2. 1956 Directory, NFS, NFS Records, Supp. II, box 49, fol. 1, SWHAC.

3. 1966–67 Directory, NFS, NFS Records, Supp. II, box 49, fol. 3, SWHAC.

4. 1979–80 Directory, UNCA, NFS Records, Supp. II, box 49, fol. 4, SWHAC.

1. RESIDENTS IN LOW-INCOME NEIGHBORHOODS: SETTLEMENT HOUSE WORKERS FROM 1886 TO 1945

1. Jeffrey Scheuer, *Legacy of Light: University Settlement's First Century* (New York: University Settlement, 1986), p. 9.

2. *Ibid.*, p. 13.

3. Stanton Coit, *Neighborhood Guilds: An Instrument of Social Reform* (London: Sonnenschein, 1891; Arno reprint, 1974).

4. Judith Ann Trolander, "Hudson Guild," in Patricia Mooney Melvin, ed., *American Community Organizations* (Westport, Conn.: Greenwood Press, 1986), pp. 84–86.

5. Graham Taylor did function as a minister as well as a settlement worker.

However, Thomas Lee Philpott in *The Slum and the Ghetto: Neighborhood Deterioration and Middle Class Reform, Chicago, 1880–1930* (New York: Oxford University Press, 1978) claimed that Taylor's political influence in his neighborhood decidedly diminished with the decline of the local Protestant population. See also Edward S. Shapiro, "Robert A. Woods and the Settlement House Impulse," *Social Service Review* (June 1978), 52:215–226; and John J. Grabowski, "From Progressive to Patrician: George Bellamy and Hiram House Social Settlement, 1896–1914," *Ohio History* (Winter 1978), 87:37–52.

6. Two articles discussing the personal reasons women had for choosing settlement house work are Stephen Kalberg, "Commitment to Career Reform: The Settlement House Leaders," *Social Service Review* (December 1975), 49:608–628, and John P. Rousmaniere, "Cultural Hybrid in the Slums: The College Woman and the Settlement House, 1889–1894," *American Quarterly* (1970), 22:45–66. See also Jane Addams' essay "The Subjective Necessity for Social Settlements," which she delivered as a lecture in 1892, then published in *Philanthropy and Social Progress* (New York: Crowell, 1893), and finally included as chapter 6 in *Twenty Years at Hull House* (New York: New American Library, 1981, originally printed 1910).

7. Sandra D. Harmon, "Florence Kelley in Illinois," *Journal of the Illinois State Historical Society* (Autumn 1981), 74:163–178. See also Kathryn Kish Sklar, "Hull House in the 1890s: A Community of Women Reformers," *Signs* (Summer 1985), 10:658–677.

8. For an early statement of these ideals, see Jane Addams, "The Objective Value of a Social Settlement," *Philanthropy and Social Progress* (New York: Crowell, 1893; Arno reprint, 1969), pp. 27–56.

9. Jane Addams, *Twenty Years at Hull House*, pp. 200–205.

10. Thomas Lee Philpott, *The Slum and the Ghetto*, p. 5.

11. Mina J. Carson, "Agnes Hamilton of Fort Wayne: The Education of a Christian Settlement Worker," *Indiana Magazine of History* (March 1984), 80:27.

12. Allen F. Davis, in *American Heroine: The Life and Legend of Jane Addams* (New York: Oxford University Press, 1973), describes Addams as a shrewd person hungry for public adulation, but has some difficulty then explaining why she courted disapproval as a peace advocate during World War I. She wasn't rewarded with the Nobel Peace Prize until 1931.

13. Robert Hunter, *Poverty: Social Conscience in the Progressive Era*, Peter d'A. Jones, ed. (New York: Harper and Row, 1965; originally published by Macmillan, 1904).

14. Kalberg, "Commitment to Career Reform," p. 612.

15. Elizabeth Gilman, "Catheryne Cooke Gilman: Social Worker," in Barbara Stuhler and Gretchen Kreuter, eds., *Women of Minnesota: Selected Biographical Essays* (St. Paul: Minnesota Historical Society, 1977), p. 206.

16. Philpott, *The Slum and the Ghetto*, p. 291.

17. Joseph P. Lash, *Eleanor and Franklin* (New York: New American Library, 1973), pp. 146–148.

18. Scheuer, *Legacy of Light*, p. 21.

19. William E. Leuchtenberg, *Franklin D. Roosevelt and the New Deal: 1932–1940* (New York: Harper Colophon Books, 1963), p. 33.

20. Judith Ann Trolander, "Twenty Years at Hiram House," *Ohio History* (Winter, 1969), 78:29.

21. Gilman, "Catheryne Cooke Gilman," p. 200.

22. Philpott devotes several chapters to settlement workers' efforts in *The Slum and the Ghetto*.

23. Allen F. Davis, *American Heroine*, pp. 121–125.

24. George Cary White, "Social Settlements and Immigrant Neighbors, 1886–1914," *Social Service Review* (March 1959), 33:55–66.

25. Letty Santiago, "From Settlement House to Poverty Program," *Social Work* (July 1972), p. 75.

26. Winifred Bolin, "Heating Up the Melting Pot: Settlement Work and Americanization in Northeast Minneapolis," *Minnesota History* (Summer 1976), 45:60.

27. Rivka Lissak, "Myth and Reality: The Pattern of Relationship Between the Hull House Circle and the 'New Immigrants' on Chicago's West Side, 1890–1919," *Journal of American Ethnic History* (Spring 1983), 2:34.

28. Trolander, "Twenty Years," p. 31.

29. Ronald J. Butera, "A Settlement House and the Urban Challenge: Kingsley House in Pittsburgh, Pennsylvania, 1893–1920," *Western Pennsylvania Historical Magazine* (January 1983), 66:36.

30. Grabowski, "From Progressive to Patrician," p. 37.

31. Gilman, "Catheryne Cooke Gilman," p. 192.

32. Taylor, quoted in Philpott, *The Slum and the Ghetto*, p. 62.

33. Gilbert Osofsky, *Harlem: The Making of a Ghetto*, 2d ed. (New York: Harper Torchbooks, 1971), p. 61.

34. Philpott, *The Slum and the Ghetto*, p. 316.

35. Butera, "A Settlement House and the Urban Challenge," p. 46.

36. Philpott, *The Slum and the Ghetto*, p. 338.

37. Judith Ann Trolander, *Settlement Houses and the Great Depression* (Detroit: Wayne State University Press, 1975), pp. 141–143. See also Howard Jacob Karger, "Phyllis Wheatley House: A History of the Minneapolis Black Settlement House, 1924 to 1940," *Phylon* (Spring 1986), 47:79–90.

38. *Ibid.*, pp. 91–106. See also Judith Ann Trolander, "The Response of Settlements to the Great Depression," *Social Work* (September 1973), 18:92–102.

39. Clarke Chambers, *Seedtime to Reform: American Social Service and Social Action, 1918–1933* (Minneapolis: University of Minnesota Press, 1963), pp. 121–123.

40. Trolander, *Settlement Houses*, p. 47.

41. *Ibid.*, p. 87.

42. Board minutes, July 2, 1942 and May 19, 1943, both in University Settlement Records, box 1, fol. 1, WRHS.

43. Ben Stoddard, settlement worker, to Frederick Crosby, board president, 18 March 1943, Neighborhood House Association Records, box 1, MHS.

44. Gertrude Owen, executive director, South Orange Community House, South Orange, New Jersey, to Lillie Peck, executive secretary, NFS Records, fol. 123, SWHAC.

45. "Settlement Papers: Community Studies and Related Documents—Books, Reports, Articles, Statements—from the HSS Files, 1933–1958," NSF Records, fol. 132, SWHAC, cites an article by Helen Hall, "Red Cross Under the Southern Cross," *Survey Graphic* (January 1944), describing Hall's work in the South Pacific.

46. Trolander, *Settlement Houses*, p. 84.

47. Robbins Gilman, "Annual Report of the Head Worker," 1942, Northeast Neighborhood House Records, box 7, MHS.

48. "War Cuts Benton House Staff: Board Members Help Out," January 1944, clipping from *Advance*, Benton House Records, box 3, CHS.

49. Frederick J. Soule, "Settlements and Neighborhood Houses," in Lorene M. Pacey, ed., *Readings in the Development of Settlement Work* (New York: Association Press, 1950).

50. Board minutes, 22 Sept. 1942, University Settlement Records, box 1, fol. 1, WRHS.

51. Clinton S. Chills, director, Alexander House, "A Settlement in the Fighting Zone," *Survey Graphic* (April 1942), 31:212.

52. Owen to Peck, 4 March 1942, NFS Records, fol. 123, SWHAC.

53. "Settlements 60th Anniversary, 1886–1946," Papers of the University Settlement Society of New York City (microfilm ed., 1972), reel 13, State Historical Society of Wisconsin.

54. "Condensed Annual Report," 1942, Benton House Records, box 3, CHS.

55. "A Brief [Report] of St. Martha's House: 1901–1964," March 1964, St. Martha's House/Houston Community Center Records, box 1, Urb A.

56. Trolander, *Settlement Houses*, p. 18.

57. John Selby, *Beyond Civil Rights* (Cleveland: World, 1966), p. 129.

58. "Aspects of War-Time Day Care Programs," *21st Conference Notebook*, 18–21 May 1944, p. 1, NFS Records, fol. 90, SWHAC.

59. United Neighborhood Houses, "The Case for the Child Day Care Center Program," December 1948, NFS Records, fol. 217, SWHAC.

60. Press release, "Settlement Head Asks for State Hearing on Child Care," 11 Jan. 1948, NSF Records, fol. 217, SWHAC.

2. THE TRADITIONAL SETTLEMENT HOUSE PROFESSIONALIZES: AN OVERVIEW OF CHANGING METHODS

1. Gwendolyn Wright, *Building the Dream: A Social History of Housing in America* (New York: Pantheon, 1981), p. 128.

2. Fern Colborn, NFS staff, to Allen Bacon, head, Germantown Settlement, 24 Feb. 1960, Germantown Settlement Records, box 1, Urb A. See

also Sophie Wojeiechowski, "Mental Health at Manhattanville Community Centers," *Round Table* (November–December 1956), pp. 4–6, Ephemera, SWHAC.

3. William H. Brueckner to Jean Maxwell, NFS staff, 4 June 1951, NFS Supp. Records, fol. 29:5, SWHAC.

4. Jean Maxwell to William Brueckner, 3 August 1951, NFS Supp. Records, fol. 29:5, SWHAC.

5. "A New Approach to Problem Ridden Families," Germantown Settlement Records, box 2, Urb A.

6. AJK, "The Settlement as Agent and Instrument," 1947, pp. 41–42, AJK Papers, fol. 33, SWHAC.

7. Helen Hall, report on "Residents at the Settlement and in the Neighborhood," presented to Henry Street board, 9 Jan. 1967, HSS Papers, fol. 37:11, SWHAC.

8. "An Overview of Hull House in 1946," p. 5, Russell Ballard Papers, fol. 30, U of Ill., C. The first woman to hold a cabinet post, Frances Perkins, was also a resident for a brief time at Hull House during the Progressive Era. However, neither Weaver nor Perkins seems to have gotten significantly involved in settlement house activities.

9. Board minutes, 31 Oct. 1947, HH Records, fol. 7, U of Ill., C.

10. John McDowell to William Brueckner, 2 Sept. 1955, CC Records, box 39, CHS.

11. Service report, 1958, p. 22, CC Records, box 5A, CHS.

12. William Brueckner to Mrs. Willing, board president, 19 Sept. 1955, CC Records, box 39, CHS.

13. "Proposed Revisions for Criteria for Admission to Agency Membership in the NFS," 17 April 1969, NFS Supp., fol. 16:2, SWHAC.

14. Willette Cragin Pierce, "A Study of the Contribution of Student Residents in the Settlement Program and Its Resulting Value to the Student," M.S. thesis, School of Social Work, Boston University, 1950, p. 44, in NFS Records, fol. 192, SWHAC.

15. Robbins Gilman, "Report of the Head Worker," August and September 1940, Northeast Neighborhood House Records, box 7, MHS.

16. For an account of Hiram House's early years, see Judith Ann Trolander, "Twenty Years at Hiram House," *Ohio History* (Winter 1969), 78:25–37, 69–71.

17. AJK, "Why and How of Settlement Federations" [1947], AJK Papers, fol. 19, SWHAC.

18. John McDowell, "Settlement and Neighborhood Houses," *Social Work Year Book* New York: Russell Sage Foundation, 1949), pp. 463–468.

19. Service report, 1963–64, CC Records, box 5A, CHS.

20. Milton A. Brown, secretary for Personnel, NFS, to "Executives of Member Agencies," 20 April 1959, NFS Supp. Records, fol. 19:1, SWHAC.

21. Robert Armstrong, program director, "Ethics and Society," 7 June 1959, Erie Neighborhood House Records, box 2, CHS.

22. Trolander, "Twenty Years at Hiram House," p. 30.

23. Clarke Chambers, "Helen Hall, 1892–1982," 1983, draft of an essay for the Helen Hall memorial service pamphlet, SWHAC.

24. Interview with Tony Wagner, Pillsbury United Neighborhood Services; Joe Holewa, East Side Neighborhood Services; Jim Storm, Loring-Nicollet-Bethlehem Community Center; Jim Cook, Sabathani Community Center; and Camillo DeSantis, United Way, 16 May 1984, Pillsbury House, Minneapolis.

25. Bertram M. Beck, "Settlements in the United States—Past and Future," *Social Work* (July 1976), 21(4):269.

26. Board minutes, 30 Oct. 1940, University Settlement Records, box 1, fol. 1, WRHS.

27. Kathleen L. Kosuda, librarian, Gloversville Free Library, to Judith Ann Trolander, 12 Sept. 1975. See also "Lillie Peck," *Dictionary of American Biography*, Supp. 6 (New York: Scribner's 1980), pp. 499–500.

28. William Brueckner to Marietta Stevenson, director, Division of Social Welfare Administration, University of Illinois, 3 May 1948, CC Records, box 31, CHS.

29. Board minutes, 16 Sept. 1961, University of Chicago Settlement Records, box 2, CHS.

30. William Brueckner, "Meeting at Como Inn," 16 Feb. 1954, CC Records, box 37, CHS.

31. Executive Council of Chicago Federation of Settlements minutes, 18 Nov. 1947, LT Papers, box 12, CHS.

32. Atkins Preston, résumé, November 1966, MFY Records, "HSS" fol., Columbia University.

33. Tony Wagner et al., interview, 16 May 1984.

34. Interview with Camillo DeSantis, director of Management and Leadership Development, United Way, 2 Feb. 1984, United Way, Minneapolis.

35. John H. Ehrenreich, *The Altruistic Imagination: A History of Social Work and Social Policy in the United States* (Ithaca: Cornell University Press, 1985), p. 53.

36. Ann Withorn, *Serving the People: Social Services and Social Change* (New York: Columbia University Press, 1984), p. 125.

37. Margaret E. Berry, *One Hundred Years on Urban Frontiers: The Settlement Movement, 1886–1986* (Washington, D.C.: UNCA, 1986).

38. "Announcements," 18 Aug. 1967, NFS Training Center Records, CHS.

39. AJK, "Interview with David Rosenstein," Papers of the University Settlement Society of New York City (microfilm ed., 1972), reel 13, State Historical Society of Wisconsin.

40. Margaret Berry to "Executive," 3 July 1969, NFS Supp. Records, fol. 33:1, SWHAC.

3. FROM FEMALE TO MALE SETTLEMENT HOUSE WORKERS

1. Clarke Chambers, "Women in the Creation of the Profession of Social Work," *Social Service Review* (March 1986), p. 12. A 1946 NFS directory may be found in UNH Records, fol. 590; a 1953 directory in NFS Records, fol. 127; a 1960 directory in Five Towns Community House Records, fol. 453; a 1966–67 directory and a 1973 one both in NFS Supp. Records, fol. 16:9. All these collections are in the SWHAC. I was unable to determine from the name of the worker his or her sex in five cases in 1946, four in 1953, eight in 1960, five in 1966–67, and one in 1973. Also not counted were three settlements that had both male and female codirectors in 1946 and Karamu House, the only settlement a married couple headed.

2. John McDowell, executive director, NFS, "Report to Kingsley House Study Committee . . ." [1948], p. 15, Wilbur I. Newsletter Papers, box 7, University of Pittsburgh.

3. "Statistics on Professional Employees in Member Agencies of the NFS . . . ," 1957–58, NFS Supp. Records, fol. 19:7, SWHAC.

4. LuAnn Sweeney, one of Clarke Chambers' graduate students, at the University of Minnesota, was preparing a paper on this subject in spring 1983.

5. Board minutes, 18 June 1958, UNH Supp. Records, fol. 3:1, SWHAC.

6. Alfred Kadushin, "Men in a Woman's Profession," *Social Work* (November 1976), 21(6):440.

7. Nina Toren, "Semi-Professionalism and Social Work: A Theoretical Perspective," in Amitai Etzioni, ed., *The Semi-Professions and Their Organization* (New York: Free Press, 1969), p. 157.

8. Helen Hall, "Settlements as a First Line of Defense," 25 May 1954, pp. 1–2, NFS Records, fol. 132, SWHAC.

9. Besides Hall's autobiography, *Unfinished Business in Neighborhood and Nation* (New York: Macmillan, 1971), see Judith Ann Trolander, *Settlement Houses and the Great Depression* (Detroit: Wayne State University Press, 1975), and Clarke Chambers, *Paul U. Kellogg and "The Survey"* (Minneapolis: University of Minnesota Press, 1971).

10. For a discussion of fact and fiction, see Allen F. Davis, *American Heroine: The Life and Legend of Jane Addams* (New York: Oxford University Press, 1973), pp. 157–175. An example of Addams' outspoken feminism is recounted in Trolander, *Settlement Houses*, p. 42. When Addams saw a 1930 newspaper article quoting a male head worker as saying women make better head workers than men, she remarked that the National Federation of Settlement "might consider disciplining this young man." It was a sign of changing times that the NFS sidestepped the issue instead.

11. Minutes, Program Committee, 14 Feb. 1949, CC Records, box 22, CHS.

12. "Service Report, 1963–64," CC Records, box 5A, CHS.

13. Mrs. Brueckner to Helen Hall, 1 Sept. 1968, Helen Hall Records, fol.

7:4, and Mrs. Brueckner to Helen Hall, 12 Nov. 1978, Helen Hall Records, fol. 8:7, SWHAC.

14. Mrs. Brueckner to Helen Hall, 29 Dec. 1976, Helen Hall Records, fol. 8:5, SWHAC.

15. Mrs. Brueckner to Helen Hall, 12 Nov. 1978, Helen Hall Records, fol. 8:7, SWHAC.

16. Interview with Camillo DeSantis, 2 February 1984.

17. Margaret Berry, "On Being a Professional—and Being a Woman," January 1982, NFS Supp. Records, fol. 35:6, SWHAC. Unless otherwise indicated, this is the document referred to in subsequent paragraphs.

18. AJK, "The Settlement Heritage," *Selected Conference Papers*, 1953, p. 14, NFS microfilm, reel 5, SWHAC.

19. P. David Finks, *The Radical Vision of Saul Alinsky* (New York: Paulist Press, 1984), p. 101.

20. Herbert J. Gans, *The Urban Villagers: Group and Class in the Life of Italian-Americans* (New York: Free Press of Glencoe, 1962), pp. 152–153.

21. Kenneth E. Boulding, "Alienation and Economic Development: The Larger Background of the Settlement Movement," *Neighborhood Goals in a Rapidly Changing World* (New York: NFS, 1958), pp. 62–63.

22. Anne Wilson Schaef, *Women's Reality: An Emerging Female System in the White Male Society* (Minneapolis: Winston Press, 1981), p. 134.

23. Kadushin, "Men in a Woman's Profession," p. 444.

24. Kenneth E. Boulding, "Man vs. Woman," *Neighborhood Goals in a Rapidly Changing World* (New York: NFS, 1958), p. 2.

25. Dee Garrison, "The Tender Technicians: The Feminization of Public Librarianship, 1876–1905," in Mary Hartman and Lois W. Banner, eds., *Clio's Consciousness Raised: New Perspectives on the History of Women* (New York: Harper and Row, 1974), p. 166.

26. Interview with Walter Smart, 12 April 1983.

27. Interview with Camillo DeSantis, 2 Feb. 1984.

4. CHANGING NEIGHBORHOODS

1. Board minutes, 7 Dec. 1939, University Settlement Records, box 1, fol. 1, WRHS. The settlement head was Wilbur A. Joseph.

2. Dolly Lowther, Laundry Workers' Union, Amalgamated Clothing Workers of America, "Propaganda for Democracy," *Round Table* (November 1941), p. 11, NFS Records, fol. 204, SWHAC.

3. NFS, "For Action Now," 1944, Phyllis Wheatley Settlement House Records, box 10, MHS.

4. "Resolutions," 1944, NFS Records, fol. 27, SWHAC.

5. "Platform of Action Adopted by the Delegate Body at the Annual Meeting," 14 Sept. 1947, NFS Records, fol. 27, SWHAC.

6. Chicago Federation of Settlements, "Statement on Present Strike Situation," 5 Feb. 1946, LT Papers, box 11, CHS; and Chicago Federation of

Settlements, "Resolution Adopted on March 16, 1948," NFS Records, fol. 209, SWHAC.

7. Annual report, 1948, p. 2, University of Chicago Settlement Records, box 19, CHS.

8. Saul Alinsky, chairman, Chicago Committee on Emergency Aid to Packinghouse Workers' Families, to Courtenay Barber, board members of the same committee, 10 June 1948, Russell Ballard Papers, Supp. II, fol. 38, U of Ill., C.

9. Board minutes, University of Chicago Settlement, 14 June 1948, Mary McDowell Papers, fol. 31, CHS.

10. Lucy Carner, "Some Shortcomings in Chicago Settlements Today," August 1945, Phyllis Wheatley Settlement House Records, box 10, MHS.

11. Carner, "Today's Work Keystone for the Future," 1951, p. 7, NFS Records, fol. 95, SWHAC.

12. Business meeting minutes, NFS Conference, 12 May 1951, NFS Records, fol. 95, SWHAC.

13. Board minutes, 21 Oct. 1946, Mary McDowell Papers, fol. 30, CHS.

14. Julius J. Manson, Arbitration Award Between HSS and Local 1707, Community and Social Agency Employees Union, 30 Dec. 1965, HSS Records, fol. 91:10, SWHAC.

15. Don Haynes, "Hull House Assn. Workers To Strike for Higher Pay," Chicago Sun-Times, 11 Oct. 1982, p. 60; "Strikers Go Back at Hull," Chicago Sun-Times, 20 Oct. 1982, p. 36.

16. Interview with Tony Wagner, executive director, Pillsbury United Neighborhood Services, 16 May 1984.

17. Anna D. Bramble, head, House of Industry, "Report to the Board of Managers," 13 Sept. 1943, United Neighborhood Association Records, box 1, Urb A.

18. "The New Americans Club," September 1941, CC Records, box 4, CHS.

19. Annual report, 1940–41, p. 13, CC Records, box 4, CHS.

20. "Program Survey," May 1958, pp. 7–8, East End Neighborhood House Records, box 6, fol. 2, WRHS.

21. John McDowell, NFS director, to Julian Greifer, Neighborhood Center, 31 March 1949, University Settlement Records, box 14, Urb A.

22. Clipping, "St. Martha's House Now Houston Center," Bulletin, 20 March 1965, St. Martha's House/Houston Community Center Records, box 1, Urb A.

23. Board minutes, 23 Aug. 1960, Baden Street Settlement Records, fol. 5, SWHAC.

24. Board minutes, 10 April 1961, p. 1, Association House Records, box 4, CHS.

25. "A Mexican Settlement Speaks," Round Table (April 1941), p. 7, NFS Records, fol. 204, SWHAC.

26. "Evening Program," University of Chicago Settlement, November 1947, box 19, CHS.

27. L. Stanton, "Eagles," 20 Jan. 1942, pp. 1–2, CC Records, box 7, CHS.

28. Annual report, 1939–40, p. 2, CC Records, box 5, CHS.

29. Chicago Federation of Settlements to "Friend," October 1954, NFS Records, fol. 211, SWHAC.

30. "Report on Case Study," 12 Aug. 1948, NFS Records, fol. 145, SWHAC.

31. Board minutes, 17 May 1940, CC Records, box 20, CHS.

32. Clipping, "Urge Vigilance to Keep Homes in Slums Safe," *Chicago Daily News,* 9 Dec. 1943, CC Records, box 29, CHS.

33. Clipping, "Jury Blames Owners for Fire Fatal to Six," *Chicago Sun-Times,* 21 Oct. 1950, CC Records, box 34, CHS.

34. "Neighborhood News," November 1954, United Neighbors Association Records, box 21, Urb A.

35. Minutes of the executive board of United Neighborhood Houses, 8 Oct. 1940, University Settlement Society of New York City Records (microfilm ed., 1972), reel 13, State Historical Society of Wisconsin.

36. Lillie Peck, executive secretary, NFS, quoting Franklin Harbach, settlement head, to "Representatives of City Federations of Settlement," 20 Jan. 1945, Phyllis Wheatley House Records, box 10, MHS.

37. "Minutes of Meeting of United Neighborhood Houses In-Service Training Course—Social Action Workshop—Oct. 24, 1945," NFS Records, fol. 217, SWHAC.

38. Minutes, Executive Council, Chicago Federation of Settlements, 17 June 1947 and 15 July 1947, LT Papers, box 12, CHS.

39. Marjorie Main, executive secretary, Chicago Federation of Settlements, "City Federation Report for the Board of Directors of the National Federation of Settlements," January 1948, NFS Records, fol. 209, SWHAC.

40. Response to a questionnaire describing the NFS, 1953, p. 5, NFS microfilm, reel 4, SWHAC.

41. "Benton House Report," January 1950, Benton House Records, box 3, CHS.

42. Minutes, Study and Planning Committee, 14 April 1950, p. 3, CC Records, box 22, CHS.

43. John McDowell and Fern Colborn to Ernest J. Bohn, chairman, Subcommittee on Housing for Low-Income Families, Advisory Committee on Government Housing Policies and Programs, 13 Oct. 1953, NFS Records, fol. 47, SWHAC.

44. Elizabeth Wood, "Public Housing and Mrs. McGee," *Round Table* (March–April 1957), p. 3, NFS Records, fol. 205, SWHAC. General Kean, who promised to be more tractable than Wood, replaced her as head of the Chicago Housing Authority. LT, in a letter dated 30 Aug. 1954 to "Mr. Fugard" of the Chicago Housing Authority board, praised Wood's honesty and protested her dismissal. See CC Records, box 38, CHS.

45. Fern Colborn, "Settlement on Housing for Presentation to [U.S. housing official] Albert M. Cole, July 23, 1953," NFS Records, fol. 138, SWHAC.

46. Board minutes, 18 May 1949 and 12 April 1950, United Neighbor-

hood Houses Records, fol. 32, SWHAC. The reference is to the Austin-Wicks Bill.

47. Telegram, Helen Hall to Robert Weisberger, New York City Council, 13 Feb. 1951, HSS House Records, box 59, SWHAC.

48. Robert C. Weaver, *The Urban Complex* (Garden City, N.Y.: Anchor Books, 1966), p. 254.

49. Robert C. Weaver, *Dilemma of Urban America* (New York: Atheneum, 1969), p. 90.

50. NFS, "A New Look at Public Housing," 1958 pamphlet in NFS Records, fol. 55, SWHAC.

51. "Contract for Relocation Services by and Between the Boston Redevelopment Authority and United South End Settlement Inc.," 21 March 1962, GPFS Records, box 3, Urb A.

52. United South End Settlements, "Castle Square Residential Relocation Program: Final Report," 1 Feb. 1964, HSS Records, box 59, SWHAC.

53. Albert Boer, *The Development of USES: A Chronology of the United South End Settlements, 1891–1966* (Boston: USES, 1966), p. 52.

54. NFS, "Report of Low Rent Public Housing in Twenty-Three Cities of the United States," 1955, HSS Records, box 37, SWHAC.

55. Annual report, 14 Jan. 1940, Wharton Centre Records, box 1, Urb A.

56. "Adult Education in Settlements" [1947?], pp. 4–5, NFS Records, fol. 4, SWHAC.

57. "Report of Walter I. Smart on Settlement Services" [1958], Germantown Settlement Records, box 1, Urb A.

58. Annual meeting, 3 May 1953, New York Settlement Records, Acc. 155, box 1, Urb A.

59. Mildred W. Guinessy, executive director, Delaware Valley Settlement Alliance, "Helping the Poor Housekeeping Family in Public Housing," NFS Training Center Records, "Various Files," CHS.

60. "Notes on General Staff Meeting," 26 March 1959, HSS Records, fol. 29:13, SWHAC.

61. "Digest of Action—Board of Directors Meeting," 18 April 1948, NFS Records, fol. 27, SWHAC; Fern Colborn, "Statement on Housing for Presentation to Albert Cole, July 22, 1953," NFS Records, fol. 138, SWHAC; John McDowell and Fern Colborn to Ernest Bohn, 13 Oct. 1953, NFS Records, fol. 47, SWHAC.

62. "Recommendations for the Conduct of Community and Leisure-Time Activities in Public Housing Projects in New York City," 9 July 1942, UNH Records, fol. 25, SWHAC.

63. Helen Hall to Lawrence J. Tolbert, Neighborhood House, Columbus, Ohio, 4 Aug. 1958, HSS Records, box 52, SWHAC.

64. "Report to the Authority on the Community Activities Program," 13 Jan. 1959, Helen Hall Papers, fol. 485, SWHAC.

65. Summary of H. Daniel Carpenter's speech attached to the minutes of

the Philadelphia Association of Settlements and Neighborhood Houses, 22 Nov. 1950, GPFS General Files, fol. 11/I/104 in Urb A.

66. Interview with Howard Karger, social work professor, and Marcy Shapiro, community organizer, 27 Dec. 1983, in Duluth, Minnesota.

67. Michael Harrington, *The Other America* (New York: Macmillan, 1962), pp. 160–163. The community building was deeded to the city and remodeled as the recreation building for the Chelsea Housing Project, then rented back to Hudson Guild for $1.00 per year. See "Notes on Settlement People and Things" [1942], UNH Records, fol. 25, SWHAC.

68. Devereux Bowly, Jr., *The Poorhouse: Subsidized Housing in Chicago, 1895–1976* (Carbondale: University of Southern Illinois Press, 1978), p. 129.

69. "Digest of Action—Board of Directors," 8–11 Nov. 1945, NFS Records, fol. 27, SWHAC.

70. "Statement of Need for a Continuation of the State Financed Low-Rent Public Housing Program," 19 Dec. 1962, UNH Supp. Records, fol. 53:9, SWHAC.

71. "Resolution of the Executive Committee" [of the Metropolitan Housing and Planning Council], 15 Sept. 1967, LT Papers, box 18, CHS.

72. Albert Boer, *The Development of USES*, p. 54.

73. "Reprint from the *Philadelphia Independent*," 20 Sept. 1952, NFS Records, fol. 44, SWHAC.

74. Educational Alliance, "Seventy Years and Still Pioneering," 1961, HSS Records, fol. 98:2, SWHAC.

75. "Hudson Guild First!—a Building for Aged," *Round Table* (Feb. 1961), p. 7, NFS Records, fol. 205, SWHAC.

76. Woods Run Settlement Director's Report, 1954, Neighborhood Centers Association, box 2, University of Pittsburgh Libraries.

77. "Report of Committee of Federation of Social Agencies on Woods Run Settlement, Lawrenceville Neighborhood House, and Soho Public Baths at Request of Mayor David L. Lawrence," 2 Dec. 1947, Neighborhood Center Association Records, box 6, University of Pittsburgh Libraries.

78. Judith Ann Trolander, *Settlement Houses and the Great Depression* (Detroit: Wayne State University Press, 1975), p. 153.

79. Boer, *The Development of USES* p. 44.

80. Mary West Jorgensen, "F.O.B. Detroit" [1950?], p. 6, NFS Records, fol. 29, SWHAC.

81. NFS board minutes, 17 May 1957, LT Papers, box 7, CHS.

82. Service report, 20 Nov. 1957, p. 2, CC Records, box 52, CHS.

83. Allen F. Davis and Mary Lynn McCree, *Eighty Years at Hull-House* (Chicago: Quadrangle, 1969), pp. 215–217.

84. Meeting between representatives of Waite House board and the Chest Budget and Distribution Committee, 5 Nov. 1964, United Way of Minneapolis, box 20, SWHAC.

85. Minutes of New Directions Committee, 29 June 1968, NFS Supp. Records, fol. 33:1, SWHAC.

86. Interview with Camillo DeSantis, 2 Feb. 1984. The mergers were E.F. Waite House in 1959 and Pillsbury-Waite in 1967. In 1984, Pillsbury-Waite merged again to become Pillsbury United Neighborhood Services, with facilities in neighborhoods in north and south Minneapolis.

87. HH annual report, May 1977, Homer Bishop Papers, fol. 26, SWHAC.

88. Interview with Tony Wagner, head, Pillsbury United Neighborhood Services, 16 May 1984.

5. BLACKS, EQUAL RIGHTS, AND INTEGRATION

1. William English Walling was a journalist and former settlement worker; Mary White Ovington was a former settlement worker who had been unsuccessful in establishing a house for blacks; and Henry Moskowitz was head worker at Madison House. See Judith Ann Trolander, *Settlement Houses and the Great Depression* (Detroit: Wayne State University Press, 1975), p. 25. See also Thomas Lee Philpott, *The Slum and the Ghetto: Neighborhood Deterioration and Middle Class Reform, 1880–1930* (New York: Oxford University Press, 1978).

2. Trolander, *Settlement Houses and the Great Depression*, pp. 134–147, *passim*.

3. NFS, "For Action Now," 1944, Phyllis Wheatley Settlement House Records, box 10, MHS.

4. Clyde E. Murray, "New Horizons for the Settlement Movement" (New York: NFS, 1944), p. 4, Phyllis Wheatley Settlement House Records, box 10, MHS.

5. "Report of the Committee on Intercultural and Interracial Relations," 1942–43, p. 11, NFS Supp. Records, fol. 33:8, SWHAC.

6. These included Rankin Christian Center in Pittsburgh, Five Towns Community House outside New York City, Cleveland's Friendly Inn, CC, and South Chicago Community Center. See Elbert R. Tingley, director, Rankin Christian Center, to AJK, 11 Sept. 1945, AJK Papers, fol. 95, SWHAC; "Factual Data Regarding Applicants for Agency Membership," 25 Oct. 1945, NFS Records, fol. 27, SWHAC; board minutes, 27 Oct. 1944, Friendly Inn Records, box 1, fol. 1, WRHS; William Brueckner, director, CC, to Mrs, Faith Jefferson Jones, director, Parkway Community House, 22 Dec. 1949, CC Records, box 33, CHS (Mrs. Jones was the first black to serve on the prestigious CC board, the director of a black settlement, and the widow of Dewey Jones, who had led integration efforts at Hull House in the late 1930s); and "Some Questions on Agency Policy and Practice in Minority Group Relationships" [at South Chicago Community Center], March 1948, Welfare Council Records, box 402, CHS.

7. "Commission on Interracial and Intercultural Relations," 7 Jan. 1943, AJK Papers, fol. 47, SWHAC.

8. Mrs. Clara L. Plevinsky to AJK, 6 July 1945, AJK Papers, fol. 99, SWHAC.

9. John Ramey, interview with Lillie Lynem, director, Henry Booth House of HH, 1965, p. 9, Hull House Training Center, "Various Files," CHS.

10. St. Clair Drake, *Race Relations in a Time of Rapid Social Change* (New York: NFS, 1966), p. 43.

11. [Interviewer not identified], "More About South Side Settlement and Support of Fair Housing During Interview with Homer Bishop" [1965], NFS Training Center Records, "Various Files," CHS.

12. Drake, *Race Relations*, p. 44.

13. "Settlements 6oth Anniversary, 1886–1946," University Settlement Society of New York City Records (microfilm ed., 1972), reel 13, State Historical Society of Wisconsin.

14. "Report of the Committee on Intercultural and Interracial Relations—NFS," 1942–43, NFS Supp. Records, fol. 33:8, SWHAC.

15. "Commission on Interracial and Intercultural Relations," 7 March 1943, AJK Papers, fol. 48, SWHAC.

16. Milton Brown, United Neighbors Association of Philadelphia, "Presentation of a Case Study . . . ," in *Today's Work—Keystone for the Future*, mimeographed, 30 Nov. 1951, p. 40, NFS Records, fol. 95, SWHAC.

17. Goldie Gibson Edwards, "Why Settlement Work Is My Profession," in *Today's Work—Keystone for the Future*, mimeographed, 1951, p. 29, NFS Records, fol. 95, SWHAC.

18. Hamilton-Madison House board minutes, 8 Jan. 1963, HSS Records, fol. 71:7, SWHAC.

19. [Murtis Taylor], interview with Al Alissi, Alta House director [1965], p. 3, NFS Training Center Records, "Various Files," CHS.

20. "What Happened to Negro Staff Member" [1965], NFS Training Center Records, "Various Files," CHS.

21. [Taylor], interview with Al Alissi, pp. 1–2.

22. Allen F. Davis and Mary Lynn McCree, eds., *Eighty Years at Hull-House* (Chicago: Quardrangle, 1969), p. 226.

23. Lillie Peck, executive secretary, NFS, to J. A. Wolf, head worker, Neighborhood Association, St. Louis, 23 Nov. 1942, AJK Papers, fol. 79, SWHAC.

24. J. A. Wolf, executive director, Neighborhood Association, to AJK, 13 July 1945, AJK Papers, fol. 79, SWHAC.

25. Edna Hansen to "Board Members," 5 December 1946, Henry Booth House Records, fol. 12, Special Collections, U of Ill., C.

26. Drake, *Race Relations*, p. 30. The actual figure was 34.16 percent.

27. *Ibid.*, p. 31.

28. Minutes of New Directions Committee, 29 June 1958, NFS Supp., fol. 33:1.

29. Margaret Berry to John Austin, NFS president, 11 July 1968, p. 3, NFS Supp., fol. 3:6, SWHAC.

30. Lillie Peck, "Report of Detroit Field Visit," 1944, p. 12, NFS Records, fol. 215, SWHAC.

31. John McDowell, NFS staff, "Record of Visit to Columbus," 15–16 July 1943, AJK Papers, fol. 49, SWHAC.

32. Trolander, *Settlement Houses*, p. 145.

33. John McDowell, "Record of Visit to Columbus . . ." and "Record of Visit to Toledo," 28 July 1943, AJK Papers, fol. 49, SWHAC.

34. Factual Information of the William Byrd Community House," September 1943, AJK Papers, fol. 101, SWHAC.

35. William McCarthy, "At Sophie Wright Settlement," *Round Table* (October 1940), p. 8, NFS, fol. 203, SWHAC.

36. LT to Dr. Horace Cayton, head of Parkway Community House, 7 May 1946, CC Records, box 30, CHS.

37. Annual report, CC Association, 1945–46, CC Records, box 5, CHS.

38. Marion Barkwell, girls' worker, "January Report 1946," CC Records, box 7, CHS.

39. Paul Weinandy, "Interracial Discussion," 18 May 1946, NFS Records, fol. 91, SWHAC.

40. "Commission on Interracial and Intercultural Relations," 7 March 1943, pp. 9–11, 13, AJK Papers, fol. 48, SWHAC.

41. Louis Berkowitz, director, Five Towns Community House, to William Brueckner, director, Emerson House, 9 Nov. 1949, CC Records, box 33, CHS.

42. Joseph Deitch, "Negro on the March: Interracial Living as Worked Out in Philadelphia," *Christian Science Monitor Weekly Magazine Section*, 19 Oct. 1946, p. 10.

43. Elizabeth Handasyde, *City or Community* (London: National Council of Social Service, 1949), pp. 36–37.

44. Chicago Federation of Settlements Committee on Minority Group Relationships minutes, 1 Oct. 1948, CC Records, box 32, CHS.

45. Chicago Federation of Settlements Executive Council minutes, 20 Jan. 1948, p. 1, LT Papers, box 12, CHS.

46. "Memorandum on Interracial Program: Soho Community House," 1941–42, AJK Papers, fol. 47, SWHAC.

47. "Commission on Interracial and Intercultural Relations," 7 March 1943, AJK Papers, fol. 48, SWHAC.

48. Minutes of the Study and Planning Committee, 28 April 1950, CC Records, box 22, CHS.

49. John H. Ramey, director, Hyde Park Neighborhood Club, "On with the Dance," 18 May 1956, NFS Training Center Records, Race Relations file, CHS.

50. Hamilton-Madison House board minutes, 9 Feb. 1960, HSS Records, fol. 71:5, SWHAC.

51. Board minutes, 28 March 1952, HH Records, fol. 10, Special Collections, U of Ill., C.

52. First Evaluation Report of the Community Services Center," November 1961, NFS Training Center Records, Race Relations file, CHS.

53. Chester R. Leighty, "People Working Together," NFS pamphlet, 1960, pp. 16–17, NFS Records, fol. 59, SWHAC.

54. Summary of membership application, 28 Jan. 1953, NFS Records, fol. 46, SWHAC.

55. "Findings of a Survey Undertaken by Kingsley House and New Orleans Day Nursery Association Between August 23, 1963, and October 25, 1963," NFS Training Center Records, Race Relations file, CHS.

56. Drake, *Race Relations,* p. 113.

57. *Ibid.,* p. 115.

58. Arthur Hillman to Mrs. Opal Jones, NFS Training Center, 17 Feb. 1965, Race Relations file, NFS Training Center Records, CHS.

59. Helen Mandlebaum, "Bethlehem Center, Atlanta, Georgia," 13 Jan. 1965, NFS Training Center Records, CHS.

60. Drake, *Race Relations,* p. 118.

61. "One delegated by many" to Mr. Sarle, 13 March 1941, Benton House Records, box 3, CHS.

62. LT, "Interview Joe Brindisi," 17 Nov. 1947, CC Records, box 31, CHS.

63. Glenford Lawrence, "Notes on an Interview with Father Alex . . . Nov. 24, 1953," CC Records, box 36, CHS.

64. "Record concerning visit with Alderman Mathew Biszcat . . . November 5, 1957," CC Records, box 43, CHS.

65. "Notes on the Orientation Sessions for Summer Staff . . . June 19 and 20, 1950," p. 4, CC Records, box 33, CHS.

66. "Swimming Pool Incident," 1965, University Settlements Records, Acc. 155, box 1, Urb A.

67. "Report of the Secretary to the Corporation of the Good Shepherd Community Center," 19 June 1941, Parkway Community House Papers, box 1, CHS.

68. Horace R. Cayton, director, to J. E. Stamps, president of the board, 4 Aug. 1948, Parkway Community Center Papers, box 2, CHS.

69. Horace R. Cayton to the board of Parkway Community House, 6 Oct. 1943, Parkway Community Center Papers, box 1, CHS.

70. St. Clair Drake and Horace R. Cayton, *Black Metropolis: A Study of Negro Life in a Northern City* (New York: Harcourt, Brace, 1945).

71. Nancy Weiss, *The National Urban League, 1910–1940* (New York: Oxford University Press, 1974), p. 168.

72. Billing for dues, May 1948, UNH Records, fol. 402, SWHAC; "Report of the Committee on Intercultural and Interracial Relations-NFS," 1942–43, p. 12, NFS Supp. 33:8, SWHAC.

73. Robert L. Neal, Welfare Council, to Gaines T. Bradford, acting executive secretary, Urban League of Pittsburgh, 16 March 1949, Welfare Council Records, box 243, CHS.

74. Robert L. Neal, "Memo to File," 6 Oct. 1948, Welfare Council Records, box 243, CHS.

75. "The South Side Settlement House," 12 Feb. 1948, Welfare Council Records, box 243, CHS.

76. C. Francis Stradford, board president, Ada S. McKinley Community House, to William Brueckner, 25 Oct. 1949, CC Records, box 33, CHS.

77. "Ada S. McKinley Community House," 22 Jan. 1960, Welfare Council Records, box 243, CHS.

78. Charles F. Wright, Welfare Council, to Alexander Ropehan, 11 Sept. 1964, Welfare Council Records, box 243, CHS.

79. Ada S. McKinley Community Services, "Service Report," 26 Sept. 1966, Welfare Council Records, box 243, CHS.

80. "Digest of Action—Board of Directors Meeting," 24–25 Jan. 1958, NFS Records, fol. 32, SWHAC.

81. Helen G. Laue, Welfare Council, "Memo to Files Re: Prairie Courts," 12 July 1955, Welfare Council Records, box 243, CHS.

82. "Report of the Interracial and Intercultural Commission" [early 1940s], AJK Papers, fol. 47, SWHAC.

83. AJK, "Why and How of Settlement Federations" [1944], AJK papers, fol. 19, SWHAC.

84. LT, head of CC, to her sister, Katharine Taylor, 13 May 1944, CC Records, box 29, CHS.

85. "Re: 647 N. Morgan Street," 2 April 1945, CC Records, box 30, CHS.

86. LT to John Joseph Ryan, director, Rental Division, OPA, 11 May 1946, CC Records, box 30, CHS.

87. LT to Edwin R. Embree, chairman, Mayor's Committee on Race Relations, 9 Feb. 1946, LT Papers, box 20, CHS.

88. Minutes, Housing Committee of the Commission on Human Relations, 5 Aug. 1948, LT Papers, box 20, CHS.

89. LT, "My Faith and My Neighbors: CC," *Christian Century* (7 May 1952), 69:553–554.

90. "The Fire at 940–942 West Ohio Street, Midnight Thursday, October 9, 1947," CC Records, box 20, CHS.

91. Board minutes, 17 Dec. 1947, CC Papers, box 20, CHS.

92. "Neighbors Protest Themselves," *Round Table* (November 1953), vol. 17.

93. Board minutes, 10 June 1959, University Settlement Records, box 1, WRHS.

94. "Methods of Work in Interracial and Intercultural Relations," 23–27 Sept. 1942, AJK Papers, fol. 49, pp. 1–8 *passim*, fol. 49, SWHAC.

95. Elbert R. Tingley, director, Rankin Christian Center, to AJK, 11 Sept. 1945, AJK Papers, fol. 95, SWHAC.

96. Joseph W. Lee, adult education worker, CC, "Erie-Morgan Playlot," 30 June 1949, pp. 10–11, CC Records, box 32, CHS.

97. Drake, *Race Relations*, p. 1.

98. *Ibid.*, p. 167.

99. *Ibid.*, p. 26.

6. PROFESSIONAL REFORM—SETTLEMENT HOUSE STYLE

1. Taped interview with a director of South Side Settlement, Columbus, Ohio, 1965, p. 1, NFS Training Center Papers, "Various Files," CHS.

2. See Clarke Chambers, *Seedtime of Reform: American Social Service and Social Action: 1918–1933* (Minneapolis: University of Minnesota Press, 1963).

3. Press release, 2 Feb. 1968, UNH Supp., fol. 45:9, SWHAC.

4. "Digest of Action—Board of Directors Meeting," 2–3 Dec. 1949, NFS Records, fol. 29, SWHAC.

5. "Making Ends Meet on Less than $2,000 a Year: A Communication to the Joint Committee on the Economic Report from the Conference Group of Nine Voluntary Organizations Convened by the National Social Welfare Assembly" (Washington, D.C.: PO, 1951). Hall chaired the conference group, which included representatives from the Salvation Army, National Urban League, Travelers Aid, Catholic Charities, National Child Labor Committee, Family Service Association, Council of Jewish Federations and Welfare Funds, and the American Association of Social Work.

6. "Some Facts About Public Assistance Budget Reductions," p. 2, LT Papers, box 12, CHS.

7. Board minutes, 20 Feb. 1950, University of Chicago Settlements, McDowell Records, fol. 32, CHS.

8. Board minutes, 30–31 May 1953, NFS Records, fol. 30, SWHAC.

9. Committee on Policies and Procedures minutes, 3 April 1958, NFS Records, fol. 55, SWHAC.

10. Margaret Berry, executive director, NFS to "NFS Board Members," 20 Oct. 1961, NFS Records, fol. 33, SWHAC.

11. "Kingsley House Executive Quits," *New Orleans Times-Picayune*, 13 April 1949.

12. Emeric Kurtagh to Helen Hall, 26 May 1949, HSS Records, fol. 32:1, SWHAC.

13. Minutes, NFS Conference, 12 May 1951, reel 4, SWHAC.

14. NFS business meeting, "Resolutions," 12 May 1951, p. 3, NFS Records, reel 4, SWHAC.

15. Board minutes, 21 Jan. 1953, UNH Records, fol. 35, SWHAC.

16. *Ibid.,* 18 Feb. 1953.

17. William B. Whiteside, Amherst College, to Helen Hall, 3 June 1953, HSS Records, box 33, SWHAC.

18. See Judith Ann Trolander, *Settlement Houses and the Great Depression* (Detroit: Wayne State University Press, 1975), pp. 92–106.

19. LT to Rep. Joseph L. Rategan, Springfield, 4 April 1941, CC Records, box 38, CHS.

20. "Recommendations Pending Legislation," 19 May 1941, McDowell Papers, fol. 28, CHS.

21. "Selected Replies of Recent Questionnaire Sent to Member Houses in

Various Cities," 1961, Phyllis Wheatley Settlement House Records, box 10, MHS.

22. "Testimony of Fern M. Colborn Before Ways and Means Committee, House of Representatives," 17 Feb. 1961, Phyllis Wheatley Settlement House Records, box 10, MHS.

23. Elizabeth Handasyde, *City or Community* (London: National Council of Social Service, 1949), p. 29.

24. Board minutes, 4–5 Feb. 1949, NFS Records, fol. 28, SWHAC.

25. Helen Hall, "Speak from Experience: Tips for Agencies at Public Hearings," *Round Table* January–February 1953).

26. Helen Hall, "Empty Pay Envelopes—and Peace," *Survey Graphic* (October 1945), pp. 394–395.

27. Hall to Representative Leonard Farbstein, 24 June 1966, HSS Records, fol. 98:9, SWHAC. See also Helen Hall, *Unfinished Business* (New York: Macmillan, 1971), p. 165.

28. Hall, "To the Editor," *New York Times,* 18 Feb. 1967.

29. Board of Directors Resolutions, 18–21 May 1944, NFS Records, fol. 90, SWHAC.

30. Helen Hall, "Statement for the Committee on Ways and Means, U.S. House of Representatives, Re: H.R. 3920, Hospital Insurance Act of 1963 (otherwise known as the Anderson-King Bill)," HSS Records, box 33; Hall, "Statement Before the Health Subcommittee of the Committee on Labor and Public Welfare, U.S. Senate, on the 'National Health Act of 1947,' S. 545, introduced by Sen. Robert A. Taft," 27 June 1947, NFS Records, fol. 132; Hall, "Statement on H.R. 4222, 'Health Insurance Benefits Act of 1961,' Before the Committee on Ways and Means, U.S. House of Representatives," 26 July 1961, Helen Hall Papers, fol. 35:14; "Statement by Miss Helen Hall . . . Before the Subcommittee on the Judiciary, U.S. Senate, 18 Dec. 1961," Hall Papers, fol. 35:15, all in SWHAC.

31. "Settlement Papers: Community Studies and Related Documents—Books, Reports, Articles, Statements—from the HSS Files, 1933–1958," NFS Records, fol. 132, SWHAC.

32. President's Commission on the Health Needs of the Nation, *Building America's Health,* vol. 4 (Washington, D.C.: PO, ca. 1952). The study also was published in *Survey.* See Hall, "When Sickness Strikes a Family," *Survey* (January 1952), 88:26–27, 29.

33. "Health Costs and How Met," 1954, NFS Records, fol. 49, SWHAC.

34. Typescript, George W. Goetschius, "The National Health Service in Great Britain: Some Consumer Reactions," HSS Records, box 52, SWHAC.

35. "Case Studies on How the Aged Meet Hospital Bills," 18 July 1961, HSS Records, fol. 87:1, SWHAC.

36. HSS, "Medicine Show," October 1939, HSS Records, Paige box 2, SWHAC.

37. Staff minutes, 1 May 1963, HSS Records, fol. 29:14, SWHAC.

38. Executive Committee minutes, 8 April 1961, NFS Records, fol. 33, SWHAC.

39. NFS annual report, 1965–66, NFS Supp. Records, fol. 4:1, SWHAC.

40. "Statement of Chicago Federation of Settlements and Neighborhood Centers to Illinois Public Aid Commission Regarding Public Assistance Cuts," 3 March 1950, NFS Supp. Records, fol. 21:3, SWHAC.

41. Board minutes, 28 Nov. 1962, HH Records, fol. 16, U of Ill., C.

42. William Braden, "Do Settlements Have a Role Today?" press release for *Chicago Sun-Times*, May 10, 11, 12, 1964, Neighborhood House Association Records, box 1, U of Ill., C.

43. "Herbert Lehman's association with the settlements . . . ," September 1951, Helen Hall Papers, fol. 12:8, SWHAC.

44. UNH press release, "Hunger and Despair in Home Relief Families, Settlement Workers Find," 27 Nov. 1946, NFS Records, fol. 217, SWHAC.

45. Board minutes, 3 May 1946, Goodrich Social Settlement Records, box 2, fol. 1, WRHS.

46. Elizabeth Handasyde, *City or Community* (London: National Council of Social Service, 1949), p. 30.

47. Board minutes, 17 March 1970, GPFS Records, Acc. 258, Urb A.

48. "Hull House at the 50th Year," 1940, HH Records, fol. 363, U of Ill., C.

49. "People Are Our Business," annual report of Irene Kaufman Settlement, 22 Jan. 1950, Neighborhood Center Association Records, box 11, University of Pittsburgh Libraries.

50. "Taped Interview with a Director of a Settlement House" [South Side Settlement House, Columbus, 1965], NFS Training Center Records, "Various Files," CHS.

51. "Report of the Head Worker for April 1943," Northeast Neighborhood House Records, box 7, MHS.

52. John McDowell to "Executive Director," Reed Street Neighborhood House, 1949, Reed Street Neighborhood House Records, box 9, Urb A.

53. Board minutes, 9 Dec. 1949, Abraham Lincoln Centre Records, CHS.

54. Board minutes, 11 Dec. 1942, Newberry Records, box 99, Marcy-Newberry Records, U of Ill., C.

55. Board minutes, 18 Feb. 1958, Marcy Center, box 8, Marcy-Newberry Records, U of Ill., C.

56. "Service Report," September 1961, Henry Booth House Records, fol. 26, U of Ill., C.

57. "Kingdom House—Summary II" [1960s], NFS Training Center Records, Race Relations file, CHS.

58. Board minutes, 7 Nov. 1965, Neighborhood House Association Records, box 2, MHS.

59. Stanley Isaacs, president, UNH, to Coverly Fischer, president, Welfare and Health Council, 26 Jan. 1953, HSS Records, fol. 92:5, SWHAC.

60. Board minutes, 30 Nov. 1961, HH Records, fol. 15, U of Ill., C; board minutes, 18 April 1962, Abraham Lincoln Centre Records, CHS.

61. Board minutes, 11 March 1965, St. Martha's House/Houston Community Center Records, box 1, Urb A. This settlement objected to the pro-birth control stand, not the delay, of the NFS.

62. [Paul Jans?], "Determining Settlement Function," 1958, pp. 9–10, HH Records, fol. 208, U of Ill., C. According to Arthur Hillman, in *Neighborhood Centers Today, Action, Programs for a Rapidly Changing World: Report of a Survey* (New York: NFS, 1960), p. 176, Meals-on-Wheels was patterned after a World War II civil defense program in England.

63. Lighthouse annual report, 1957, HH Records, fol. 218, U of Ill., C.

64. Robert H. MacRae, executive director, Welfare Council of Metropolitan Chicago, to James C. Brown IV, Chicago Community Trust, 27 April 1960, Welfare Council Records, box 243, CHS.

65. *Christopher News* (30 March 1962), (3):1–2, Christopher House Records, box 3, and Sister Mary William to Rt. Rev. Msgr. Vincent W. Cooke, archdiocesan supervisor of charities, 6 Feb. 1964, Marillac House Records, box 2, both in the CHS.

66. Minutes, Greater Cleveland Neighborhood Centers, 25 Feb. 1964, East End Neighborhood House Records, box 4, fol. 2, WRHS.

67. Sister Mary William to Mr. Faye Robinson, Cook County Department of Public Aid, 18 May 1965, Marillac House Records, box 2, CHS.

68. "Neighbors at Work," 17 Jan. 1964, Marillac House Records, box 2, CHS.

69. "Report of the Head Worker," February 1942, Northeast Neighborhood House, box 7, MHS.

70. Board minutes, 9–10 Dec. 1939, NFS microfilm, reel 3, SWHAC.

7. SETTLEMENT HOUSES LOSE INFLUENCE: THE SOCIOLOGICAL ATTACK

1. Among other sources, Alinsky stated his ideas in *Reveille for Radicals* (New York: Vintage, 1969; originally published by the University of Chicago Press in 1946) and *Rules for Radicals: A Practical Primer for Realistic Radicals* (New York: Random House, 1971).

2. Sidney Dillick, secretary, Group Work Division, Providence Council of Social Agencies, "Some Problems of Social Work Practice in Community Organization," 9 April 1949, Wilbur I. Newstetter Papers, box 14, University of Pittsburgh Libraries.

3. Francis Bosworth, executive director, Friends Neighborhood Guild, "Organization in the Neighborhood or Small Community," paper presented at the National Conference on Social Welfare, Minneapolis, 18 May 1961, in Friends Neighborhood Guild Records, box 66, fol. 263, Urb A.

4. Alinsky, *Reveille for Radicals*, p. 67.

5. Saul Alinsky and Marion K. Sanders, *The Professional Radical: Conversations with Saul Alinsky* (Evanston: Harper and Row, 1970), pp. 41–42.

6. Clipping, " 'United Neighbors' Put Areas on Road to Self-Betterment," *Philadelphia Evening Bulletin,* 8 Nov. 1956, in United Neighbors Association Records, box 21, SWHAC.

7. Community Workers Committee Minutes, 23 Jan. 1957, GPFS Records, fol. II/I/44, Urb A.

8. Board minutes, 25 April 1958, p. 3, HH Records, fol. 13, U of Ill., C.

9. "Community Organization Unit Conference," 2 Nov. [1961?], Friends Neighborhood Guide Records, box 66, Urb A.

10. Annual report, Manhattanville Community Centers, 1958–59, p. 6, Ephemera Collection, "New York–Manhattanville Community Centers" fol., SWHAC.

11. "The Settlement Approach to Neighborhoods" [ca. 1960], NFS Training Center Records, Neighborhood Organization file, CHS.

12. Board minutes, 6 Jan. 1943, Goodrich Social Settlement Records, box 2, fol. 1, WRHS.

13. John McDowell, "The Cleveland Settlement Study," 1946, p. 25, University Settlement Records, box 7, fol. 1, WRHS.

14. Neighborhood Services Section of the Community Chest minutes, 7 Jan. 1959, GPFS Records, box 2, Urb A.

15. Board minutes, 22 Oct. 1965, Friendly Inn, box 10, fol. 3, WRHS.

16. Welfare Federation of Metropolitan Chicago, "Special Report on Chicago Community Councils," January 1953, CC Records, box 36, CHS.

17. Marguerite Sylla, head, monthly report, November 1939, p. 1, University of Chicago Settlement Records, box 19, CHS.

18. Lucy Carner to Ernest W. Burgess, 5 April 1943, Gads Hill Center Records, box 14, CHS.

19. Minutes of a meeting between representatives of the Back of the Yards Council and University of Chicago Settlement called by the Council of Social Agencies, 30 Aug. 1944, Mary McDowell Papers, fol. 29, CHS.

20. Board minutes, 2 April 1945, Mary McDowell Papers, fol. 30, CHS.

21. "A Statement by the Board of Directors of the University of Chicago Settlement," September 1945, Mary McDowell Papers, fol. 30, CHS.

22. Board minutes, 17 Jan. 1949, Mary McDowell Papers, fol. 31, CHS.

23. Fern Colborn, NFS, "Confidential Report on 'Back of the Yards Area Council,'" 15 Jan. 1955, NFS Records, fol. 211, SWHAC.

24. "Afternoon Program," November 1947, p. 1, University of Chicago Settlement Records, box 19, CHS.

25. Board minutes, 20 Oct. 1947, Mary McDowell Papers, fol. 30, CHS.

26. Joseph B. Meegan, executive secretary, Back of the Yards Neighborhood Council, to Jacob Logan Fox, board chairman, Mary McDowell Settlement, 8 Jan. 1962, University of Chicago Settlement Records, box 3, CHS.

27. Board minutes, 16 Dec. 1963, University of Chicago Settlement Records, box 2, CHS.

28. David Finks, *The Radical Vision of Saul Alinsky* (Ramsey, N.J.: Paulist Press, 1984), p. 95.

29. *Ibid.*, pp. 95–100.

30. Joan E. Lancourt, *Confront or Concede: The Alinsky Citizen-Action Organization* (Lexington, Mass.: D.C. Health, 1979), p. 128.

31. "The Following Material Has Been Prepared by H. Daniel Carpenter, the Executive Director of Hudson Guild, and the Director of the Chelsea Citizen Participation Project from September 1956 to September 1958" [1965], GPFS Records, Acc. 258, box 1, Urb A. See also Lancourt, *Confront or Concede*, pp. 7–8, 128–29, 137. A 1957 NFS publication on how to bring about citizen participation quoted Dan Carpenter at length, but never mentioned Alinsky or his methods. The pamphlet contained such advice as "Avoid calling large meetings unless (1) they are needed for general education purposes, or (2) you are prepared to help people dissipate hostility and project their feelings constructively." Instead of Carpenter being ousted, Finks claims Carpenter walked out after failing to oust Father Dunn (Finks, *The Radical Vision*, p. 105).

32. Saul D. Alinsky to W. H. Brueckner, 16 Nov. 1961, NFS Training Center Records, Neighborhood Organization file, CHS.

33. Hillel Black, "This Is War," 25 Jan. 1964, *Post*, NFS Training Center Records, Neighborhood Organization file, CHS.

34. William H. Brueckner to "Members of the Board of Directors," 2 Feb. 1965, CC Records, box 46, CHS.

35. Near Northwest Side Planning Commission minutes, 7 Nov. 1962, CC Records, box 51, CHS.

36. Brueckner to "Members of the Board of Directors," 2 Feb. 1965, CC Records, box 26, CHS.

37. John H. Ramey, "Interview with William H. Brueckner," ca. 1965, NFS Training Center Records, Race Relations file, CHS.

38. Lancourt, *Confront or Concede*, pp. 11–14, 123, 151.

39. Conversation with Frank Seever, Minneapolis, 1 May 1986.

40. "Rochester, New York—Information Prepared by Mrs. DeLeslie (Loma) Allen About Baden Street Settlement and the FIGHT Organization," 10 Feb. 1966, GPFS Records, Acc. 258, box 1, Urb A. See also Lancourt, *Confront or Concede*, p. 66.

41. Sidney J. Lindenberg, executive director, Baden Street Settlement, to Arthur Hillman, director of NFS Training Center, 10 March 1967, NFS Training Center Records, Neighborhood Organization file, CHS.

42. "Rochester, New York—Information Prepared by Mrs. DeLeslie (Loma) Allen About Baden Street Settlement and the FIGHT Organization,"

43. "Workshop IV—'Boards and Board Committees,' " 13 Jan. 1967, NFS Training Center Records, Neighborhood Organization file, CHS.

44. The kit and related materials may be found in NFS Supp. Records, fols. 32:1–2, SWHAC.

45. George Brager and Harry Specht, *Community Organizing* (Columbia University Press, 1973), p. 274.

46. Board minutes, Hamilton-Madison House, 12 Dec. 1961, in HSS Records, fol. 71:6, SWHAC.

47. Trolander, *Settlement Houses and the Great Depression* (Detroit: Wayne State University Press, 1975), p. 152.

48. William F. Whyte, *Street Corner Society: The Social Structure of an Italian Slum,* 2d ed. (Chicago: University of Chicago Press, 1955), p. 103.

49. Herbert J. Gans, "The Settlement House and the Attack on Urban Poverty," paper presented to the Northeastern Regional Conference, NFS, 3 May 1963, University House (Philadelphia), *passim,* University Settlement Records, Acc. 155, box 1, "Annual meeting, 1963" fol., Urb A.

50. Herbert J. Gans, "Redefining the Settlement's Function for the War on Poverty," *Social Work* (October 1964), 9:5.

51. *Ibid.,* p. 6.

52. *Ibid.,* p. 12.

53. *Ibid.,* p. 7.

54. Gans, "The Settlement House."

55. Herbert Gans, *The Urban Villagers: Group and Class in the Life of Italian Americans* (New York: Free Press of Glencoe, 1962), pp. 150–53.

56. Margaret Berry to Herbert J. Gans, 25 July 1963, NFS Supp. Records, fol. 35:5, SWHAC.

57. Margaret Berry, "Points and Viewpoints: Mr. Gans Is Challenged," *Social Work* (January 1965), pp. 104–107.

58. Wilbur Cohen, "L'Envoi," in "Flowers from Arden House," 1958, UNH Supp. Records, fol. 59:15, SWHAC.

59. Clipping, "Miss Carr Blames Hull House Board," *New York Times,* 5 Jan. 1943, NFS Records, fol. 294, SWHAC.

60. LT, head of CC, to Lillie Peck, executive secretary, NFS Records, fol. 294, SWHAC. Taylor soon hired Brueckner to direct Emerson House.

61. Margaret Berry, comments on Lloyd Ohlin's paper "The Problem of Conformity in American Society Today," National Conference on Social Welfare, 1957, p. 3, in NFS Supp. Records, fol. 34:10, SWHAC.

62. Interview with Howard Karger, social work professor, and Marcy Shapiro, community organizer, 27 Dec. 1983, in Duluth, Minnesota.

63. Philip L. Holstein, "The Social Settlement Movement and Neighborhood Social Services: Past, Present, and Future" (senior paper, Hampshire College, 1976), p. 81, in SWHAC.

64. Margaret Berry to Judith Ann Trolander, 23 April 1986.

65. "Report of Consultation on Development Plans for Federations," 1–2 Feb. 1959, NFS Supp. Records, fol. 30:13, SWHAC.

66. Interview with Camillo DeSantis, director of Management and Leadership Development, United Way of Minneapolis, 2 Feb. 1984.

67. UNH, "Planning a Citywide Fund-Raising Campaign for Settlement Houses," 19 Nov. 1971, Hall Ephemera, SWHAC.

8. FIGHTING THE EFFECTS OF POVERTY: FROM JUVENILE DELINQUENCY
TO THE GREAT SOCIETY

1. Rex M. Johnson, Council of Social Agencies, Rochester, "Present Day Settlement Ojectives" [1950?], pp. 3–4, NFS Records, fol. 207 SWHAC.

2. Clifford Manshardt, director, Bethlehem House, *Out of Bethlehem* (October 1945), p. 2, Bethlehem-Howell Records, Bethlehem, box 31, U of Ill., C.

3. Allen F. Davis and Mary Lynn McCree, eds., *Eighty Years at Hull-House* (Chicago: Quadrangle, 1969), p. 214.

4. Board minutes, 10 Oct. 1946, University Settlement Records, box 1, fol. 1, WRHS.

5. Board minutes, 15 March 1951, University Settlement Records, box 1, fol. 2, WRHS.

6. Russell Ballard, testimony before Finance Committee, U.S. Senate, on H.R. 6000, 26 Jan. 1950, Ballard Papers, Supp. I, fol. 18, U of Ill., C. Ballard had given similar testimony before congressional committees in 1946 and 1949.

7. Irving M. Kriegsfeld, testimony representing the NFS at a hearing before the Senate Subcommittee on Juvenile Delinquency, 22 Jan. 1954, NFS Records, fol. 51, pp. 6–7, SWHAC.

8. John McDowell testifying for the NFS before the U.S. Senate Special Subcommittee on Juvenile Delinquency, 17 Nov. 1955, NFS Records, fol. 53, SWHAC.

9. Fern M. Colborn, "Testimony for the Subcommittee on Juvenile Delinquency of the Senate Committee on Labor and Public Welfare," 29 April 1959, NFS Records, fol. 57, SWHAC.

10. William H. Brueckner, "Testimony for the Special Subcommittee on Education, U.S. House of Representatives," 17 July 1961, NFS Supp., fol. 60:10, SWHAC.

11. "Resolutions Adopted at the Annual Meeting," 18 May 1957.

12. Family Division of the Health and Welfare Council, "Report of the Committee on Inter-Agency Referrals," June 1960, pp. 4–5, GPFS Records, box 4, Urb A.

13. Friendly Inn to Unreached Youth Advisory Committee, 4 May 1955, Friendly Inn Records, box 7, fol. 4, WRHS.

14. "Termination Report on Jaguar Club," 11 Aug. 1959, Friendly Inn Records, box 7, fol. 4, WRHS.

15. Judith R. Arnold, "Register: The Friendly Inn Social Settlement," 7 May 1973 [Friendly Inn Records?], WRHS.

16. Service report, CC Association, 1 Sept. 1960, p. 9, CC Records, box 5A, CHS.

17. "Service Report for Association House," October 1964, pp. 1125f., Association House Records, box 4, CHS.

18. Robert Parkhurst, "Report on the Special Youth Project," June 1965–

January 1966, University Settlements Records, Acc. 155, box 1, Urb A. The two settlements employing New York City workers were University Settlement and Dixon House.

19. Brueckner to Gideon W. Fryer, School of Social Work, University of Tennessee, 14 Feb. 1955, CC Records, box 38, CHS.

20. Board minutes, 27 April 1954, CC Records, box 21, CHS.

21. Brueckner to Fryer, 14 Feb. 1955.

22. Robert M. Johnston, Jr., "The Street—a Social Worker's Office," "Chicago Life" section of the *Chicago Daily News,* March 1962, pp. 4–6.

23. Service report, 20 Nov. 1957, pp. 8–9; service report, 1958, p. 3; service report, 1 Sept. 1960, p. 2; all in CC Records, box 52, CHS.

24. "Breaking Through Barriers," 4 June 1959, CC Records, box 21, CHS.

25. Beverly Luther and Harold H. Weissman, "Adolescent Service Centers," in Harold H. Weissman, ed., *Individual and Group Services in the MFY Experience* (New York: Association Press, 1969), pp. 163, 165–168.

26. "Mayfield-Murray Hill District Council Newsletter," May 1969, Alta Social Settlement, box 5, fol. 3, WRHS.

27. Helen Hall, *Unfinished Business* (New York: Macmillan, 1971), p. 248.

28. Janet P. Murray, assistant executive director, UNH, to John N. Haddad, executive director, St. Christopher House, Toronto, 1 May 1958, UNH Supp. Records, fol. 60:10, SWHAC.

29. Jacob Markowitz, justice, New York County Court House, to Grove Press, 30 Dec. 1964, HSS Records, Paige box 1, SWHAC.

30. Board minutes, 21 July 1969, p. 2, Association House Records, box 4, CHS. Association House helped finance the clinic at Erie.

31. Hall, *Unfinished Business,* p. 249.

32. Ruth S. Tefferteller, "Delinquency Prevention Through Revitalizing Parent-Child Relations," *Annals of the American Academy of Political and Social Science* (March 1959), 322:69–78 *passim.*

33. "Pre-delinquent Gang Project, 1956–1966," p. 1, HSS Records, fol. 66:10, SWHAC.

34. "Friends Neighborhood Guild—Functional Services" [1967?], Friends Neighborhood Guild Records, box 21, fol. 48, Urb A.

35. "Service Report for Association House," 1965, Association House Records, box 4, CHS.

36. Joseph Helfgot, *Professional Reforming* (Lexington, Mass.: Heath, 1983), p. 16.

37. "MFY: Working Paper—Draft No. 2," 17 July 1957, HSS Records, fol. 79:5, SWHAC.

38. Minutes, Hamilton-Madison board, 9 Sept. 1958, HSS, box 32, SWHAC.

39. Helen Hall, "A Note on the Inception and Impact of MFY," 10 March 1967, p. 3, HSS Records, fol. 80:4, SWHAC.

40. Joseph Weisheba, "James E. McCarthy: Youth Project Official," *New York Post,* 11 Jan. 1960.

41. Board minutes, of Hamilton-Madison House, 10 Jan. 1961, HSS Records, fol. 71:6, SWHAC.

42. Helen Hall to Jacob Kaplan of the Kaplan Foundation, 9 July 1959, HSS Records, fol. 25:15, SWHAC.

43. Helen Hall, "A Note on the Inception and Impact of MFY," p. 4.

44. Helfgot, *Professional Reforming*, pp. 32–33.

45. *Ibid.*, p. 28.

46. Henry Heifetz, "Introduction," in Harold H. Weissman, ed., *Community Development in the MFY Experience* (New York: Association Press, 1969), p. 19. According to Will Dodge, who had classes from Ohlin and Merton, Cloward and Ohlin got the theory from the sociologist Merton, who in turn got it from Emile Durkheim's work on suicide.

47. Helen Hall, "A Note on the Inception and Impact of MFY," p. 3. Currier and his wealthy wife established a foundation, the Taconic, which they named by combining parts of the names of their three children. The foundation probably would have achieved more fame, but the Curriers' generosity was cut short by Mr. and Mrs. Stephen Currier's untimely death in a plane crash.

48. "MFY, Sept. 8, 1959," pp. 51–52, HSS Records, fol. 79:11, SWHAC.

49. Hall, "A Note on the Inception and Impact of MFY," pp. 4–5.

50. "MFY, Sept. 8, 1959," p. 58, HSS Records, fol. 79:11, SWHAC.

51. Judith Ann Trolander, *Settlement Houses and the Great Depression* (Detroit: Wayne State University Press, 1975), p. 194.

52. "A Proposal for the Relationship Between the City of New York and MFY," 1 Sept. 1961, HSS Records, fol. 79:12, SWHAC.

53. Helfgot, *Professional Reforming*, p. 26.

54. Board minutes of Hamilton-Madison House, 12 Dec. 1961, HSS Records, fol. 71:6, SWHAC.

55. Beverly Luther, "Overview of Group Services," in Harold H. Weissman, ed., *Individual and Group Services in the MFY Experience* (New York: Association Press, 1969), p. 110.

56. O. Hettie Jones, "Overview of Services to Individuals and Families," in Harold H. Weissman, ed., *Individual and Group Services in the MFY Experience* (New York: Association Press, 1969), p. 28.

57. Trolander, *Settlement Houses*, p. 153.

58. "LENA Is Not a Lady" [1962?], in HSS Records, fol. 78:7, SWHAC.

59. Board minutes of Hamilton-Madison House, 12 Dec. 1961, HSS Records, fol. 71:6, SWHAC.

60. William Brueckner, "Testimony for the Special Sub-Committee on Education, U.S. House of Representatives," 17 July 1961, CC Records, box 45, CHS.

61. Service report, 1963–64, p. 7, and service report, 1964–65, p. 7, CC Records, box 5A, CHS.

62. Brueckner to Margaret Berry, 17 Dec. 1959, CC Records, box 45, CHS.

63. Richard Cloward, "A Review of Research in Conjunction with MFY," 1967, MFY Records, box 26, "Reports" fol., Columbia University.

64. Henry Heifetz, "Introduction," p. 20.

65. Helen Hall, *Unfinished Business* (New York: Macmillan, 1971), p. 98.

66. Harold H. Weissman, "Overview of the Community Development Program," in Harold Weissman, ed., *Community Development in the MFY Experience* (New York: Association Press, 1969), pp. 25–26.

67. *Ibid.*, pp. 26–27.

68. Helen Hall to Winslow Carlton, 17 Sept. 1962, in HSS Records, fol. 7:8, SWHAC. Carlton was chairman of both the Henry Street and MFY boards. However, the MFY staff did not function closely with its board, which grew to an unwieldy seventy or so members. Regarding the staff, Will Dodge, who worked for the Neighborhood Youth Corps for MFY one summer in the mid-1960s while studying for his Ph.D. at the New York School of Social Work, wrote in a note to me on 4 Jan. 1982, "My impression was that the personnel of settlements [staff] moved back and forth to MFY in a network fashion (like 'cousins' who were in the same family and therefore could be more critical of 'their own kind' ")."

69. MFY, "Parent Education" [1963?], HSS Records, Legal fol. 3:15, SWHAC.

70. Harold H. Weissman, "The Housing Program, 1962 to 1967," *Community Development in the MFY Experience* (New York: Association Press, 1969), pp. 50–51, 54–55.

71. Board minutes of Hamilton-Madison House, 12 March 1963, HSS Records, fol. 71:7, SWHAC.

72. Geoffrey Wiener, head of Hamilton-Madison, to "Mrs. Jones," a contributor, May 1963, HSS Records, box 33, SWHAC. The MFY grant was $25,000 for this program at Hamilton-Madison.

73. Ruth S. Tefferteller, Henry Street staff, to Helen Hall, 17 Feb. 1964, HSS Records, box 47, SWHAC.

74. Frances K. Kernohan, Junior League, to Helen Hall, 11 May 1964, HSS Records, fol. 82:6 SWHAC.

75. Herbert Krosney, "MFY: Feuding Over Poverty," *The Nation* (14 Dec. 1964), 199:459.

76. Frank Riessman, "Mobilizing the Poor," *Commonwealth* (21 May 1965), 82:285–289.

77. James A. Wecksler, "Fischel's Folly," *New York Post*, 7 Jan. 1965.

78. Homer Bigart, "Youth Unit Aide Ran as a Leftist," *New York Times*, 27 Aug. 1964, p. 30.

79. Riessman, "Mobilizing the Poor."

80. Krosney, "MFY: Feuding Over Poverty," p. 460.

81. Bertram Beck, "MFY: Reflections About Its Administration," in Harold H. Weissman, ed., *Justice and the Law* (New York: Association Press, 1969), p. 147.

82. Helen Hall, "A Note on the Inception and Impact of MFY," p. 6. Geoffrey Wiener, Hamilton-Madison head, in a private note to Hall (18 Sept. 1964, HSS Records, fol. 26:6, SWHAC), was hardly as gracious. He called MFY community organization efforts "a little juvenile . . . a little like cops-and-robbers . . . very dangerous and inflammatory and divisive." He also

criticized MFY staff for deliberately excluding the board from policymaking and keeping board members "ignorant of everything except carefully screened and predigested, general and positive reports."

83. Edward V. Sparer, director, Legal Services Unit, "Report on the Experiment in Settlement House Legal Clinics," 18 May 1965, HSS Records, fol. 62:4, SWHAC. The three were HSS, Educational Alliance, and University Settlement.

84. "Report on Progress and Status of Program: Integrated Pre-School and Parent Opportunity Centers," April 1967, HSS Records, box 32, SWHAC.

85. Helen Hall, "A Note on the Inception and Impact of MFY," pp. 6–7.

86. Bertram Back, "MFY: Reflections About Its Administration," p. 149.

87. "Suggested Questions for Discussion in Groups Following Wilbur Cohen's Presentation," 1958, UNH Records, 59:15, SWHAC.

88. "Citizen Participation," 18 April 1957, UNH Supp. Records, fol. 59:15, SWHAC.

89. Press release, 14 Feb. 1963, University Settlements Records, Acc. 155, box 1, "Women's Committee" fol., Urb A.

90. Board minutes, 14 Nov. 1962, UNH Supp. Records, fol. 3:5, SWHAC.

91. Annual report, July 1960–May 1961, UNH Supp. Records, fol. 2:4, SWHAC.

92. Margaret Berry to Attorney General Robert Kennedy, 4 Feb. 1963, NFS supp., fol. 29:9, SWHAC.

93. U.S. Representative Leonard Fabstein to Helen Hall, 6 May 1963, HSS Records, fol. 98:9, SWHAC.

94. "Progress Report—2nd Year of U.S. Government Health Services Demonstration Project at HSS House," 1964–65, HSS Records, fol. 58:9, SWHAC.

95. "Study Den Program" [1962], NFS Supp. Records, fol. 28:1, SWHAC.

96. "A Brief History of Houston Community Center: 1901–1969," 15 Jan. 1969, p. 4, St. Martha's House/Houston Community Center, box 1, Urb A.

97. "Firman House," September 1966, Firman House Records, fol. 7, U of Ill., C.

98. "Groups Further Aims of Team Teaching Project," *Pittsburgh Tribune,* 15 March 1962, Kingsley Association Records, box 4, University of Pittsburgh Libraries.

99. "Jobs for School Youth" [1962?], Friends Neighborhood Guild Records, box 3, fol. 207, Urb A.

100. Francis Bosworth, executive director, Friends Neighborhood Guild, to Seymour Wolfbine, 25 Jan. 1963, Friends Neighborhood Guild Records, box 53, fol. 202, Urb A.

101. Francis Bosworth to Congressman William Green, 17 Sept. 1962, requested help in getting the Opportunities Act out of the Rules Committee, Guild Records, box 63, fol. 200. Bosworth to Senator Joseph S. Clark mentioned Hubert Humphrey's support for fifty-fifty matching funds for programs like Jobs for Youth: Guild Records, box 63, fol. 202, Urb A.

102. Occupation Planning Committee, "Inventory of Youth Employment

Program, Projects, and Services in Cleveland," June 1961, pp. 4, 5, University Settlement Records, box 9, fol. 1, WRHS. The list also included projects at University Settlement and Friendly Inn.

103. "Service Report—Olivet Community Center," 1961, p. 5, Olivet Community Center Records, box 3, CHS.

104. Neighborhood House, North Richmond, California, annual report, 1962, p. 3, NFS Training Center, Race Relations file, CHS.

105. Board minutes, 16 Oct. 1963, UNH Supp. Records, fol. 3:6, SWHAC.

106. "Statement of Helen M. Harris . . . Before the Subcommittee on Employment and Manpower, Senate Committee on Labor and Public Welfare on S. 2036, the Youth Employment Opportunities Act of 1961," 23 June 1961, UNH Supp. Records, fol. 4:12, SWHAC.

107. Mrs. Elizabeth Day, field secretary, NFS, to Robert E. Shrider, Bethlehem Community Center, 13 Nov. 1962, NFS Supp., fol. 58:9, SWHAC.

108. Minutes of the Study and Planning Committee, 28 April 1950, CC Records, box 22, CHS.

109. Board minutes, Hamilton-Madison House, 14 April 1959, in HSS Records, fol. 71:5, SWHAC.

110. Antoinette Fried, director of Group Work, James Weldon Johnson Community Center, "The Youth March for Integrated Schools—the News Behind the Headlines," *Round Table* (Summer 1959), pp. 5–6, NFS Records, fol. 205, SWHAC.

111. Laurel Bolgiano, Teen Program supervisor, Hamilton-Madison House, "Social Issues and Teenagers," 7 Dec. 1960, HSS House Records, fol. 71:10–11, SWHAC.

112. Ann Tompkins, Junior Program supervisor, Hamilton-Madison House, "Social Issues and Young Adults," 7 Dec. 1960, HSS records, fol. 71:10–11, SWHAC.

113. Hudson Guild, "Newsletter," May 1960, HSS Records, box 38, SWHAC.

114. United Neighborhood Houses, "Settlements Join March on Washington," 25 Aug. 1963, UNH Records, Supp. 3, Paige box 16, "Washington Rally" fol., SWHAC.

115. Board minutes, Hamilton-Madison House, 10 Sept. 1963, HSS Records, fol. 71:7, SWHAC.

116. David M. Goldenburg, executive director, Hamilton-Madison House, to "Board Member," 7 Aug. 1964, HSS Records, fol. 72:1, SWHAC.

117. William E. Leuchtenburg, *A Troubled Feast* (Boston: Little, Brown. 1973), p. 160.

118. Helen M. Harris, executive director, United Neighborhood Houses, to her Executive Division and Youth Program staff [Fall 1964], UNH Records, Supp. 3, Paige box 16, "Schwerner Memorial" fol., SWHAC.

119. Daniel G. Karue, principal, P.S. 175M, to Stanley Isaacs, president, United Neighborhood Houses, 15 Dec. 1961, and Milton Yale, executive director, Harlem Neighborhoods Association, to Isaacs, 19 Dec. 1961, both

in UNH Records, Supp. 3, Paige box, 1, "Harlem Neighborhoods Association" fol., SWHAC.

120. Stanley Isaacs to Milton Yale, 2 Jan. 1962, UNH Records, Supp. 3, Paige box 1, "Harlem Neighborhoods Association" fol., SWHAC.

121. Kenneth B. Clark, *Dark Ghetto: Dilemmas of Social Power* (New York: Harper and Row, 1965), p. xiii.

9. THE WAR ON POVERTY "SAVES" THE SETTLEMENTS

1. Richard A. Cloward, "The War on Poverty: Are the Poor Left Out?" *The Nation*, 2 Aug. 1965, pp. 59–60.

2. Helen Harris to Mrs. May Taylor Thomas, Eugene, Oregon, author of a letter to *The Nation* criticizing Cloward's attitude toward the settlements, 9 Aug. 1965, UNH Supp., fol. 45:8, SWHAC.

3. Cloward, "The War on Poverty," p. 59.

4. Juliet Brudney to James G. Patton, National Farmers Union, 8 Nov. 1965, UNH Supp. Records, fol. 35:5, SWHAC.

5. Board minutes, 19 Jan. 1966, UNH Supp. Records, fol. 3:9, SWHAC.

6. Staff meeting minutes, 28 June 1966, UNH Supp. Records, fol. 3:9, SWHAC.

7. Board minutes, 27 Oct. 1966, UNH Supp. Records, fol. 3:9, SWHAC.

8. Cloward, "The War on Poverty," p. 58.

9. Conversation with Will Dodge, 5 Jan. 1982.

10. Annual report, NFS, 1965–66, HSS Records, box 8, SWHAC.

11. Richard Cosswiller, "Hull House, a New Face" (1967), in Allen F. Davis and Mary Lynn McCree, eds., *Eighty Years at Hull-House* (Chicago: Quadrangle, 1969), p. 250.

12. Board minutes, 24 Sept. 1965, HH Records, fol. 18, U of Ill., C. The federal Public Health Service financed Home Delivered Meals, board minutes, 13 Sept. 1965, Olivet Community Center Records, box 3, CHS.

13. Interview with Camillo DeSantis, 2 Feb. 1984, in Minneapolis.

14. Helen Hall to Mrs. Anne M. Roberts, staff director, Antipoverty Operations Board, 17 Aug. 1965, HSS Records, fol. 122:14, SWHAC. Hall's letter to Peterson is attached to the letter to Roberts.

15. "Newsletter," October 1964, Baden Street Settlement Records, fol. 89, SWHAC.

16. "New York City Council Against Poverty," October 1966, HSS Records, fol. 122:14, SWHAC.

17. Executive Committee minutes, 11 Nov. 1964, NFS microfilm, reel 4, SWHAC.

18. Board minutes, 29–30 Jan. 1965, NFS microfilm, reel 4, SWHAC.

19. Neighborhood House, annual report, 1964, NFS Training Center Records, Race Relations file, CHS.

20. "Philadelphia Anti-Poverty Action Committee: University Settlements

Community Action Proposal," November 1965, University Settlements Records, Acc. 155, box 2, Urb A.

21. Board minutes, 16 Dec. 1964, UNH Supp. Records, fol. 3:7, SWHAC. In the late 1930s and early 1940s, Harris was the New York City administrator of the National Youth Administration.

22. "Head of Poverty Unit Resigns," *New York Times,* 21 April 1966, p. 30.

23. Board minutes, Hamilton-Madison House, 15 Nov. 1966, HSS Records, fol. 71:9, SWHAC.

24. "Introduction to the Delaware Valley Settlement Alliance CAP," 1964, GPFS Records, box 2, Urb A.

25. DVSA Staff Committee on Community Concerns, 1 Dec. 1965, GPFS Records, Acc. 258, box 1, Urb A.

26. "The Kingsley Association: 1893–1968," Kingsley Association Records, box 4, University of Pittsburgh Libraries. According to Will Dodge, St. Paul settlements were the major agency group under the city's Community Action Program.

27. William Friedlander, "Neighborhood Organization Study—Milwaukee: Triple O–Northcott Neighborhood House," March 1967, NFS Training Center Records, Neighborhood Organization file, CHS.

28. *Delaware Valley Settlement Alliance Newsletter* (Winter 1964), GPFS Records, Acc. 258, box 1, Urb A.

29. "Neighborhood Organization Study: Summary of Major Finding and Guidelines," NFS Training Center Records, Neighborhood Organization file, CHS.

30. Delaware Valley Settlement Alliance, *DVSA Viewpoints* (March 1969), p. 1, GPFS Records, Acc. 258, box 1, Urb A.

31. "Report of the Staff Committee on Community Concerns," June 1968, GPFS Records, Acc. 258, Urb A.

32. "For Discussion and Action at the First Meeting of the GPFS," 8 April 1969, GPFS Records, Acc. 258, box 1, Urb A.

33. Board minutes, May 1968, NFS Supp. Records, fol. 2:2, SWHAC.

34. "Policy Statement of Friends Neighborhood Guild Board on the Poor People's Campaign, 1968," 1 May 1968, Friends Neighborhood Guild, box 21, fol. 49, Urb A. See also board minutes, 25 April 1968, St. Martha's House/Houston Community Center, box 1, Urb A.

35. Delegate Assembly minutes, 16 April 1968, GPFS Records, Acc. 258, box 1, Urb A.

36. "Project Report—Rat Control Program," 16 Nov. 1967, University Settlement, box 9, fol. 3, WRHS.

37. William Friedlander, "Some Aspects of Community Work of Settlement Staff," NFS Neighborhood Organization Conference, 21 March 1967, p. 4, NFS Training Center Records, Neighborhood Organization file, CHS.

38. "Freedom and Responsibility: A Committee Report to NCA of Hous-

ton and Harris County," Spring 1966, p. 7, NFS Training Center Records, Neighborhood Organization file, CHS.

39. "Negro History Month Celebrated," *DVSA Newsletter* (Spring 1967), GPFS Records, Acc. 258, box 1, Urb A.

40. "Newsletter," October 1964, Baden Street Settlement Records, fol. 89, SWHAC.

41. "Service Report to the Community Fund, September 1967–October 1968," p. 23, HH Records, fol. 399, U of Ill., C.

42. "Youth Center Director: More Changes Needed," *Minnesota Daily*, 29 July 1974.

43. United Bay Area Crusade, "Statement of Policy on Public Issues," 13 May 1964, NFS Records, Supp. 4, Paige box 1, "Civil Rights Questionnaire" fol., SWHAC.

44. Ramey, "Interview with Mrs. Onque," p. 9, Hallie Q. Brown House [1965], NFS Training Center Records, Race Relations file, CHS.

45. "Staff Freedom Aspects of Agency Policy" [1967], p. 4, NFS Training Center Records, Neighborhood Organization file, CHS.

46. Taylor, "Interview with Homer Bishop, executive director, Columbus Federation of Settlements" [1965], NFS Training Center Records, Race Relations file, CHS. The open housing advocate was Bernie Wohl of South Side Settlement.

47. Ramey, "Gads Hill Center, Chicago, Illinois," 1965, p. 2, NFS Training Center Records, Race Relations file, CHS.

48. Sister Mary William, head of Marillac, to "Richard," 11 Oct. 1965, Marillac House Records, box 3, CHS.

49. "Statement of Sister Mary William Sullivan . . . Regarding the Demonstration of June 12, 1965," Marillac House Records, box 2, CHS.

50. Mike Moore, "Fines Paid, Nuns Saved from Jail," *Chicago Daily News*, 9 Aug. 1965, p. 1. The attorney quoted was Maurice Scott, Jr. The other was Howard Geter, Jr.

51. Abra Prentice, "13 Nuns Spread Charity from High Rise to Alley," *Chicago Sun-Times*, 20 March 1966, clipping in Marillac House Records, box 3, CHS.

52. Sign-up list for King rally volunteers, 25 July 1965, Marillac House Records, box 3, CHS.

53. Press release, 1 May 1968, Marillac House Records, box 5, CHS.

54. "Statement from Hull House on School Boycott," 17 Oct. 1963, NFS Records, Supp. 4, Raige box 1, "Civil Rights Questionnaire" fol., SWHAC.

55. Ramey, "HH," 1965, NFS Training Center Records, Race Relations file, CHS.

56. St. Clair Drake, *Race Relations in a Time of Rapid Social Change* (New York: NFS, 1966), p. 45.

57. Alice Griffin, "Wharton Centre" [1965], NFS Training Center Records, Race Relations file, CHS.

58. Ramey, interview with Lillie Lynem, 1965, p. 5, NFS Training Center Records, "Race Relations" file, CHS.

59. "Confidential Memorandum to Citizens and Organizations Interested in Responding to the Needs of a Young Afro-American Organization," 29 April 1968, Germantown Settlement Records, box 1, Urb A.

60. Executive Director's Report, 21 Oct. 1968, Germantown Settlement Records, box 1, Urb A.

61. Staff minutes, 9 Dec. 1968, Germantown Settlement Records, box 2, Urb A.

62. "A Brief History of Houston Community Center: 1901–1969," 15 Jan. 1969, p. 5, St. Martha's House/Houston Community Center Records, box 1, Urb A.

63. "Federation Focus," February 1970, GPFS Records, Acc. 258, box 1, Urb A.

64. Sidney J. Lindenberg, executive director, Baden Street Settlement, to "Board and Committee Members," 28 July 1964, HSS Records, box 51, SWHAC.

65. Sidney J. Lindenberg, ed., *The Negro in the U.S.: A Guide to Understanding*, mimeographed 74-page booklet, 1964, Baden Street Settlement Records, fol. 90, SWHAC. This booklet was another example of Lindenberg's attempts to make sense out of the events.

66. "Newsletter," October 1964, Baden Street Settlement Records, fol. 89, SWHAC.

67. "Fellowship Commission—Committee on Community Tensions—Special Meeting on North Philadelphia Rioting and Looting," 3 Sept. 1964, Wharton Centre Records, box 4, fol. 58, Urb A.

68. Board minutes, 8 April 1968, Association House Records, box 4, CHS.

69. "Beacon Light," August 1966, p. 1, Uptown Center Records, U of Ill., C.

70. Sister Mary William to Charles H. Henderson, field representative, Great Lakes Region of VISTA, 2 Aug. 1966, Marillac House Records, box 4, CHS.

71. "Night Shift: July 20, 1966," Friendly Inn Records, box 6, fol. 5, WRHS.

72. Service report, 1966, Newberry Center Records, box 99, U of Ill., C.

73. Louise Larsen, executive director, Toberman Settlement House, "Volunteer Friendly Visiting Services to Families at Toberman Settlement House," *100,000 Hours a Week* (San Pedro, Calif.: NFS, 1965), pp. 31–38.

74. Sister Mary William, director of Marillac, to Mrs. Robert Allen, Marillac House Records, box 4, CHS.

75. "The Leadership Development Program," July 1967, Marillac House Records, box 4, CHS.

76. "The Marillac House Program for Neighborhood Leadership" [1966], Marillac House Records, box 4, CHS.

77. Board minutes of Greater Philadelphia Federation of Settlements, 12 Nov. 1968, GPFS Records, Acc. 258, box 1, Urb A.

78. Board minutes of University Settlement, 9 Sept. 1964, University Settlement Records, box 1, fol. 5, WRHS.

79. *Delaware Valley Settlement Alliance Newsletter* (Winter 1965), p. 1, GPFS Records, Acc. 258, box 1, Urb A.

80. Annual report, 1966–67, Germantown Settlement Records, box 1, Urb A.

81. VISTA, "The Jane Addams Training Center" [1965], Friendly Inn Records, box 13, fol. 3, WRHS. The settlements providing residence were Mary McDowell, Association House, Abraham Lincoln Centre, Benton House, Gads Hill Center, and Neighborhood Service Organization. Clarence Darrow arranged for VISTAs to live in a public housing project.

82. NFS Training Center, "Report for 1966," p. 2, NFS Training Center Records, Neighborhood Organization file, CHS.

83. Hull House press release, "HH Receives Urban Service Award from Office of Economic Opportunity," 6 Feb. 1968, UNCA office.

84. Roderick Rasmussen, VISTA volunteer, "School Drop-Outs," 8 Aug. 1966, HSS Records, fol. 130:6, SWHAC.

85. Mrs. Gallivan, VISTA volunteer, to Candido de Leon, MFY, 17 Jan. 1966, HSS Records, fol. 130:6, SWHAC.

86. "VISTA" [1966], HH Records, fol. 211, U of Ill., C.

87. "Spanish Center Plans New Program," *Spotlight* (December 1967), Paul Jans Papers, box 5, U of Ill., C.

88. Executive Committee minutes, 4 Jan. 1967, p. 2, HH Records, fol. 211, U of Ill., C.

89. Helen Hall to Mrs. Henderson [not sent but telephoned], 17 Jan. 1966, HSS Records, fol. 130:6, SWHAC; minutes of executive staff meeting, 4 Jan. 1967, p. 2, HH Records, fol. 211, U of Ill., C.

90. Minutes of executive staff meeting, 5 Oct. 1966, p. 2, HH Records, fol. 211, U of Ill., C.

91. Jim Wolf, VISTA supervisor, to Paul Jans, Hull House head, and Homer Bishop, 9 Dec. 1966, Uptown Center Records, box 7, fol. 15, U of Ill., C.

92. Board minutes, 23 May 1967, Germantown Settlement Records, box 1, Urb A.

93. Among those settlements with Head Start programs in 1965 were Olivet in Chicago (board minutes, 10 June 1965, Olivet Community Center Records, box 3, CHS), and Friendly Inn in Cleveland (board minutes, 28 May 1965, Friendly Inn Records, box 10, fol. 3, WRHS). Philadelphia called its program "Get Set," and settlements worked in cooperation with the Board of Education, *DVSA Newsletter* (Winter 1965), GPFS Records, Acc. 258, box 1, Urb A.

94. Minutes of the Delegate Assembly, 8 Dec. 1964, GPFS Records, Urb 11/1/47, Urb A. See also *DVSA Newsletter* (Summer 1965), GPFS Records, Acc. 258, box 1, Urb A, and *DVSA Newsletter* (Winter 1965), GPFS Records, Acc. 258, box 1, Urb A.

95. Forest Neighborhood House (Bronx), "Program Report," June 1967, HSS Records, fol. 99:4, SWHAC.

96. Juliet Brudney, UNH staff, to UNH member agencies, 30 Nov. 1966, UNH Supp. Records, fol. 5:15, SWHAC.

97. Board minutes, 10 June 1965, Olivet Community Center Papers, box 3, CHS.

98. *DVSA Newsletter* (Spring 1968), GPFS Records, Acc. 258, box 1, Urb A.

99. "Annual Report of Social Service Department," 1966, Marcy-Newberry Records, Marcy, box 8, U of Ill., C.

100. Philip S. How, executive director, and Frank S. Seever, consultant director, to Stephen B. Sweeney, chairman of the board, University Settlements, 24 Jan. 1966, University Settlements Records, Acc. 155, box 1, Urb A.

101. Margaret Berry, "Report on Neighborhood Service Programs Under Many Auspices," December 1967, NFS Supp. Records, fol. 2:1, SWHAC.

102. "Meeting on Agency Designs," 26 Sept. 1968, Recent NFS Ephemera, fol. 5, SWHAC.

103. Board minutes, 8 April 1968, Neighborhood House Association Records, box 2, MHS.

104. Judith Ann Trolander, *Settlement Houses and the Great Depression* (Detroit: Wayne State University Press, 1975), p. 158.

105. *News and Round Table* (April–July 1971), Northside Settlement Services Records, "NFS-1" fol., SWHAC.

106. Louis A. Zurcher et al., *From Dependency to Dignity: Individual and Social Consequences of a Neighborhood House* (New York: Behavioral Publications, 1969), *passim.*

107. "U.S. Cutback Bars Twelve New Projects To Aid City Poor," *New York Times,* 2 Jan. 1967, p. 1.

108. Board minutes, 6 Jan. 1967, p. 1, HH Records, fol. 18, U of Ill., C.

109. "Executive Director's Report to the Board of Directors of the Friends Neighborhood Guild—May-June 1968," Friends Neighborhood Guild Records, box 21, fol. 49, Urb A.

10. THE LEGACY OF THE WAR ON POVERTY: THE BLACK ASCENDANCY
WITHIN THE SETTLEMENT HOUSE MOVEMENT, FRAGMENTATION, AND
THE CONSERVATIVE SOCIAL CLIMATE

1. "Racial and Ethnic Composition of Neighborhoods Served by NFS Affiliates," 1969 NFS Supp. Records, fol. 45:3, SWHAC.

2. Interview with Jim Cook, 16 May 1984.

3. Interview with Camillo DeSantis, director, Management and Leadership Development, United Way of Minneapolis, 2 Feb. 1984.

4. Mrs. Frances Edwards Brueckner to Helen Hall, 1 Sept. 1968, Hall Papers, fol. 7:4, SWHAC.

5. Fern Colborn to Lois Buell, UNH, 29 Oct. 1965, UNH Supplement Records, fol. 59:16, SWHAC.

6. Bob Egan, former Henry Street staffer, to Helen Hall, 15 Jan. 1978, Hall Papers, fol. 8:7, SWHAC.

7. Interview with DeSantis, 2 Feb. 1984.

8. Ruby Pernell, "The Privilege of These Terrific Years," *Public Welfare* (28 July 1970), pp. 253–254.

9. "On October 17, 1966, the NFS and NC . . . ," NFS Supp. Records, fol. 16:1, SWHAC.

10. Executive Committee minutes, 25 June 1971, NFS Supp. Records, fol. 2:5, SWHAC.

11. Pernell, "The Privilege," p. 253.

12. *News and Round Table* (July–August 1969), Northside Settlement Services Records, box 1, "Hennepin County Federation of Settlements, 1967–1971" fol. SWHAC.

13. Berry to "Board Member," NFS Supp. Records, fol. 2:3, SWHAC.

14. Margaret E. Berry, "All Points of View," *NFS News and Round Table* (January 1969), Recent NFS Ephemera, fol. 3, SWHAC.

15. "Board Consensus—Black Settlement Conference" [1969], NFS Supp. Records, fol. 2:7, SWHAC.

16. "Full Agency Information for the National Budget and Consultation Committee," 1969, NFS Supp. Records, fol. 2:4, SWHAC.

17. Margaret Berry to John Austin, president, NFS, 4 March 1970, NFS Supp. Records, fol. 3:7, SWHAC.

18. *Ibid.*

19. Board minutes, February 1970, NFS Supp. Records, fol. 2:4, SWHAC.

20. Berry to Austin, 4 March 1970.

21. *Ibid.*

22. Kenneth L. Brown, head, United South End Settlements, "Notes: Northeast Regional Techni-Culture Meeting, New York City," 21 March 1970, NFS Supp. Records, fol. 45:3, SWHAC.

23. *Ibid.*

24. Clipping, "Strange Welcome: Convention Finds Policy Under Fire from Hosts," NFS Supp. Records, fol. 43:6, SWHAC.

25. Minutes of the annual meeting, 30 May 1970, NFS Supp. Records, fol. 43:6, SWHAC.

26. "Remarks of Arthur C. Logan, M.C.," 30 May 1970, UNH Supp. Records, fol. 59:17, SWHAC.

27. Clipping, "Strange Welcome: Convention Finds Policy Under Fire from Hosts." NFS Supp. Records.

28. Biographies of NFS board members, 1967, NFS Supp. Records, fol. 3:1, SWHAC.

29. "NFS Prexy Named Judge," *News and Round Table* (April–July 1971), Northside Settlement Services Records, "NFS-1" fol., SWHAC.

30. Minutes, Hennepin Country Federation of Settlements and Neigh-

borhood Centers, 1 Feb. 1971, Northside Settlement Services Records, box 1, "Hennepin County Federation of Settlements, 1967–1971" fol., SWHAC.

31. "Full Agency Information for NBC," March 1971, Recent NFS Ephemera, fol. 3, SWHAC.

32. Lindsay Miller, "Daily Closeup: Up-to-Date History," *New York Post,* 11 Feb. 1972.

33. Press release, "The NFS, founded in 1911 by Jane Addams and Lillian Wald . . ." [1971], Recent NFS Ephemera, fol. 1, SWHAC.

34. DeSantis, 2 Feb. 1984.

35. Interview with Walter Smart, 13 April 1983.

36. "Agency Prospectus," 1972–73, appendix 6, Recent NFS Ephemera, fol. 1, SWHAC.

37. Walter L. Smart, "State of the Movement" [1972], Recent NFS Ephemera, fol. 1, SWHAC; 1980 annual report, Recent NFS Ephemera, fol. 11, SWHAC.

38. Interview with Tony Wagner, head, Pillsbury United Neighborhood Services, 16 May 1984.

39. Miller, "Daily Closeup."

40. Frederick B. Taylor, president, NFS, and Walter Smart to "Executive Directors of Member Agencies and City Federations, Board Presidents," 22 Nov. 1972, Recent NFS Ephemera, fol. 10, SWHAC.

41. UNCA, *News and Round Table* (October–November 1979), Recent NFS Ephemera, fol. 1, SWHAC.

42. Smart, interview, 13 April, 1983.

43. *Ibid.*

44. Conversation with Irwin Abrams, business manager, UNCA, 13 April 1983.

45. Smart, interview, 13 April 1983.

46. "Unemployed Social Workers' Cooperative" [ca. 1976], HSS Records, fol. 127:18, SWHAC.

47. Walter L. Smart to "Members of the Executive Committee," 21 Jan. 1982, Recent NFS Ephemera, fol. 13, SWHAC.

48. Walter I. Trattner, *From Poor Law to Welfare State: A History of Social Welfare in America,* 3d ed. (New York: Free Press, 1984), pp. 319–321.

49. Interview with Jim Storm, director, Loring-Nicollet-Bethlehem Community Center, 16 May 1984.

50. Telephone conversation with Nancy Johnston, fieldwork supervisor, School of Social Work, University of Minnesota, 29 May 1984 and 19 Nov. 1986. While the school did do one graduate field placement in a settlement house in 1985–86, it did none in 1986–87.

51. Walter L. Smart to Earl Craig, Jr., president, Northside Settlement Services, Minneapolis, 25 Nov. 1974, Northside Settlement Services Records, box 2, "NFS, 1974–75" fol. SWHAC.

52. Board minutes, 1 May 1976, Recent NFS Ephemera, SWHAC.

53. Executive Committee minutes, 28 Jan. 1977, Recent NFS Ephemera, SWHAC.

54. DeSantis, 2 Feb. 1984.

55. UNH board minutes, 16 June 1981, p. 3, Hall Ephemera, SWHAC.

56. Edwin D. Abrams to Charles T. Williams, president, UNCA, 21 Dec. 1981, UNCA office.

57. Comments from Brian Mulhern, archivist, SWHAC, 18 March 1983.

58. "Report of the New Directions Committee . . . ," 24 Jan. 1969, Recent NFS Ephemera, fol. 3, SWHAC.

59. Walter L. Smart to "Presidents and Executives of Member Agencies," 7 February 1972, Recent NFS Ephemera, fol. 1, SWHAC.

60. Attachments to Mercer D. Tate, president of UNCA, to Smart, 8 Feb. 1983, UNCA office.

61. Board minutes, 22 Jan. 1970, UNH Supp. Records, fol. 4:2, SWHAC.

62. "Criteria for Agency Admission and Accreditation," 25 Jan. 1976, NFS Supp. Records, fol. 16:2, SWHAC; "Report of Re-Accreditation Study: Westminster Neighborhood Association—Los Angeles," 23 March 1982, UNCA office.

63. Bert Beck, chair, Commission on Accreditation and Membership Standards, "Accreditation: An Account of Process and Product," *News and Round Table* (February–March 1976), Recent NFS Ephemera, fol. 9, SWHAC.

64. Leslie Maitland, "At 75, Settlement House Group Still Offers a Firm Hand to Poor," *New York Times*, 30 Sept. 1975, p. 39.

65. "A Neighborhood House" [1973], Recent NFS Ephemera, SWHAC.

66. Smart, interview, 13 April 1983.

67. "U.N.H. Receives Million Dollar Grant," *News and Round Table*, 1977, Recent NFS Ephemera, fol. 8, SWHAC.

68. Smart to Clarence Boebel et al., 28 Feb. 1978, UNCA office.

69. Frederick B. Taylor, president, NFS, to Helen Hall, 11 Sept. 1973, UNCA office.

70. UNH Executive Directors Council minutes, 19 Jan. 1977, Hall Ephemera, SWHAC.

71. "California State Association of Settlements and Neighborhood Centers," August 1978, UNCA office.

72. "Outline of a Proposal for: An Albany Headquarters of the New York State Association of Settlement Houses and Neighborhood Centers," March 1975, Hall Ephemera, SWHAC.

73. UNH Executive Directors Council minutes, 14 Oct. 1981, Hall Ephemera, SWHAC.

74. Board minutes, 22–23 Oct. 1981, Recent NFS Ephemera, SWHAC.

75. Smart to Mercer D. Tate, UNCA board, 23 Feb. 1983, UNCA office.

76. Smart to Ralph Burlinham, executive director, Ada McKinley Community Services, 24 March 1983, UNCA office.

77. DeSantis, 2 Feb. 1984.

78. Jerome Stevenson, speech before the Midwest American Settlement House Centennial Conference, Minneapolis, 2 May 1986.

79. "New Members," *News and Roundtable* 50 (Fall 1986), p. 7.

80. "New Staff," *ibid.*, p. 8.

81. "Objectives and Characteristics of Settlements and Neighborhood Centers," attached as Appendix A to "Criteria for Agency Admission and Accreditation," 23 Jan. 1976, NFS Supp. Records, fol. 16:2, SWHAC.

82. "Summary of Staff and Program Activities [of the] NFS Washington Legislative Office for the First Seven Months (September 1, 1970, through March 31, 1971)," NFS Supp. Records, fol. 2:5, SWHAC.

83. "Sills Joins University of Delaware Faculty," *NFS News and Round Table* (April–July 1971), Northside Settlement Services Records, box 2, "NFS-1" fol., SWHAC.

84. Tony Wagner, interview, 16 May 1984.

85. *Ibid.*

86. "Thompson Wins in Mississippi," *News and Round Table* (March–June 1973), p. 14, Recent NFS Ephemera.

87. Smart, comment to me, 13 April 1983.

88. Judith Ann Trolander, *Settlement Houses and the Great Depression* (Detroit: Wayne State University Press, 1975), p. 42.

89. UNH board minutes, 27 Jan. 1976, Hall Ephemera, SWHAC. See also Shawn Kennedy, "Women Social Workers Decry Diminished Power in Settlement Houses," *New York Times*, 24 April 1976, p. 32.

90. UNH Women's Issues Committee, "Report: Women's Issues Conference," January 1977, Hall Ephemera, SWHAC.

91. UNH board minutes, 17 Jan. 1978, and "UNH Committees—1979–80," 15 Jan. 1980, both in Hall Ephemera, SWHAC.

92. Don Hayner, "Hull House Assn. Workers To Strike for Higher Pay," *Chicago Sun-Times*, 11 Oct. 1982, p. 60.

93. "Black Men's Focus Group" flier, 1986, in my possession. The group was meeting at Oak Park Neighborhood Center, which is part of Pillsbury United Neighborhood Services.

94. Susan Steinwall, archivist, "Inventory to Henry Street Settlement Records," 1983, p. 5, SWHAC.

CONCLUSION

1. Harry Boyte, *The Backyard Revolution* (Philadelphia: Temple University Press, 1980).

2. Jeffrey Scheuer, *Legacy of Light: University Settlement's First Century* (New York: University Settlement, 1986), pp. 24–25.

3. Interview with Jim Storm, 16 May 1984, in Minneapolis.

4. Interview with Camillo DeSantis, 16 May 1984, in Minneapolis.

INDEX